100 SONGS for KiDS

D0478236

10/13

ISBN 978-0-634-04490-8

HAL•LEONARD®
CORPORATION
7777 W. BLUEMOUND RD. P.O. BOX 13819 MILWAUKEE, WI 53213

Visit Hal Leonard Online at
www.halleonard.com

100 SONGS for KiDS

STRUM AND PICK PATTERNS

This chart contains the suggested strum and pick patterns that are referred to by number at the beginning of each song in this book. The symbols ⊓ and ∨ in the strum patterns refer to down and up strokes, respectively. The letters in the pick patterns indicate which right-hand fingers plays which strings.

p = thumb
i = index finger
m = middle finger
a = ring finger

For example; Pick Pattern 2
is played: thumb - index - middle - ring

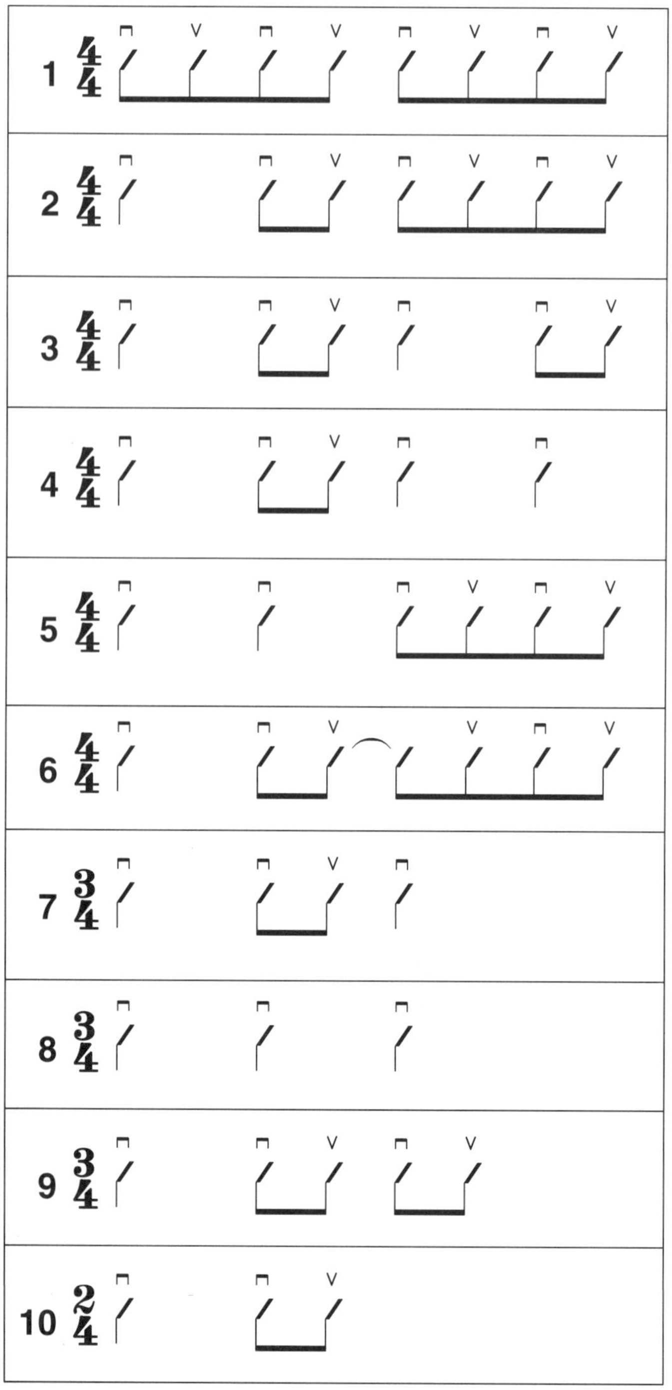

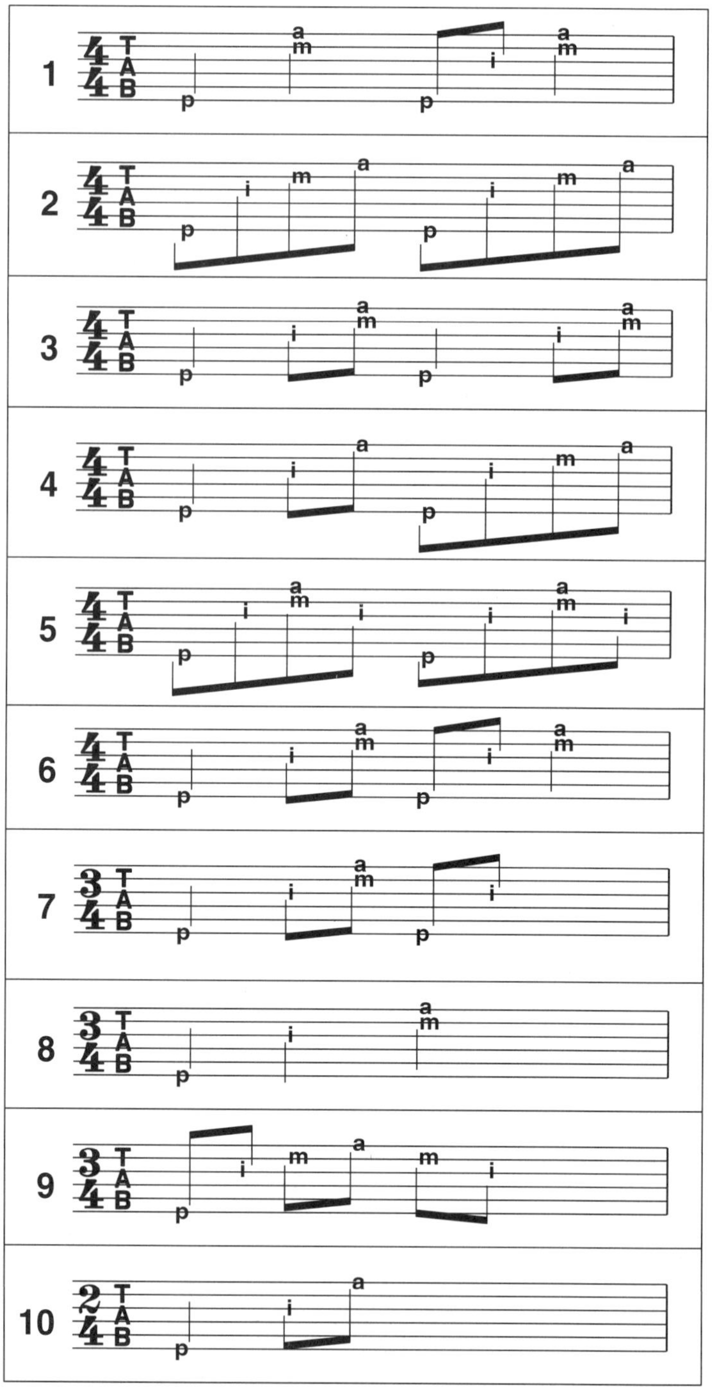

You can use the 3/4 Strum or Pick Patterns in songs written in compound meter (6/8, 9/8, 12/8, etc.).
For example, you can accompany a song in 6/8 by playing the 3/4 pattern twice in each measure.
The 4/4 Strum and Pick Patterns can be used for songs written in cut time (¢) by doubling the note time values in the patterns. Each pattern would therefore last two measures in cut time.

A-Hunting We Will Go

Traditional

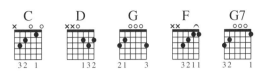

Strum Pattern: 4
Pick Pattern: 5

Moderately

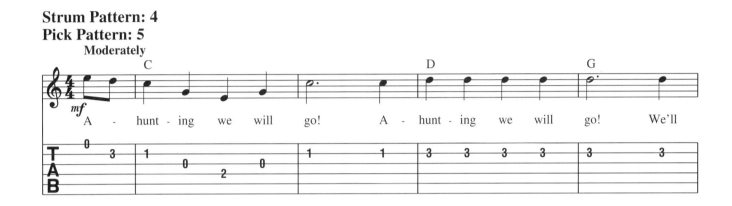

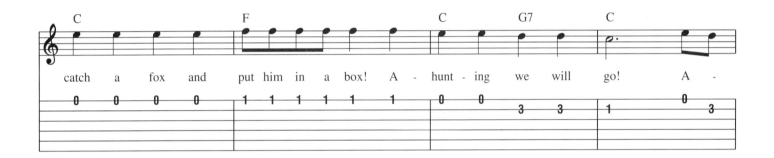

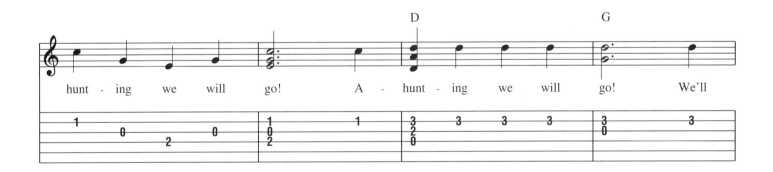

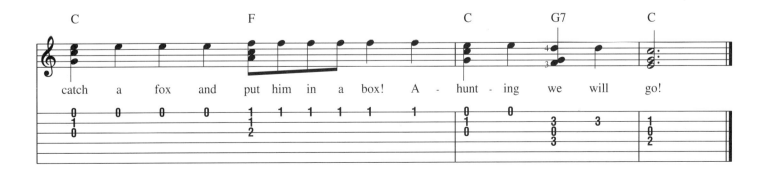

A-Tisket A-Tasket

Traditional

Strum Pattern: 10
Pick Pattern: 10

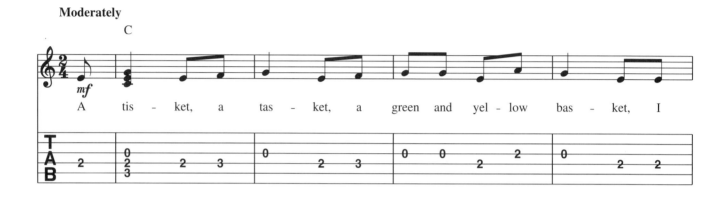

Moderately

A tis - ket, a tas - ket, a green and yel - low bas - ket, I

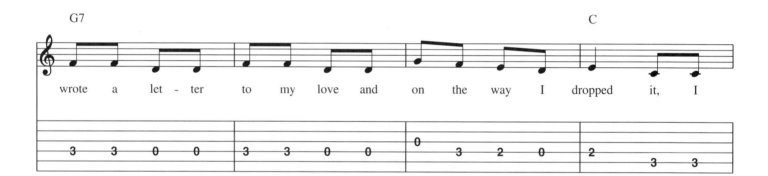

wrote a let - ter to my love and on the way I dropped it, I

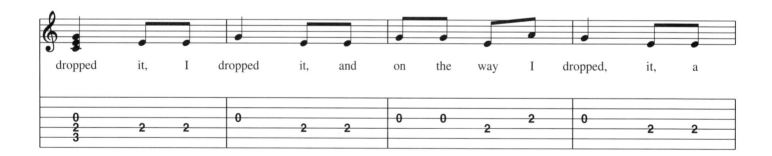

dropped it, I dropped it, and on the way I dropped, it, a

lit - tle boy picked it up and put it in his pock - et.
(girl)   (her)

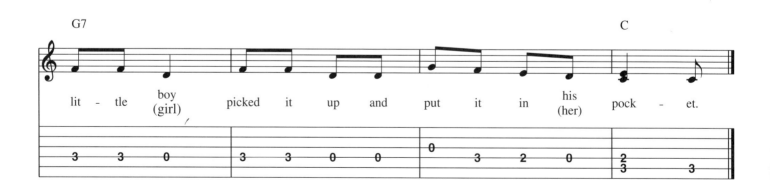

All Night, All Day

Spiritual

Strum Pattern: 4
Pick Pattern: 3

Verse
Moderately slow

1., 2. Day is dy - in' in ___ the west, an - gels watch-in' o - ver me my Lord. ___

Sleep my child and take ___ your rest, an - gels watch-in' o - ver me.

Chorus

All night, all day, an - gels watch-in' o - ver me my Lord. ___ All night, all day,

1.
2.

an - gels watch-in' o - ver me. me. An - gels watch-in' o - ver me. ___

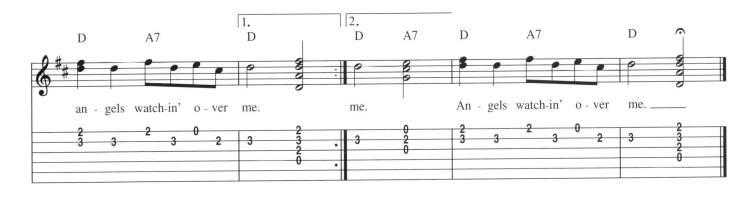

Alouette

Traditional

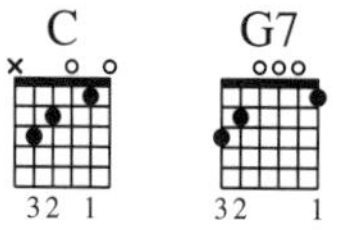

Strum Pattern: 10
Pick Pattern: 10

Chorus
Moderately

mf A - lou - et - te, gen - tille A - lou - et - te,

A - lou - et - te, je te plu - me - rai.

Verse

1., 7. Je te plu - me - rai la tête, je te plu - me - rai la tête,
2. – 6. *See additional lyrics*

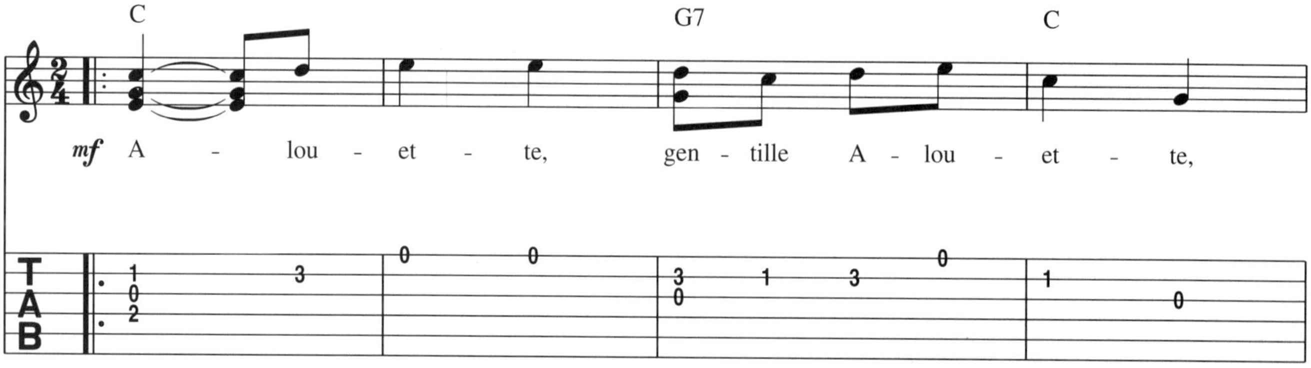

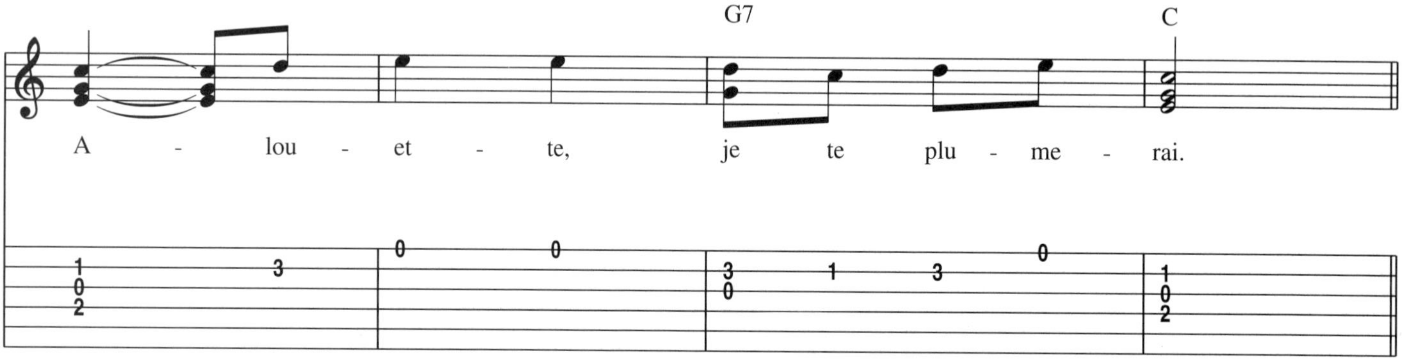

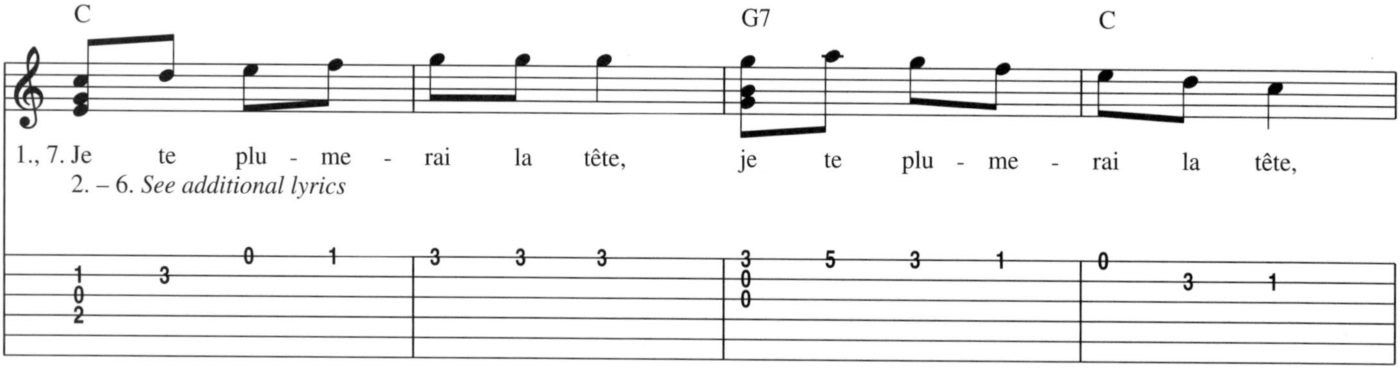

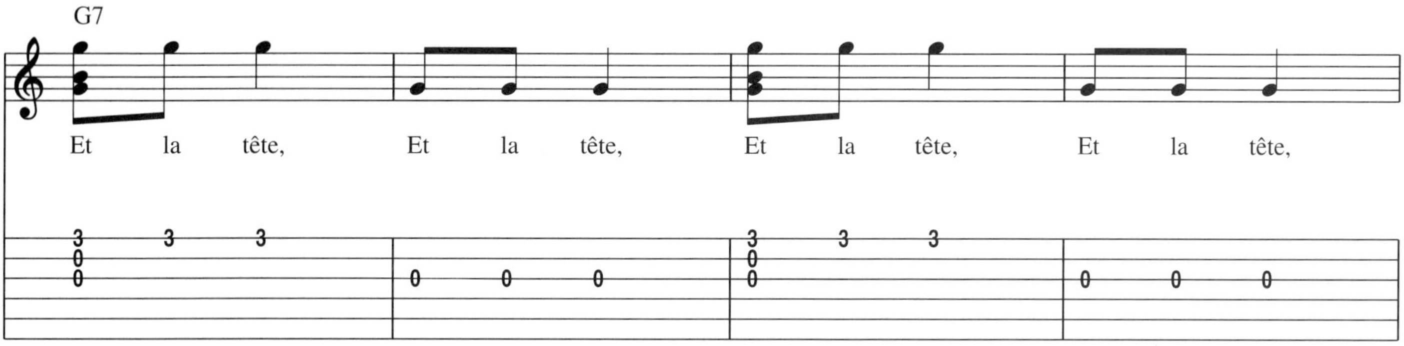

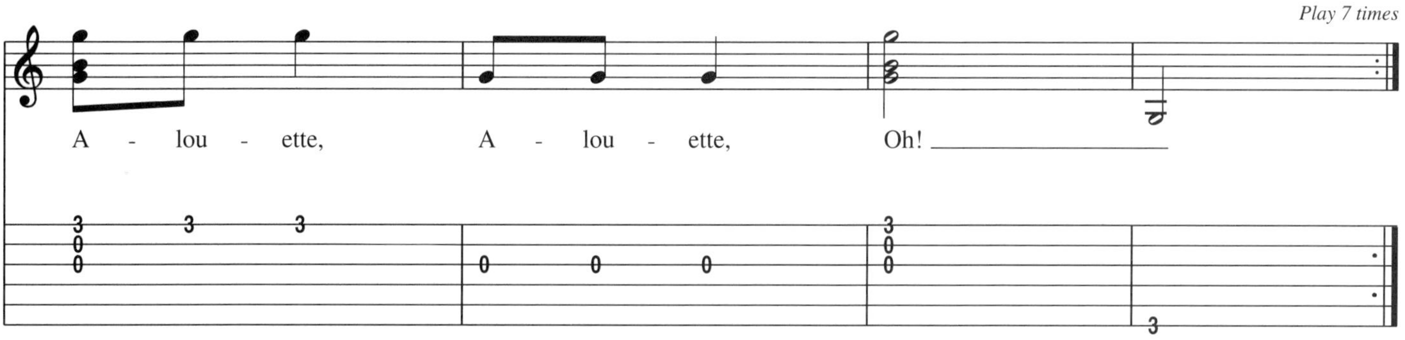

Play 7 times

Outro-Chorus

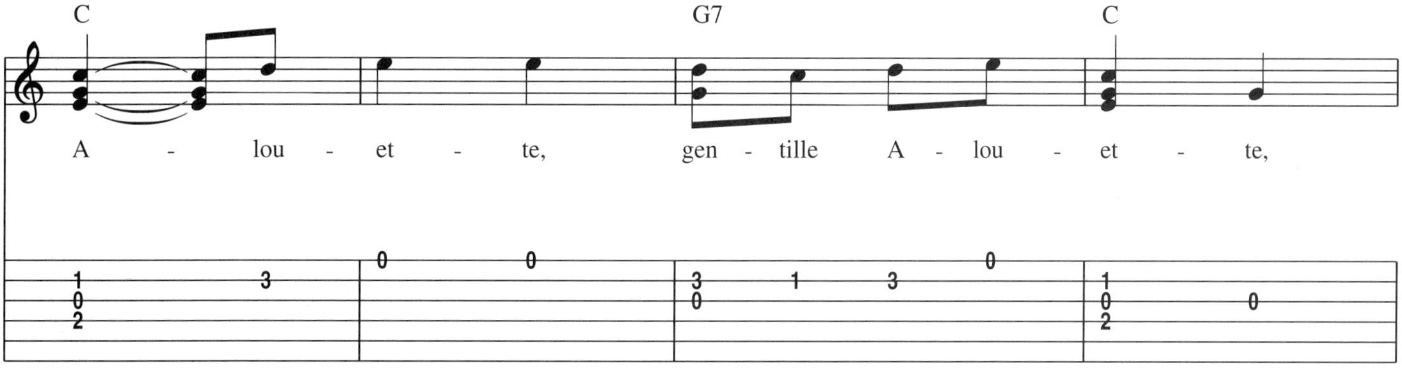

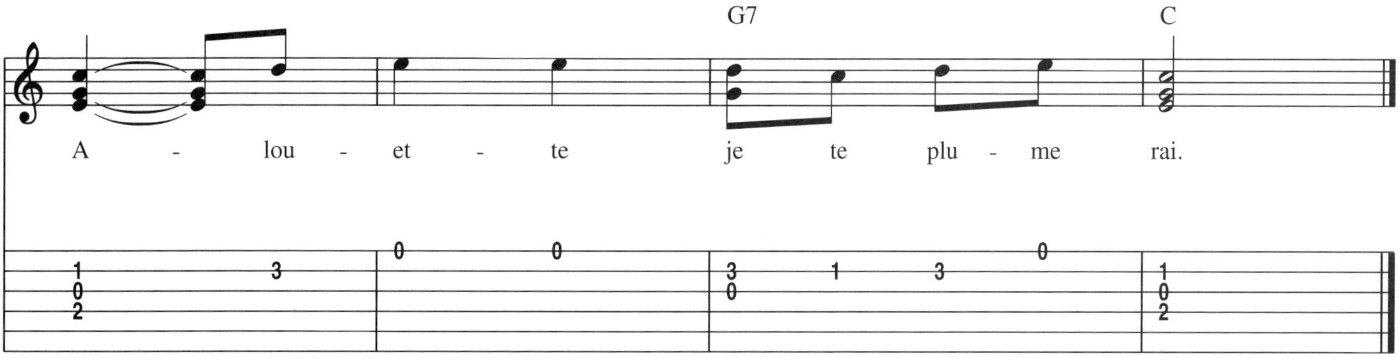

Additional Lyrics

2) le bec
3) le cou
4) les jambes
5) les pieds
6) les pattes

Alphabet Song

Traditional

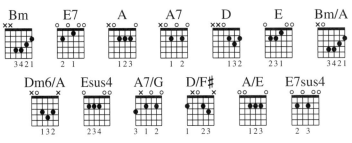

Strum Pattern: 3, 4
Pick Pattern: 3, 4

America, the Beautiful

Words by Katherine Lee Bates
Music by Samuel A. Ward

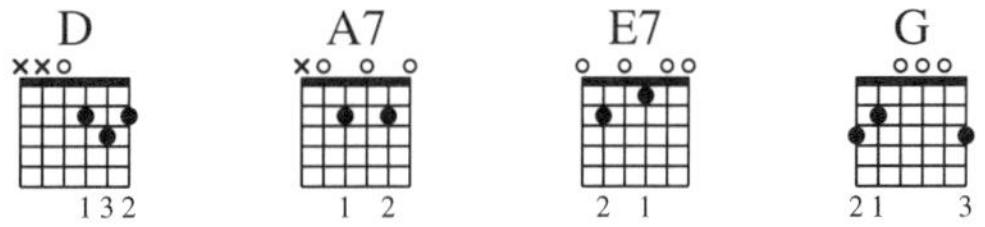

Strum Pattern: 4
Pick Pattern: 3

Additional Lyrics

2. O beautiful for patriot dream
   That sees beyond the years,
   Thine alabaster cities gleam
   Undimmed by human tears.
   America! America!
   God shed His grace on thee,
   And crown thy good with brotherhood
   From sea to shining sea.

Animal Fair

American Folksong

Strum Pattern: 8
Pick Pattern: 8

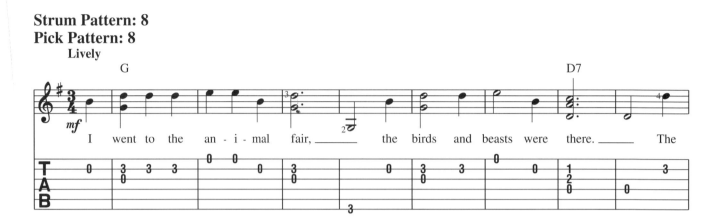

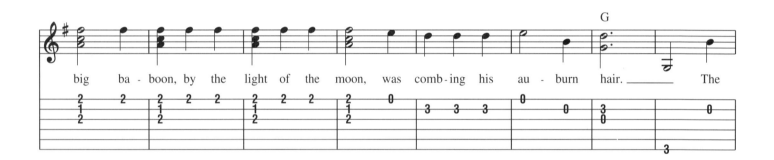

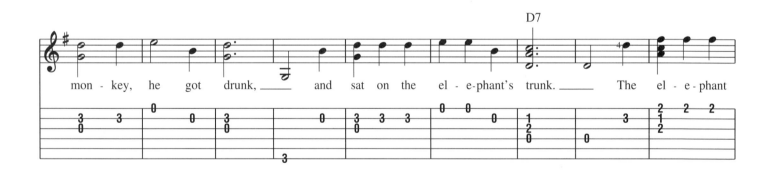

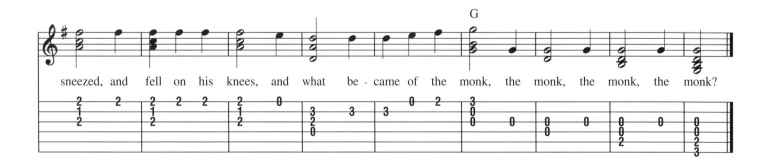

Baa Baa Black Sheep

Traditional

Strum Pattern: 10
Pick Pattern: 10

Baa, baa, black sheep have you an-y wool?

Yes, sir, yes, sir, three bags full.

One for my mas-ter, one for my dame, but

none for the lit-tle boy who cries in the lane.

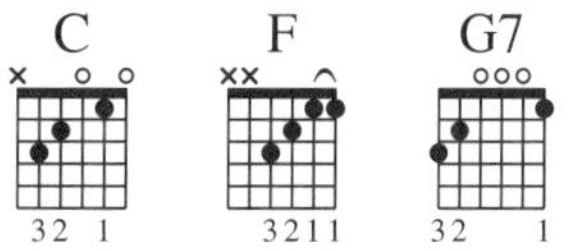

Barnyard Song

Traditional

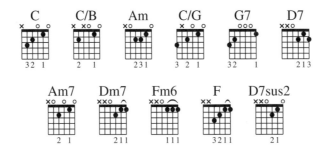

Strum Pattern: 7, 8
Pick Pattern: 7, 8

Verse
Moderately fast

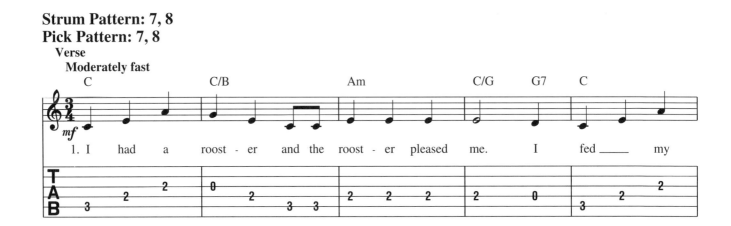

1. I had a roost-er and the roost-er pleased me. I fed ___ my

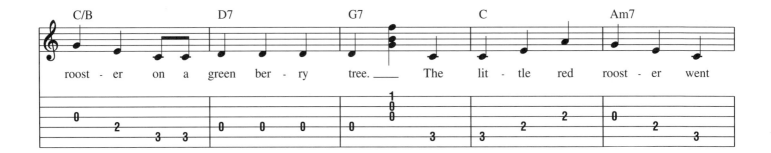

roost-er on a green ber-ry tree. ___ The lit-tle red roost-er went

"cock-a-doo-dle doo, dee doo-dle-dee, doo-dle-dee, doo-dle-dee doo." ___

Verse
C C/B Am C/G G7 C
2. I had a cat and the cat pleased me. I fed my
C/B D7 G7 C C/B
cat on a green ber - ry tree. The lit - tle cat went
Am D7sus2 G7 C Am7 Dm7 G7
"meow, meow," the lit - tle red roost - er went "cock - a - doo - dle
Am Fm6 C F G7 C
doo, dee doo - dle - dee, doo - dle - dee, doo - dle - dee doo."

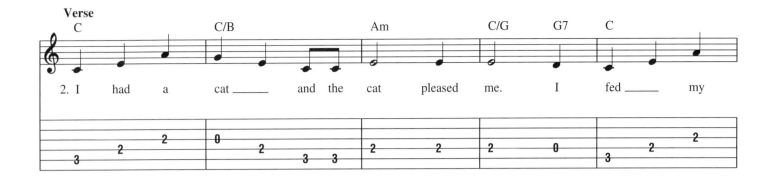

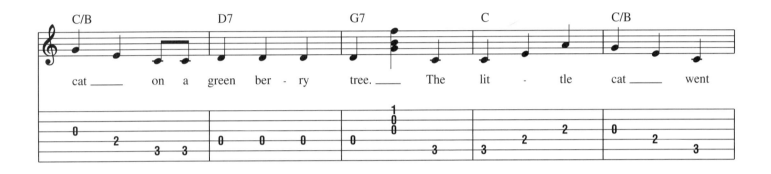

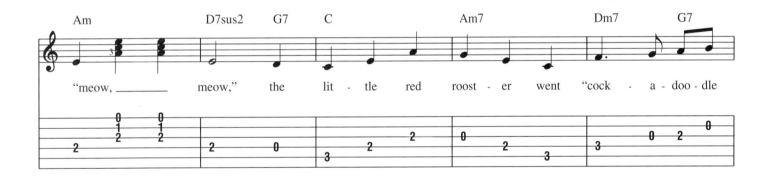

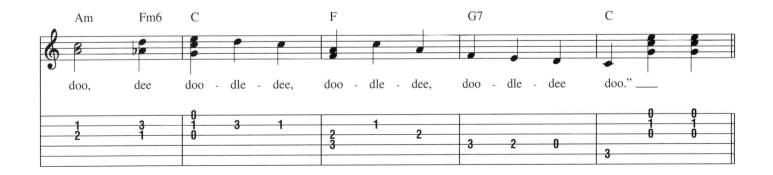

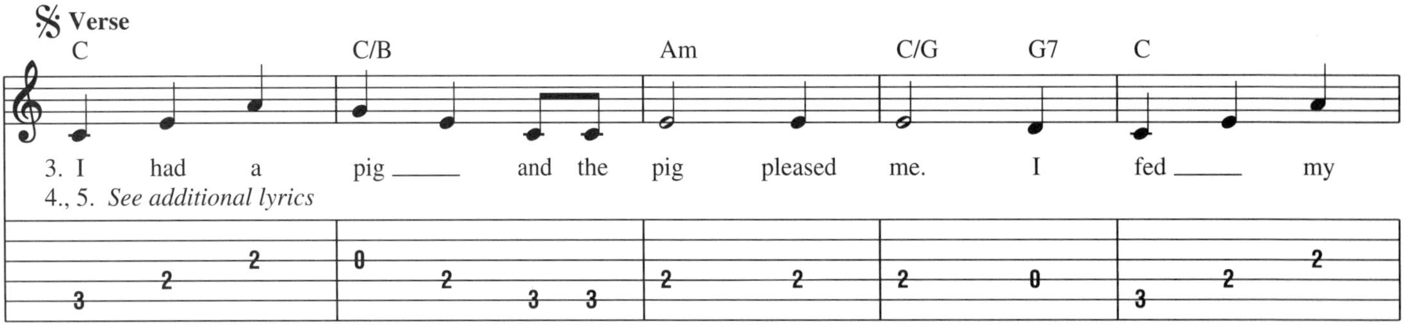

3. I had a pig _____ and the pig pleased me. I fed _____ my
4., 5. *See additional lyrics*

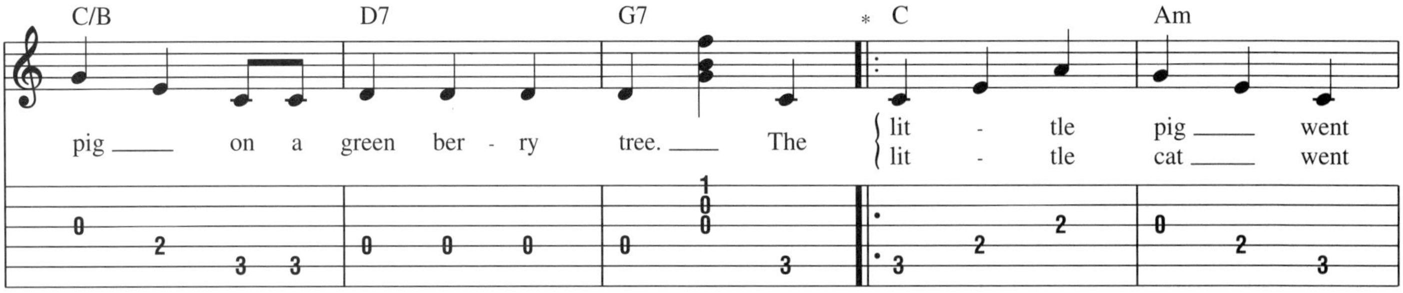

pig _____ on a green ber - ry tree. _____ The { lit - tle pig _____ went
                                                  { lit - tle cat _____ went

*Verses 4. and 5.: repeat as needed for each animal

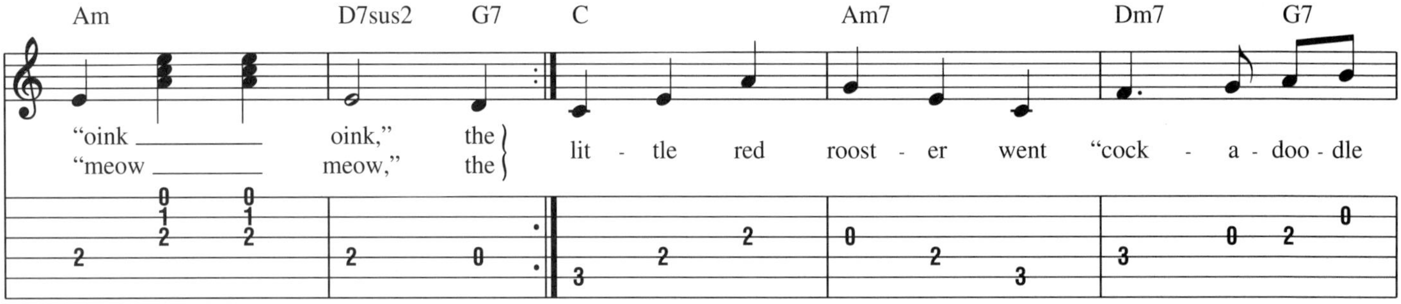

"oink _____ oink," the } lit - tle red roost - er went "cock - a - doo - dle
"meow _____ meow," the }

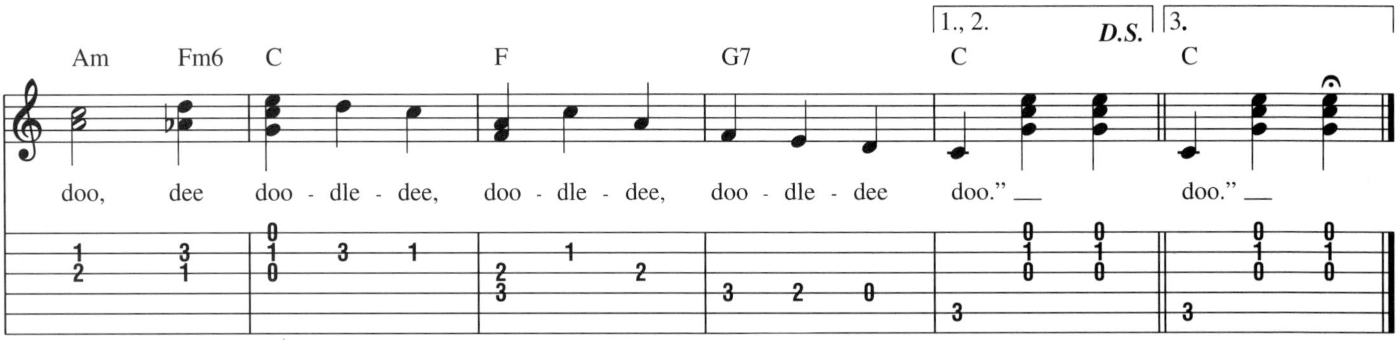

doo, dee doo - dle - dee, doo - dle - dee, doo - dle - dee doo." ___   doo." ___

Additional Lyrics

4. I had a cow and the cow pleased me.
   I fed my cow on a green berry tree.
   The little cow went "moo, moo."
   The little pig went "oink, oink."
   The little cat went "meow, meow."
   The little red rooster went "cock-a-doodle-doo,
   Dee doodle-dee, doodle-dee, doodle-dee doo."

5. I had a baby and the baby pleased me.
   I fed my baby on a green berry tree.
   The little baby went "waah, waah."
   The little cow went "moo, moo."
   The little pig went "oink, oink."
   The little cat went "meow, meow."
   The little red rooster went "cock-a-doodle-doo,
   Dee doodle-dee, doodle-dee, doodle-dee doo."

Be Kind to Your Web-Footed Friends

Traditional

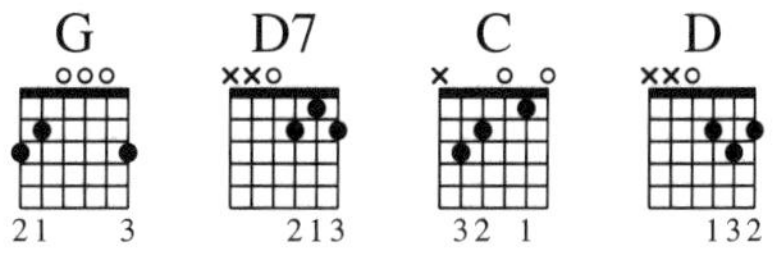

Strum Pattern: 3, 4
Pick Pattern: 1, 3
Moderate March

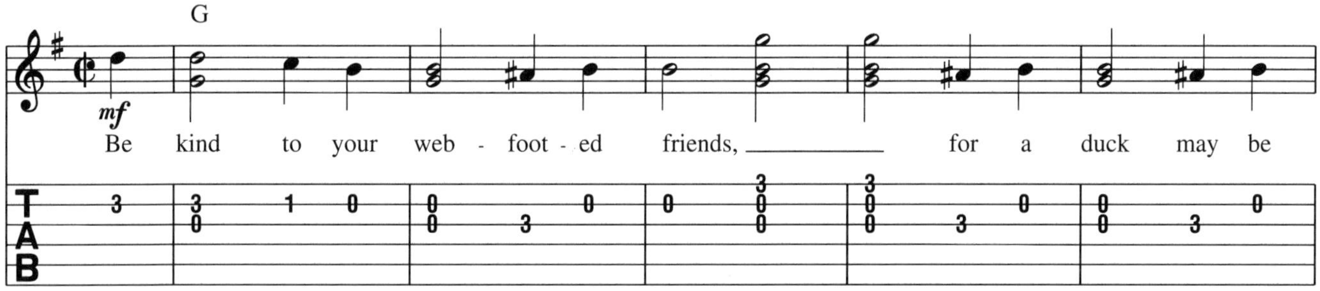

Be kind to your web - foot - ed friends, _____ for a duck may be

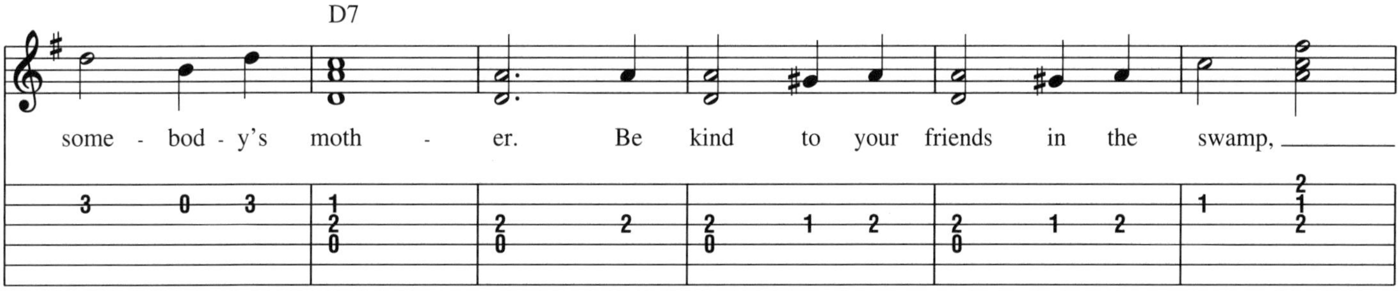

some - bod - y's moth - er. Be kind to your friends in the swamp, _____

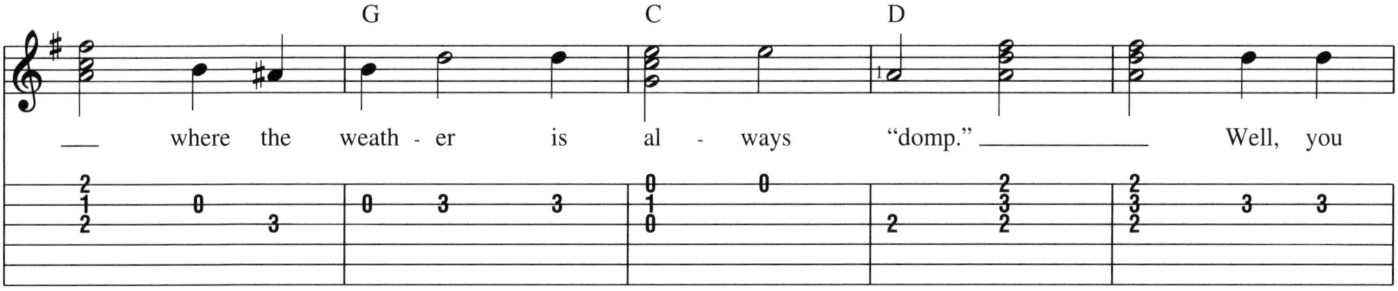

___ where the weath - er is al - ways "domp." _____ Well, you

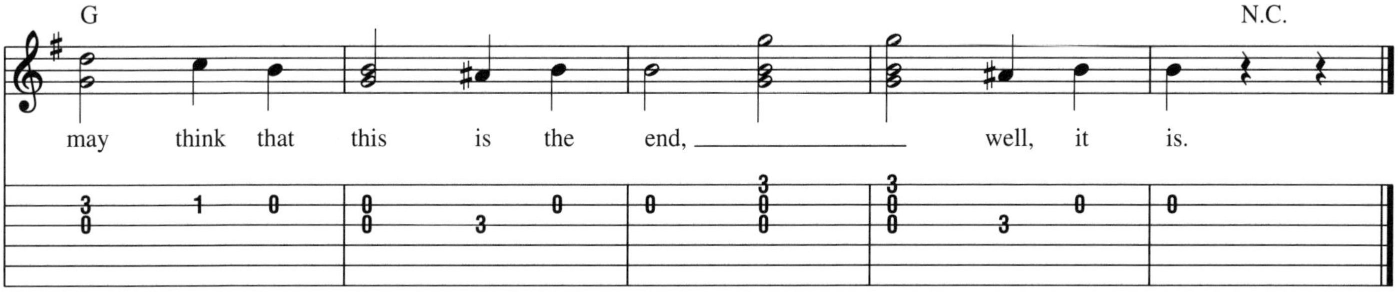

may think that this is the end, _____ well, it is.

The Bear Went Over the Mountain

Traditional

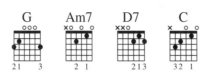

Strum Pattern: 8
Pick Pattern: 8

Verse
Brightly

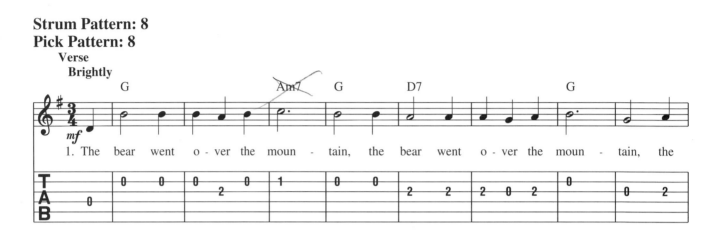

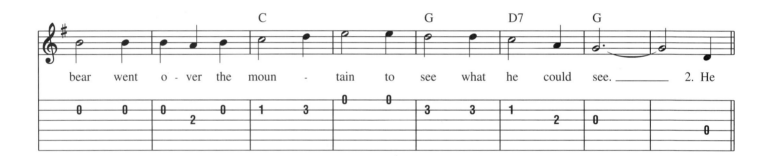

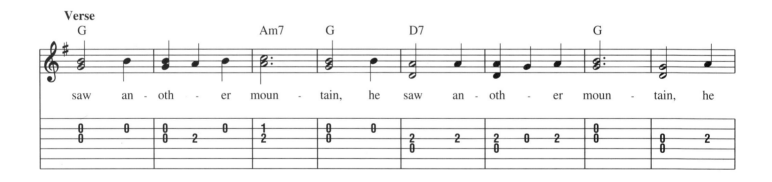

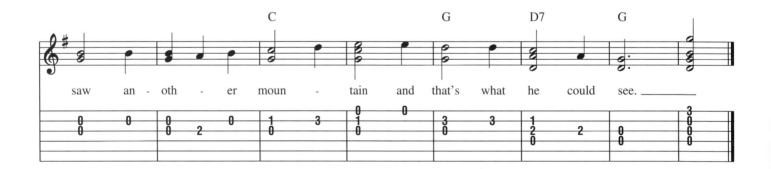

The Bluetail Fly
(Jimmy Crack Corn)

Words and Music by Daniel Decatur Emmett

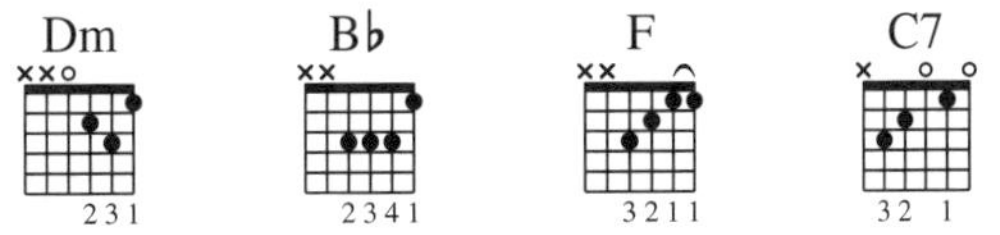

Strum Pattern: 10
Pick Pattern: 10

Verse
Rubato

1. When I was young I used to wait on Mas-ter ___ and hand him his plate, and pass the bot-tle when

2.–5. *See additional lyrics*

Chorus
A tempo

he got dry, and brush a-way the Blue-tail Fly! Jim-my crack corn, and I don't care, Jim-my crack corn, and

I don't care. Jim-my crack corn, and I don't care, my Mas-ter's gone a - way. ___ 2. And way.

Additional Lyrics

2. And when he'd ride in the afternoon,
   I'd follow after with a hickory broom;
   The pony being very shy,
   When bitten by the Bluetail Fly!

3. One day while riding round the farm,
   The flies so numerous they did swarm;
   One changed to bite him on the thigh,
   The devil take the Bluetail Fly!

4. The pony run, he jump, he kick,
   He threw my Master in the ditch;
   He died and the jury wondered why,
   The verdict was the Bluetail Fly!

5. They laid him under a 'simmon tree,
   His epitaph is there to see:
   "Beneath this stone Jim forced to lie,
   A victim of the Bluetail Fly!"

Bingo

Traditional

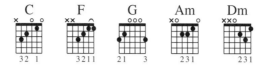

Strum Pattern: 4, 3
Pick Pattern: 2, 5

1. There was a farm-er had a dog and
3.-6. *See additional lyrics*

Bing - o was his name - o: B - I - N - G - O, B - I - N - G - O,

B - I - N - G - O and Bing - o was his name - o. 2. There was a farm-er had a dog and

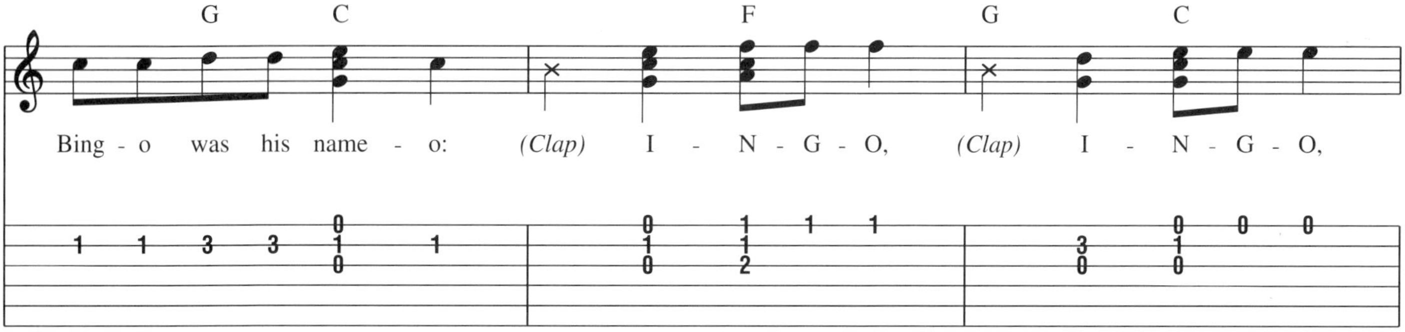

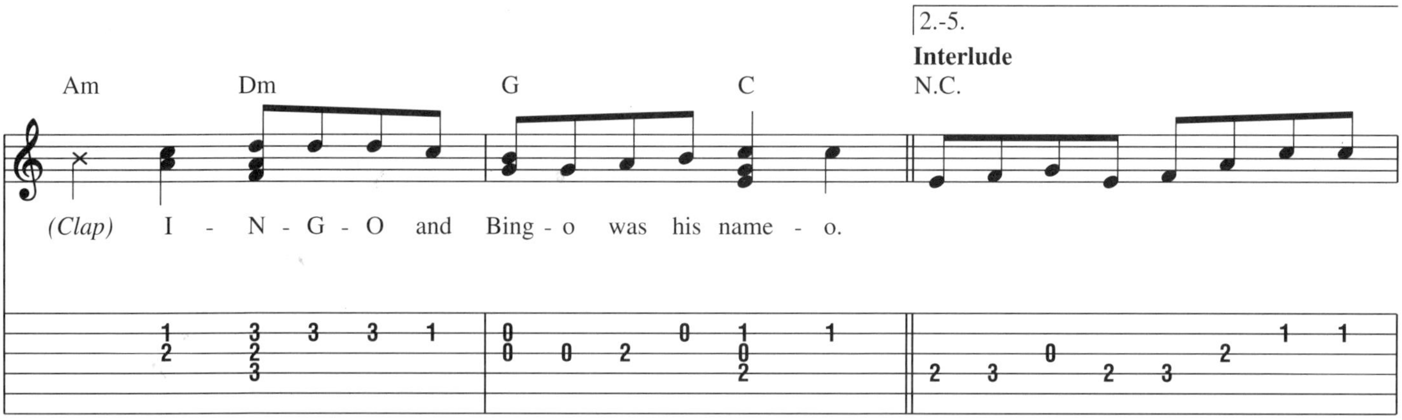

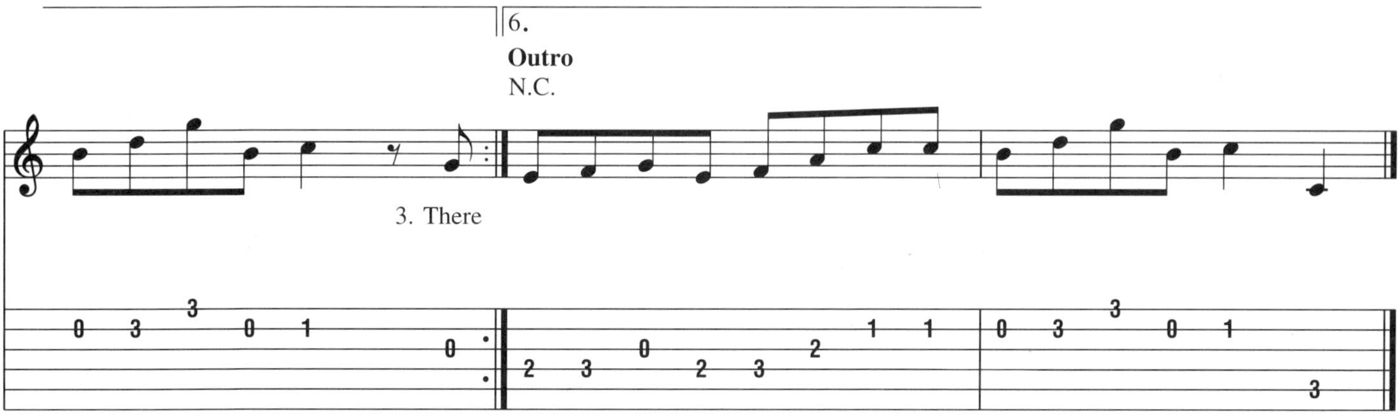

Additional Lyrics

3. There was a farmer had a dog and Bingo was his name-o:
   - - N-G-O, - - N-G-O, - - N-G-O
   And Bingo was his name-O:

4. There was a farmer had a dog and Bingo was his name-o:
   - - - G-O, - - - G-O, - - - G-O
   And Bingo was his name-O:

5. There was a farmer had a dog and Bingo was his name-o:
   - - - - O, - - - - O, - - - - O

6. There was a farmer had a dog and Bingo was his name-o:
   - - - - -, - - - - -, - - - - -
   And Bingo was his name-O:

Bye, Baby Bunting

Traditional

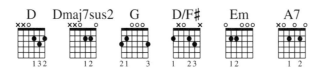

Strum Pattern: 7
Pick Pattern: 7

Verse
Quickly

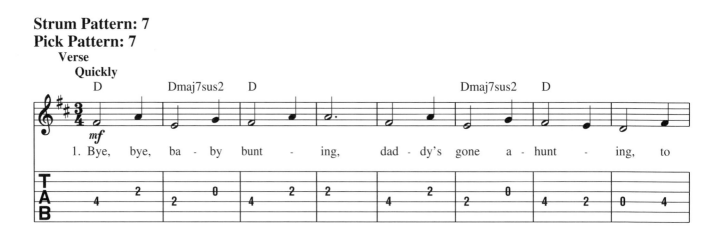

1. Bye, bye, ba - by bunt - ing, dad - dy's gone a - hunt - ing, to

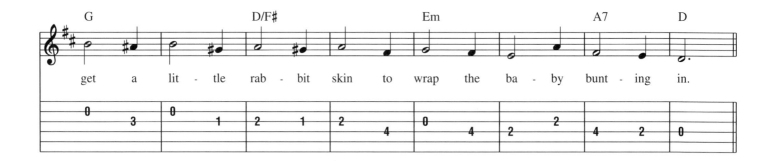

get a lit - tle rab - bit skin to wrap the ba - by bunt - ing in.

Verse

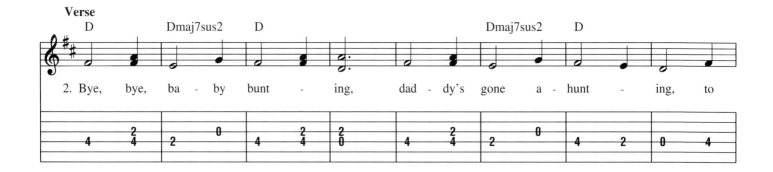

2. Bye, bye, ba - by bunt - ing, dad - dy's gone a - hunt - ing, to

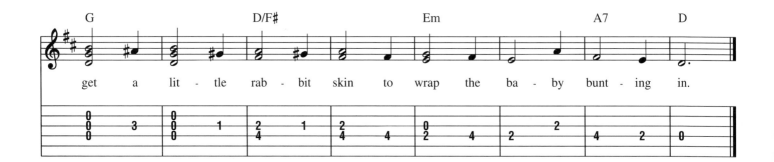

get a lit - tle rab - bit skin to wrap the ba - by bunt - ing in.

(Oh, My Darling) Clementine

Words and Music by Percy Montrose

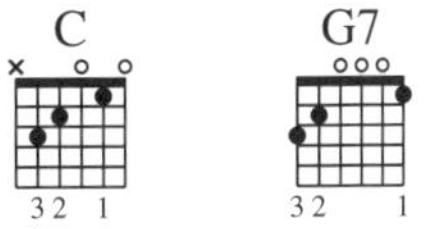

Strum Pattern: 9
Pick Pattern: 7

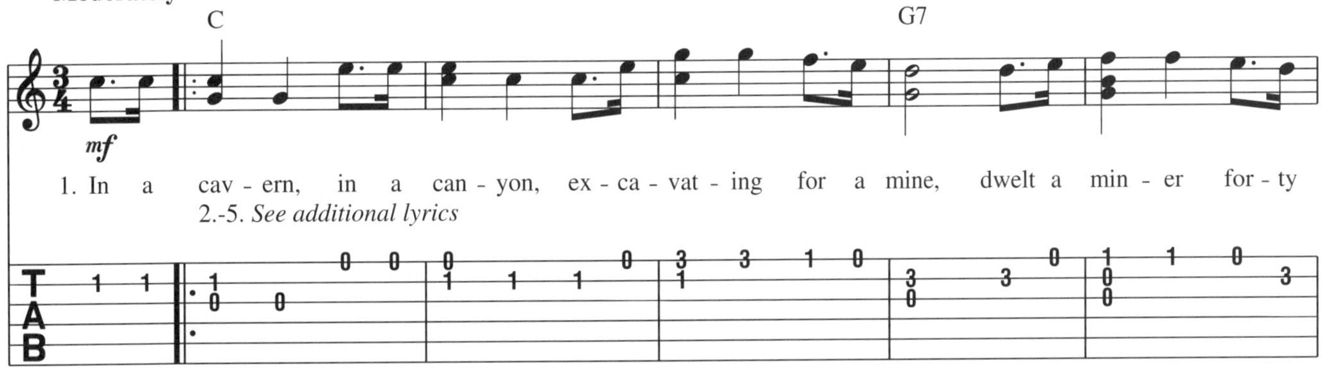

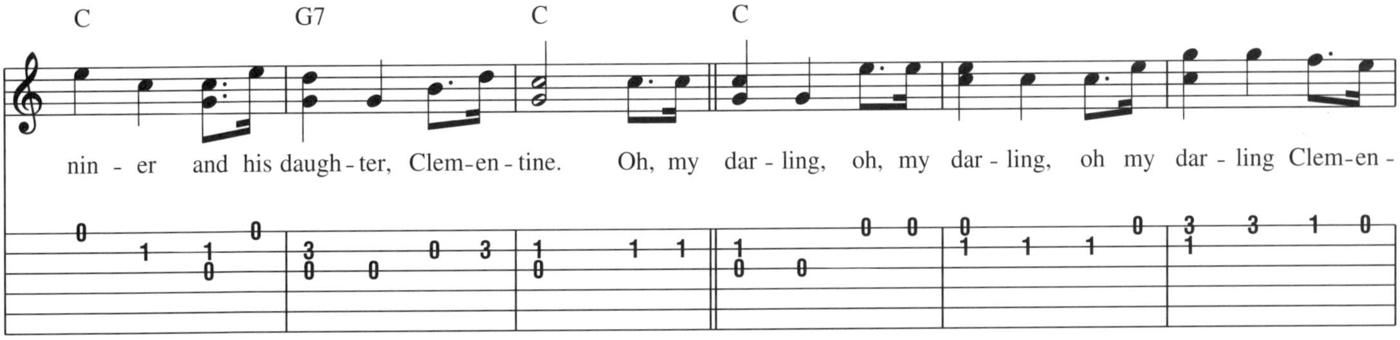

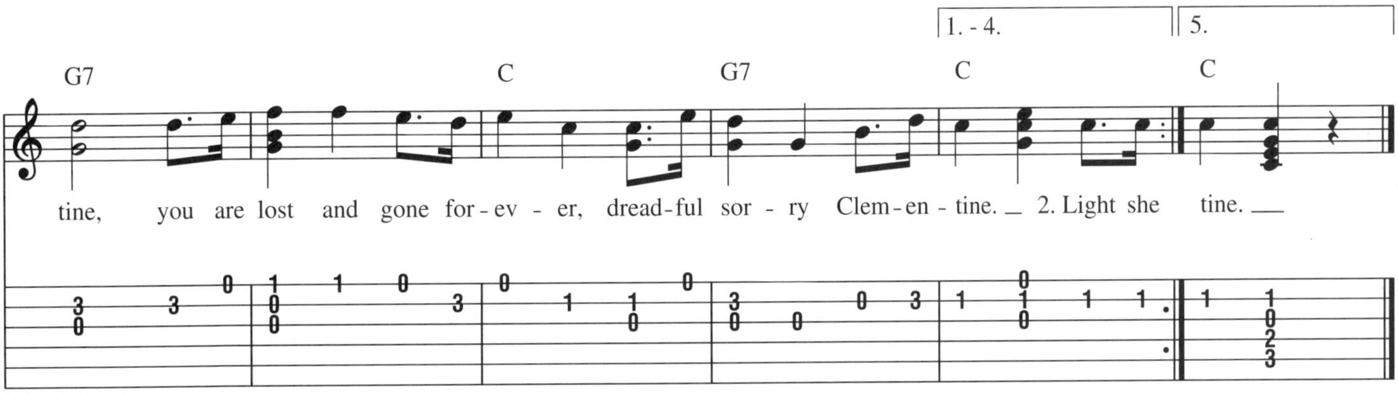

Additional Lyrics

2. Light she was and like a fairy
   And her shoes were number nine,
   Herring boxes without topses
   Sandals were for Clementine.

3. Drove she ducklings to the water
   Ev'ry morning just at nine,
   Stubbed her toe upon a splinter
   Fell into the foaming brine.

4. Ruby lips above the water
   Blowing bubbles soft and fine,
   But alas I was no swimmer
   So I lost my Clementine.

5. There's a churchyard on the hillside
   Where the flowers grow and twine,
   There grow roses 'mongst the posies
   Fertilized by Clementine.

Cock-a-Doodle-Doo

Traditional

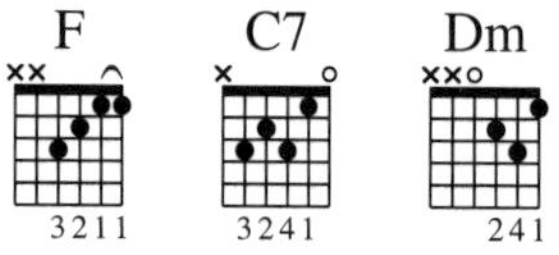

Strum Pattern: 7
Pick Pattern: 7

Verse
Moderately

1. Cock - a - doo - dle doo! My dame has lost her shoe, my mas-ter's lost his fid-dling

2. *See additional lyrics*

stick and does-n't know what to do. ___ And does-n't know what to do, ___ and does-n't kow what to

do. ___ My mas-ter's lost his fid-dling stick and does-n't know what to do. ___ shoe. ___

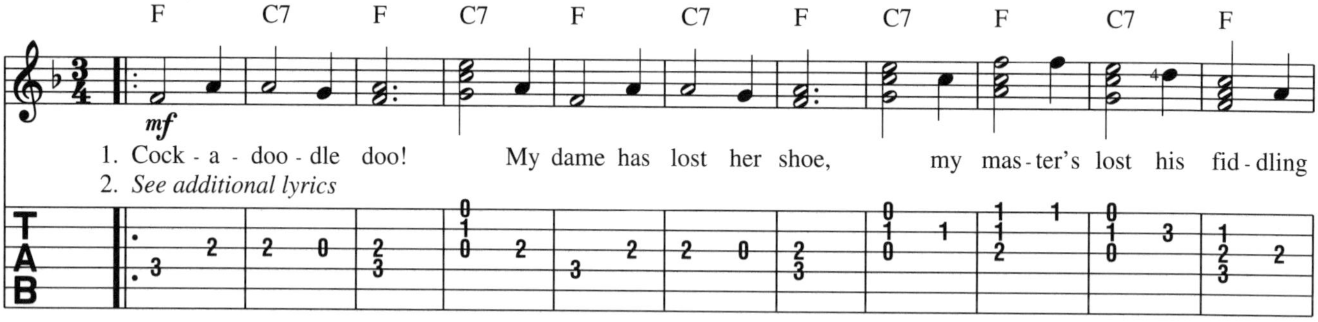

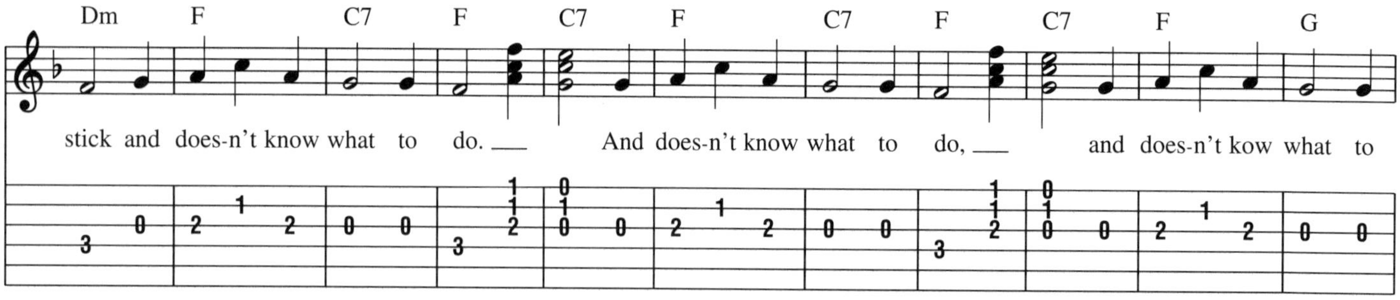

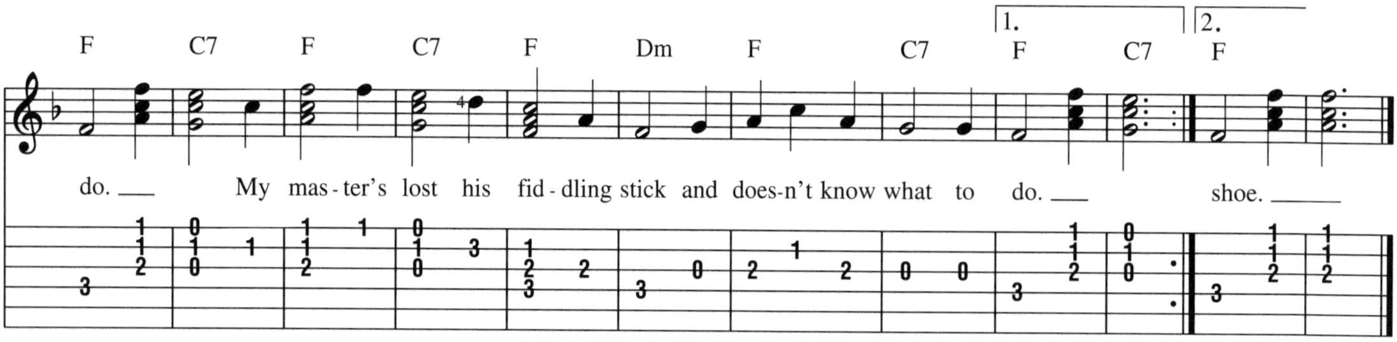

Additional Lyrics

2. Cock-a-doodle doo!
What is my dame to do?
Till master finds his fiddling stick,
She'll dance without her shoe.
She'll dance without her shoe,
She'll dance without her shoe,
Till master finds his fiddling stick,
She'll dance without her shoe.

Do Your Ears Hang Low?

Traditional

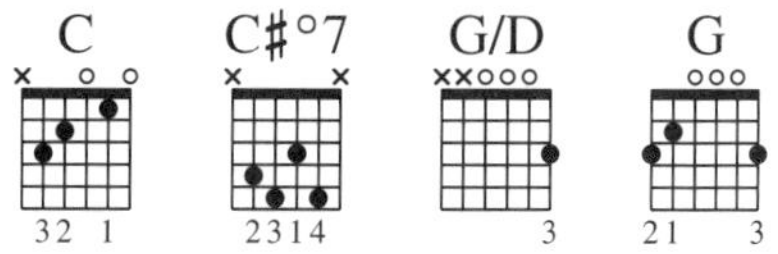

Strum Pattern: 3, 2
Pick Pattern: 4

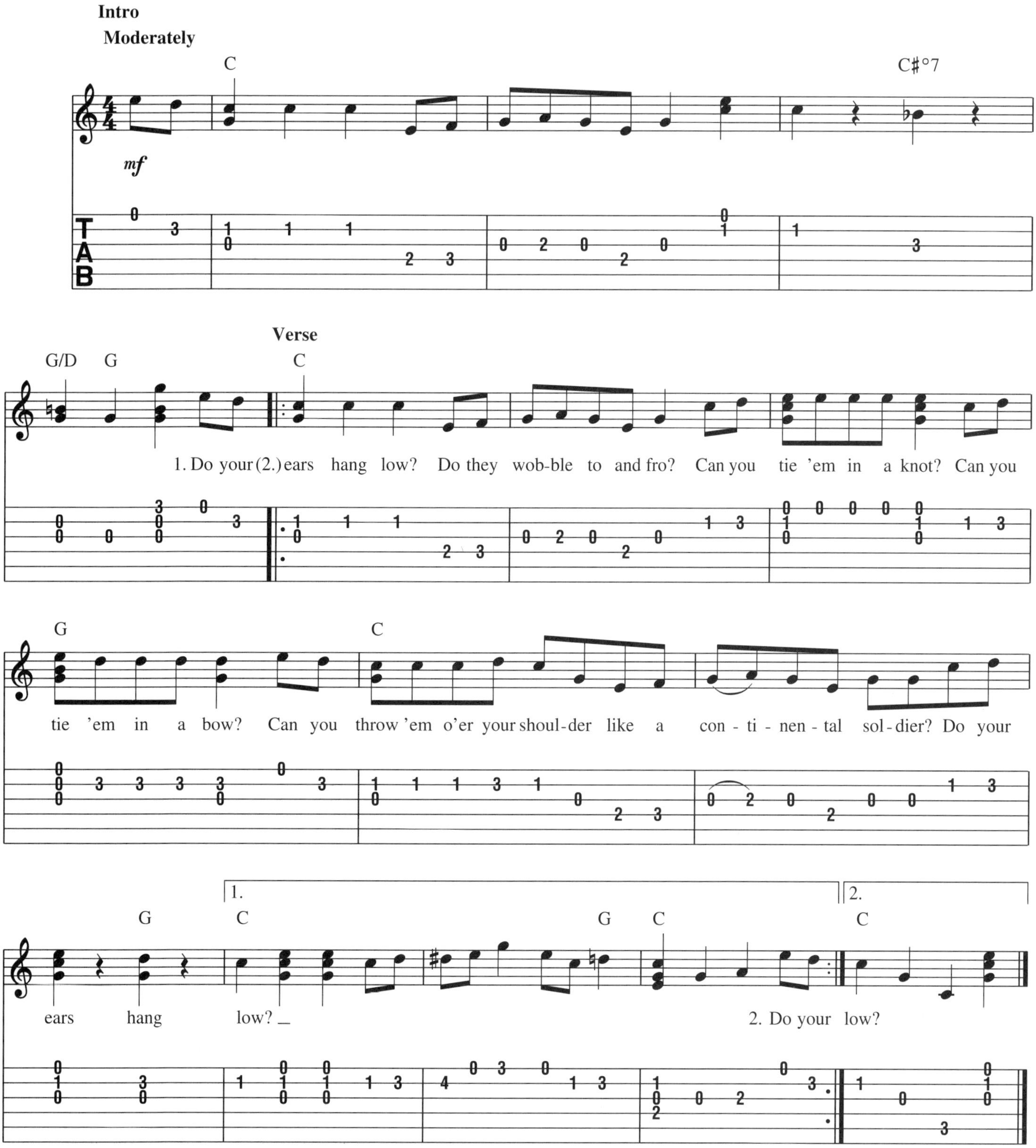

Down by the Station

Traditional

G   D7

Strum Pattern: 4
Pick Pattern: 3

Verse
Moderately

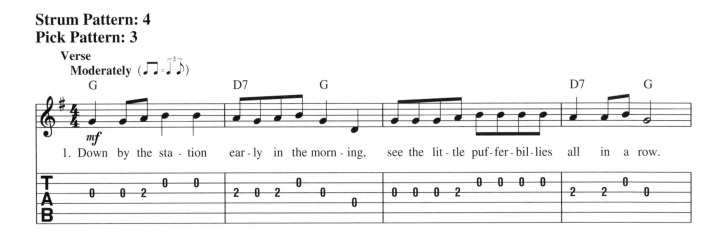

1. Down by the sta - tion ear - ly in the morn - ing, see the lit - tle puf - fer - bil - lies all in a row.

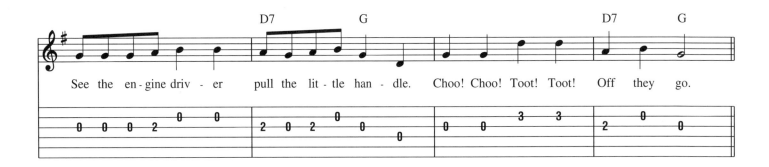

See the en - gine driv - er pull the lit - tle han - dle. Choo! Choo! Toot! Toot! Off they go.

Verse

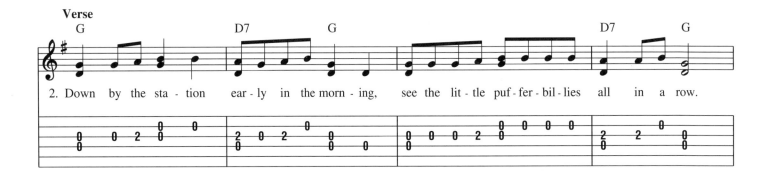

2. Down by the sta - tion ear - ly in the morn - ing, see the lit - tle puf - fer - bil - lies all in a row.

See the en - gine driv - er pull the lit - tle han - dle. Choo! Choo! Toot! Toot! Off they go.

Dry Bones

Traditional

Strum Pattern: 3
Pick Pattern: 3

E - ze - kiel cried, "Them dry bones!" E - ze - kiel cried, "Them dry bones!" E -

ze - kiel cried, "Them dry bones!" Oh, hear the word of the Lord! _____ 1. The

Verse

foot bone con - nect - ed to the leg bone, the leg bone con - nect - ed to the

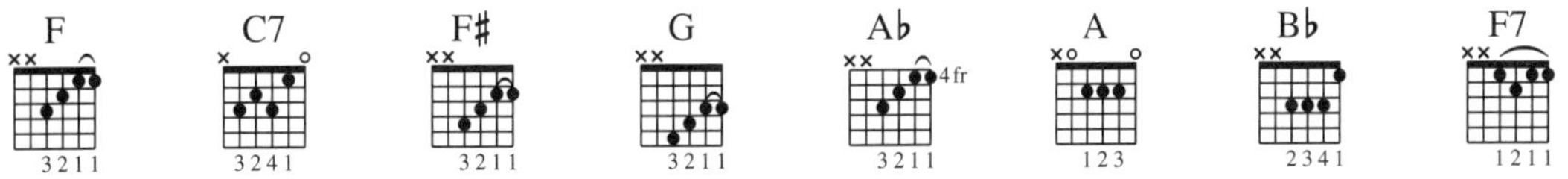

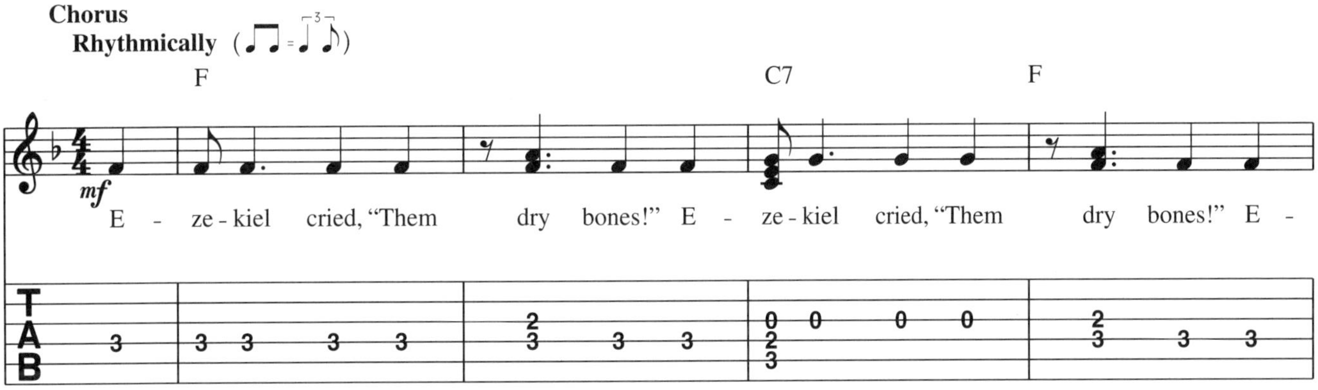

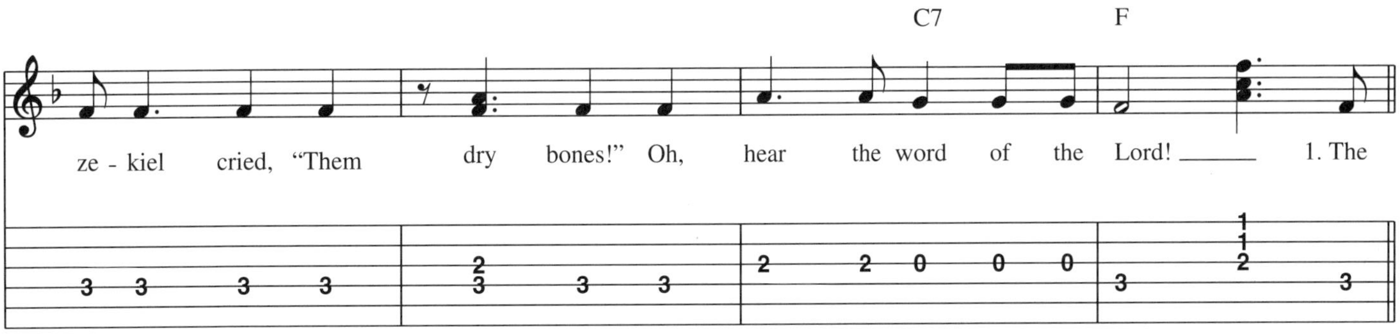

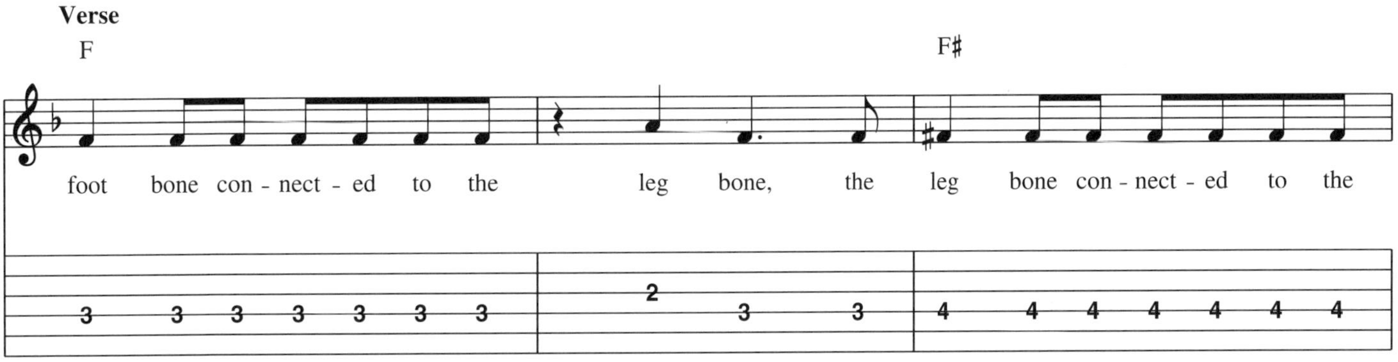

G
knee bone, the knee bone con - nect - ed to the thigh bone, the
A♭
thigh bone con - nect - ed to the back bone, the
A
back bone con - nect - ed to the
B♭
neck bone, the neck bone con-nect - ed to the head bone.
F7
Oh, hear the word of the
Chorus
B♭
Lord! Them
B♭
bones, them bones gon - na walk a - roun', them
F7
bones, them bones gon - na
B♭
walk a - roun', them bones, them bones gon - na walk a - roun'.
F7
Oh, hear the word of the

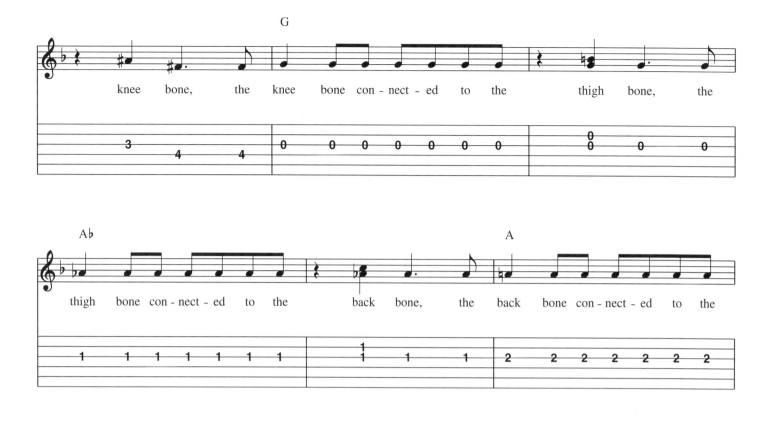

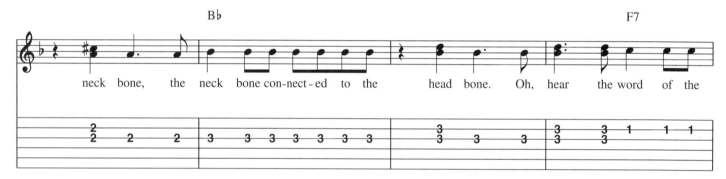

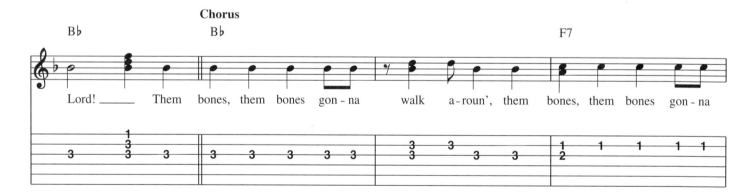

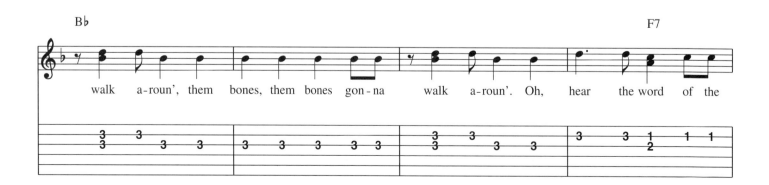

Verse
B♭ B♭ A
Lord! 2. The head bone con-ect-ed to the neck bone, the neck bone con-nect-ed to the
A♭
back bone, the back bone con-nect-ed to the thigh bone, the
G F♯
thigh bone con-nect-ed to the knee bone, the knee bone con-nect-ed to the
F
leg bone, the leg bone con-nect-ed to the foot bone. Oh,
B♭ C7 F
hear the word of the Lord!

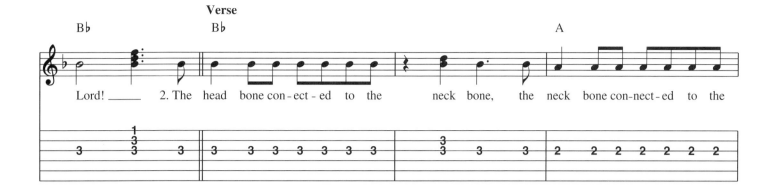

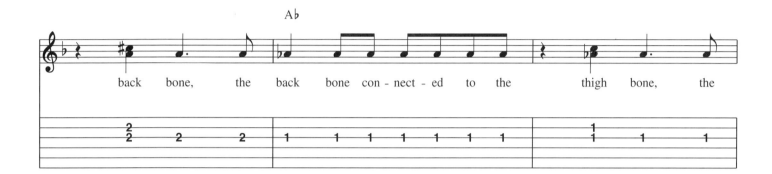

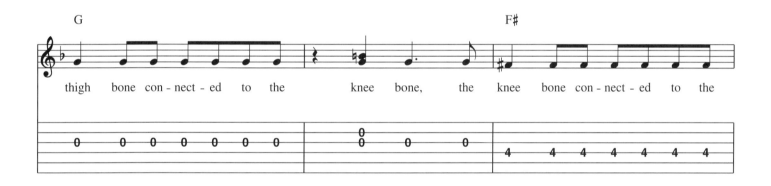

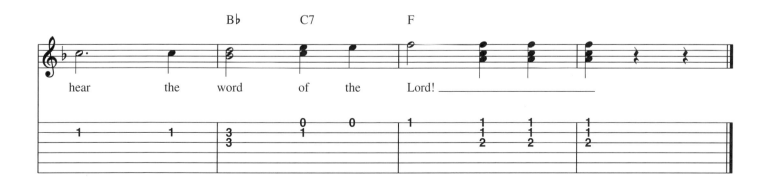

Down in My Heart

Traditional

Strum Pattern: 5, 4
Pick Pattern: 1, 3

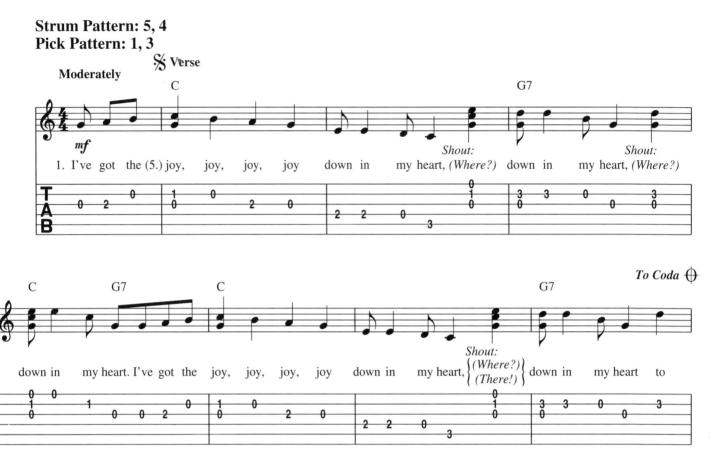

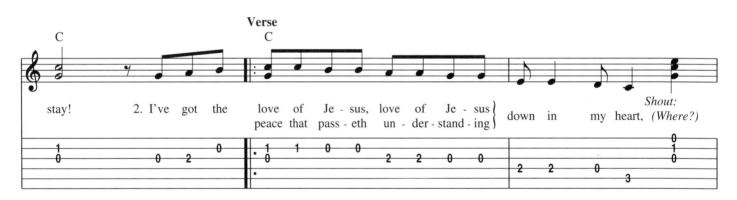

1.
2.
G7 C C
Shout:
down in my heart, (Where?) down in my heart to stay! 3. I've got the stay! 4. I've got the
Verse
C
won - der - ful love of my bless - ed Re - deem - er way down in the depths of my heart,
Shout:
(Where?)
G7 C G7
down in the depths of my heart,
Shout:
(Where?) down in the depths of my heart. I've got the
C
won - der - ful love of my bless - ed Re - deem - er way down in the depths of my heart,
Shout:
(Where?)
D.S. al Coda
Coda
G7 C C
down in the depths of my heart to stay! 5. I've got the stay!

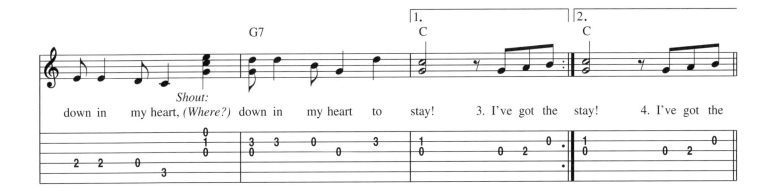

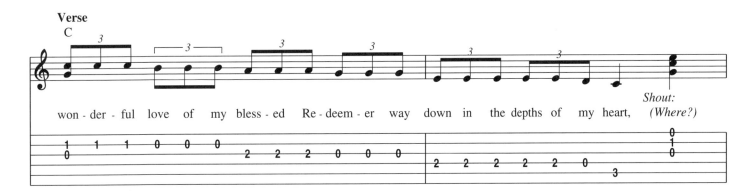

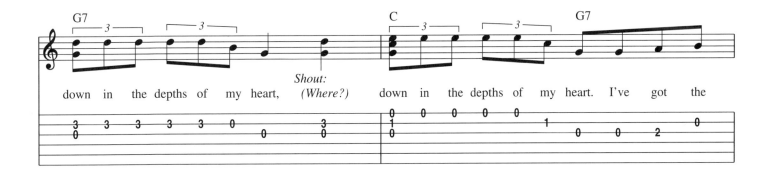

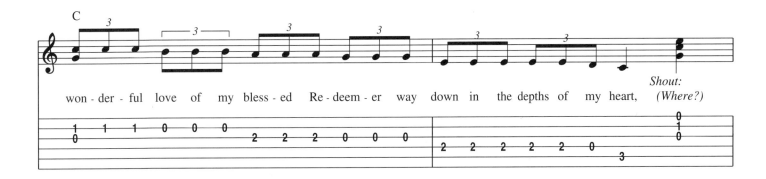

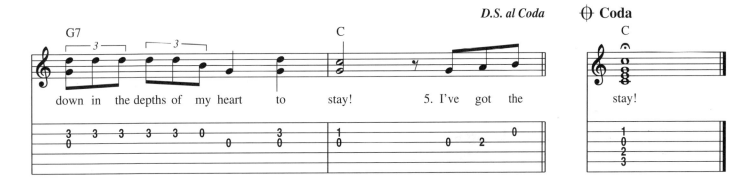

Eensy Weensy Spider

Traditional

C   G7   Am   D7

*Strum Pattern: 10
*Pick Pattern: 10

Playfully

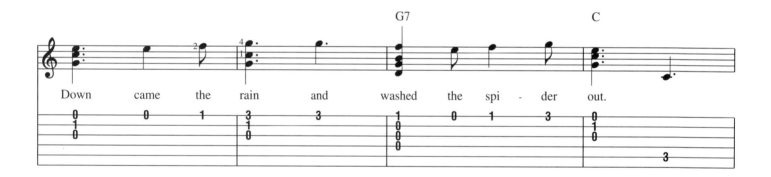

The een-sy ween-sy spi-der went up the wa-ter spout.

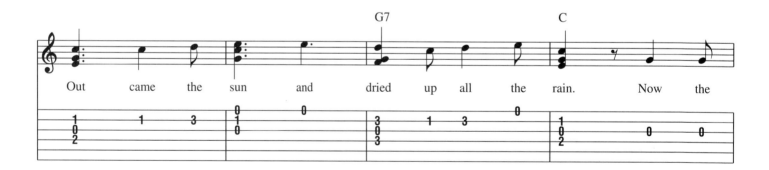

Down came the rain and washed the spi-der out.

Out came the sun and dried up all the rain. Now the

een-sy ween-sy spi-der went up the spout a-gain.

Evening Prayer

By Engelbert Humperdinck

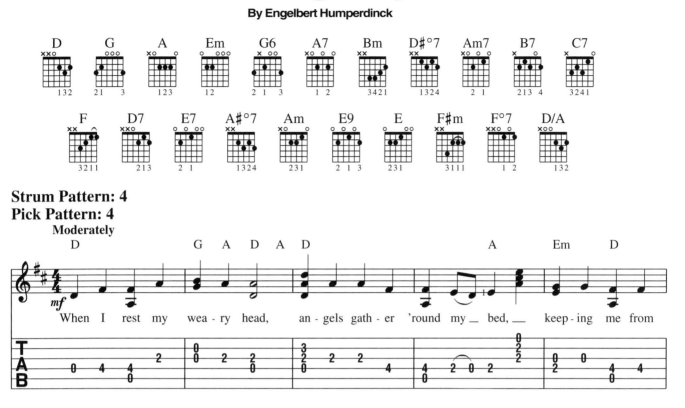

Strum Pattern: 4
Pick Pattern: 4

Moderately

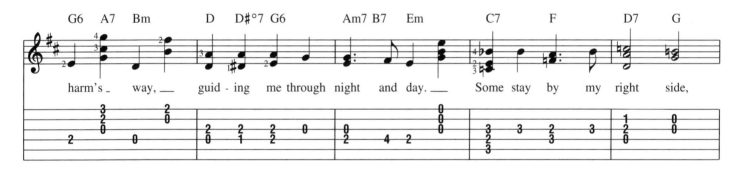

When I rest my wea-ry head, an-gels gath-er 'round my bed, keep-ing me from

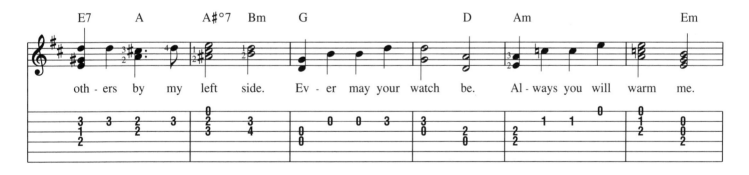

harm's way, guid-ing me through night and day. Some stay by my right side,

oth-ers by my left side. Ev-er may your watch be. Al-ways you will warm me.

An-gels ev-er with your might, please bless and guard my soul to-night.

The Farmer in the Dell

Traditional

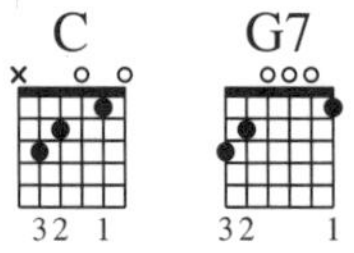

Strum Pattern: 8
Pick Pattern: 8

Verse

Fast

1. The farm - er in the dell, _____ the farm - er
2. – 9. *See additional lyrics*

in the dell. _____ Heigh ho, the der - ry

oh, the farm - er in the dell. _____ 2. The ___

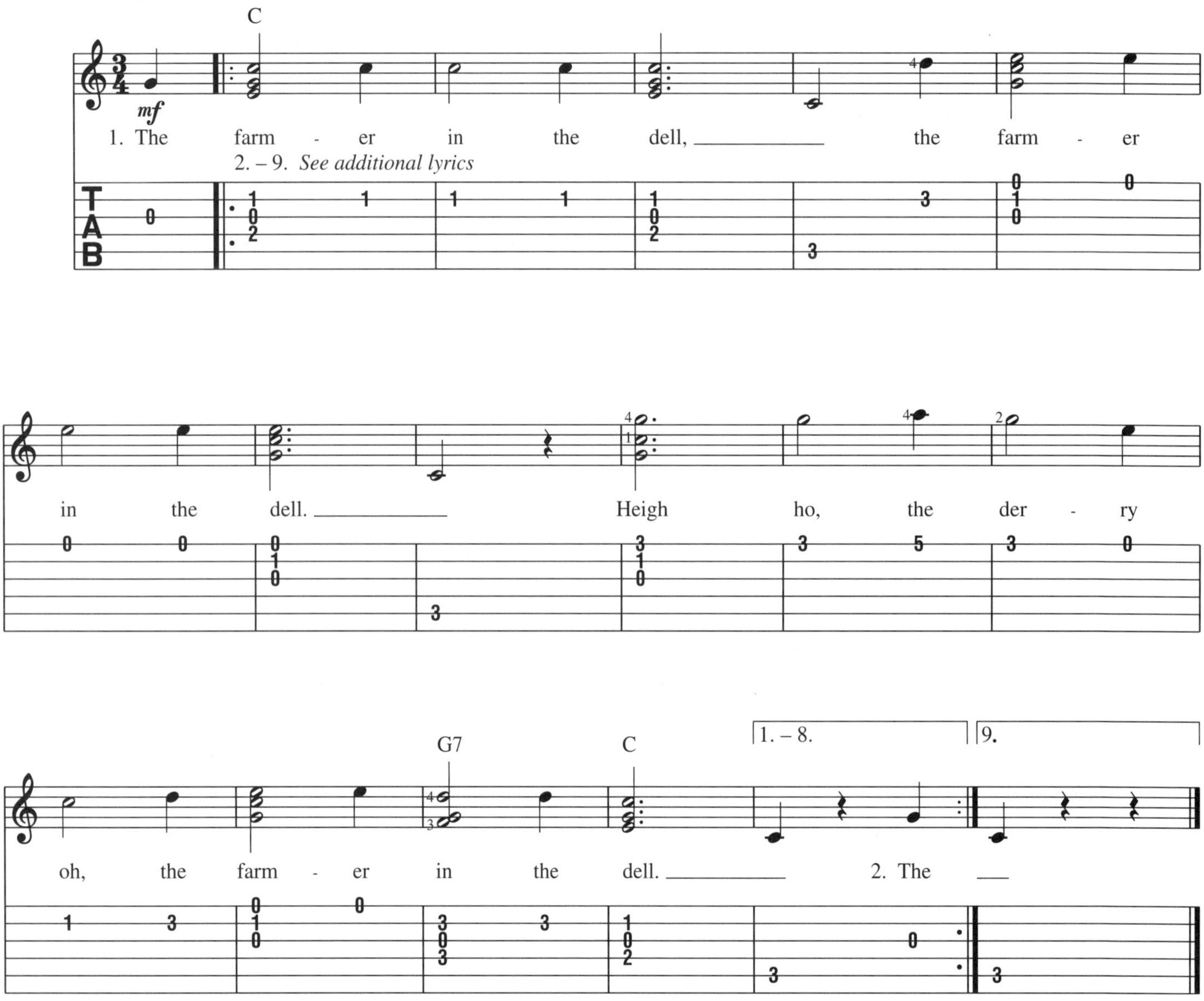

Additional Lyrics

2. The farmer takes a wife,
   The farmer takes a wife,
   Heigh ho, the derry oh,
   The farmer takes a wife.

3. The wife takes a child, etc.

4. The child takes a nurse, etc.

5. The nurse takes a dog, etc.

6. The dog takes a cat, etc.

7. The cat takes a rat, etc.

8. The rat takes the cheese, etc.

9. The cheese stands alone, etc.

Frère Jacques
(Are You Sleeping?)

Traditional

Strum Pattern: 5
Pick Pattern: 1

Verse

Moderately

1. Are you sleep-ing, are you sleep-ing, broth-er John, broth-er John?
French: Frè - re Jac - ques, Frè - re Jac - ques, dor - mez vous, dor - mez vous?

Morn-ing bells are ring - ing, morn-ing bells are ring - ing, ding ding dong, ding ding dong.
Son nez les ma - ti - nes, son-nez les - ma - ti - nes, din din don, din din don.

Verse

2. Are you sleep-ing, are you sleep-ing, broth-er John, broth-er John?
Frè - re Jac - ques, Frè - re Jac - ques, dor - mez vous, dor - mez vous?

Morn-ing bells are ring - ing, morn-ing bells are ring - ing, ding ding dong, ding ding dong.
Son - nez les ma - ti - nes, son-nez les - ma - ti - nes, din din don, din din don.

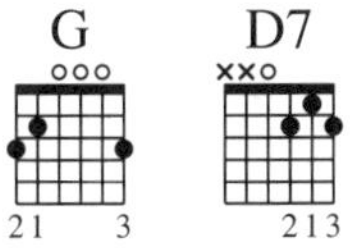

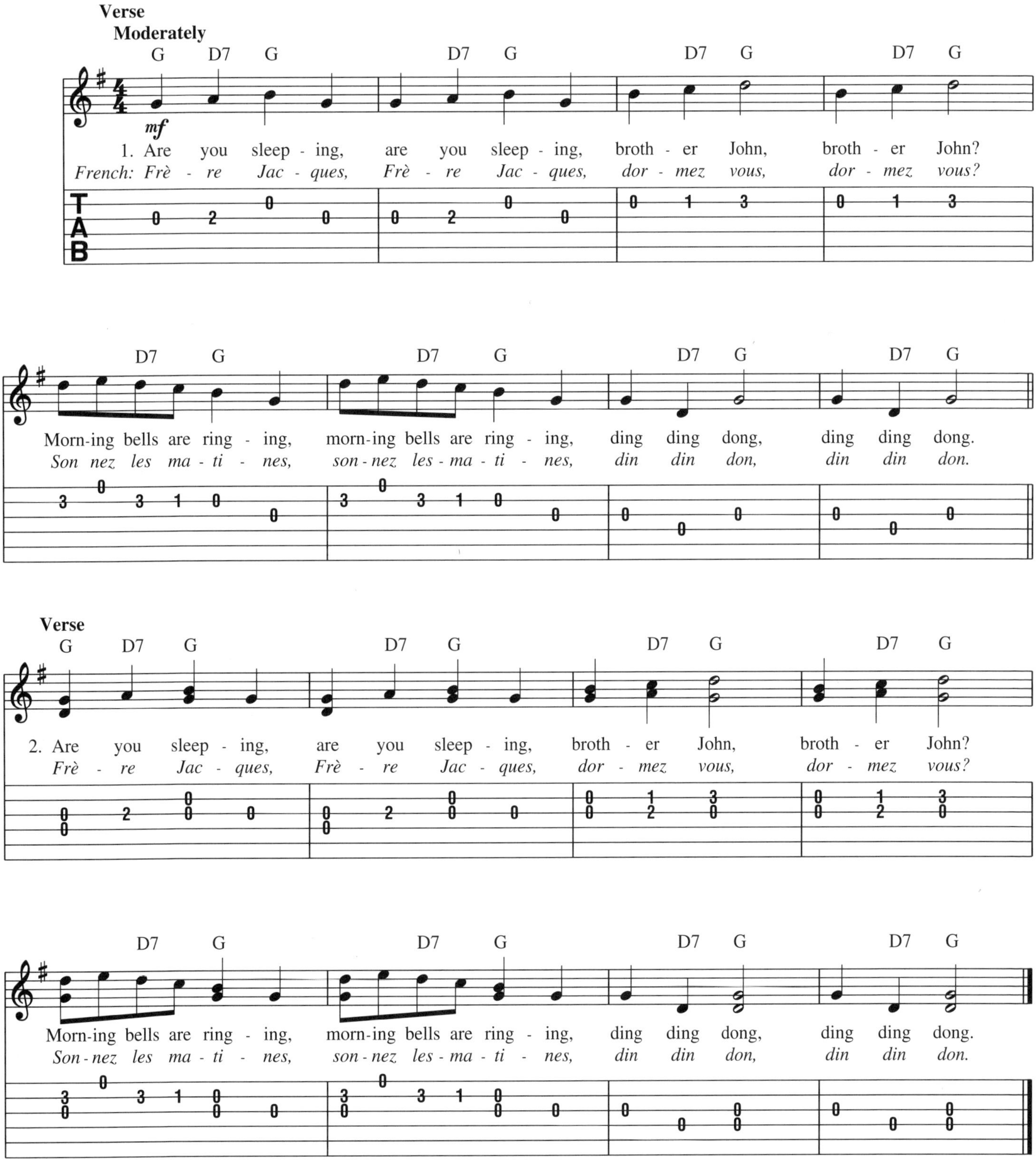

For He's a Jolly Good Fellow

Traditional

Strum Pattern: 7, 8
Pick Pattern: 8

Moderately

For he's a jol - ly good fel - low, for

he's a jol - ly good fel - low, for

he's a jol - ly good fel - low, which

no - bod - y can de - ny! _____ Which

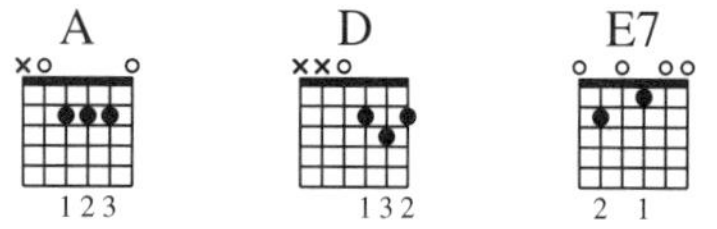

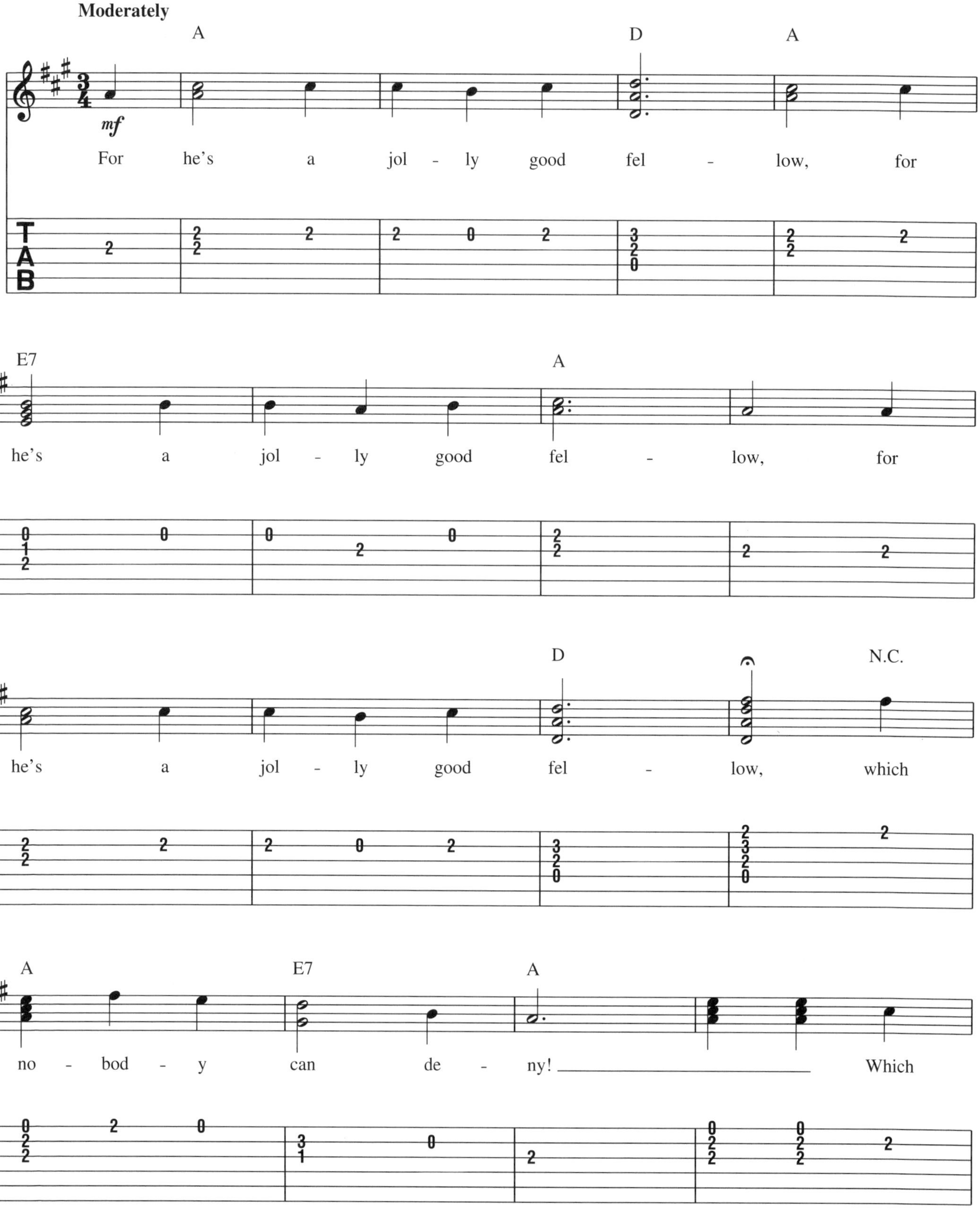

D A
no - bod - y can de - ny! Which
D A
no - bod - y can de - ny! For
D
he's a jol - ly good fel - low, which
A E7 A
no - bod - y can de - ny!

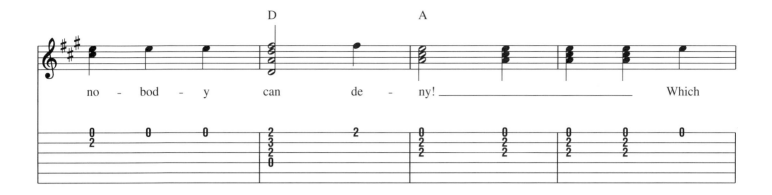

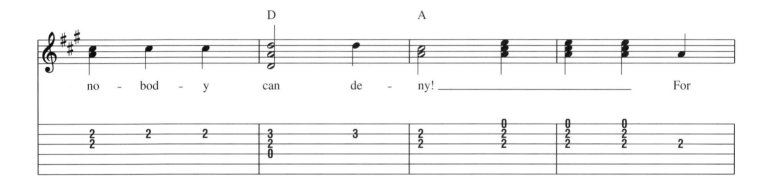

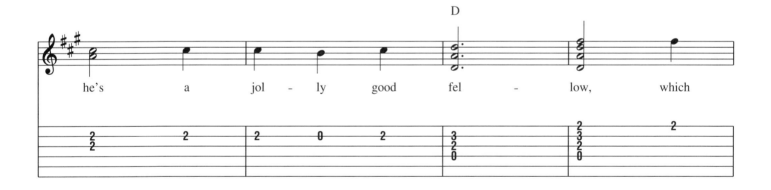

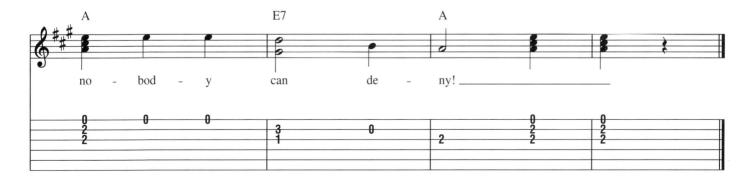

Frog Went A-Courtin'

Traditional

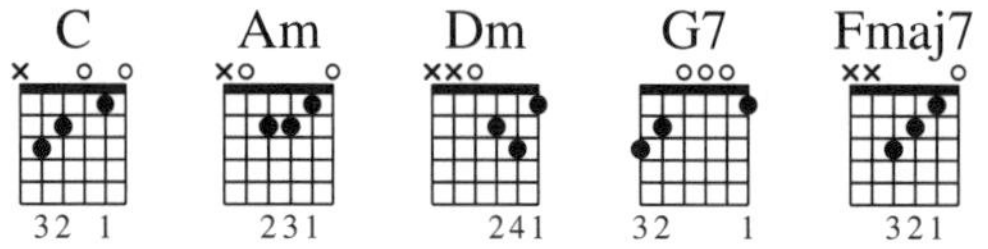

Strum Pattern: 4
Pick Pattern: 5

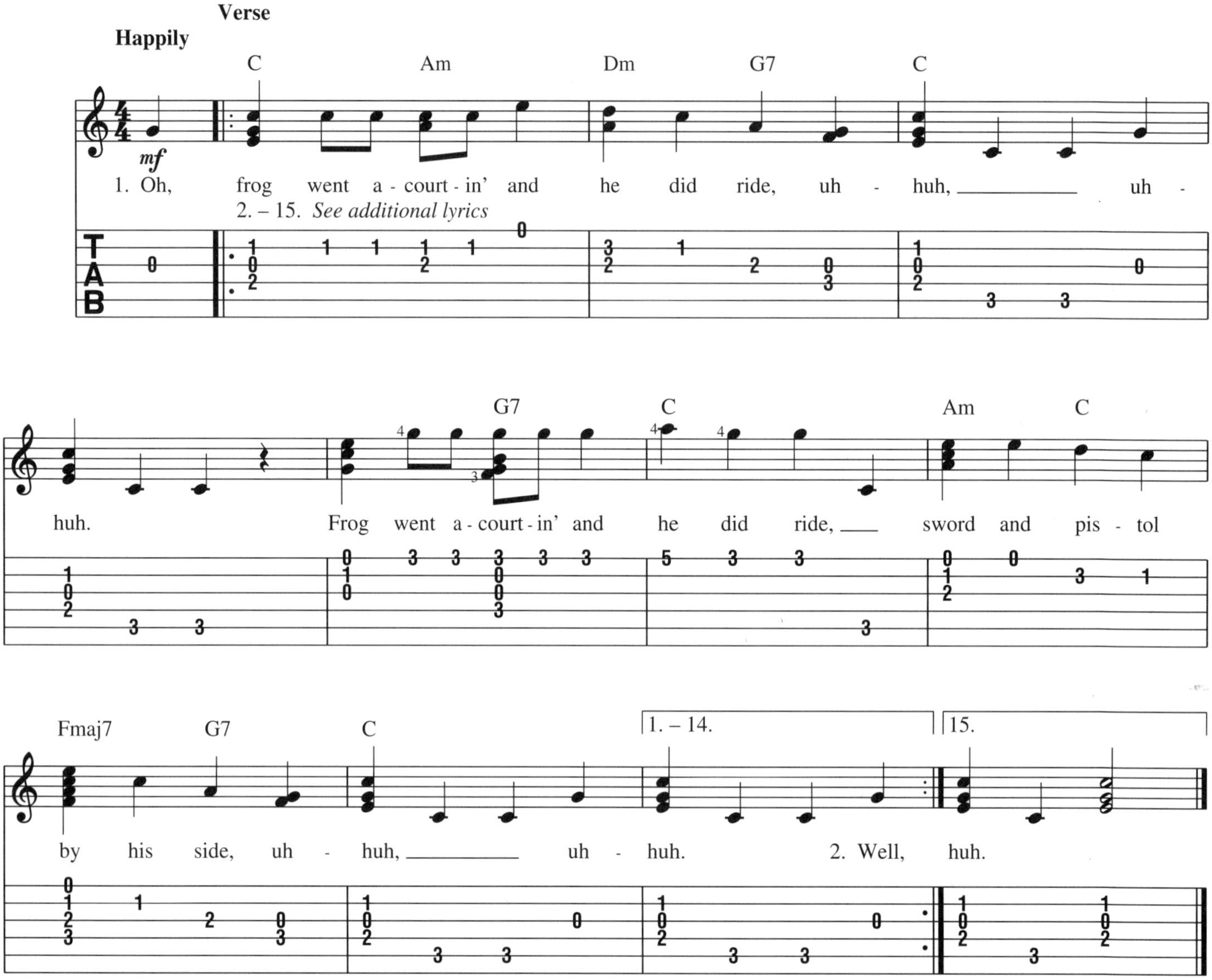

Additional Lyrics

2. Well, he rode down to Miss Mousie's door, uh-huh, uh-huh,
   Well, he rode down to Miss Mousie's door,
   Where he had often been before, uh-huh, uh-huh.

3. He took Miss Mousie on his knee, uh-huh, uh-huh,
   He took Miss Mousie on his knee,
   Said, "Miss Mousie will you marry me?" Uh-huh, uh-huh.

4. "I'll have to ask my Uncle Rat, etc.
   See what he will say to that." etc.

5. "Without my Uncle Rat's consent,
   I would not marry the President."

6. Well, Uncle Rat laughed
   And shook his fat sides,
   To think his niece would be a bride.

7. Well, Uncle Rat rode off to town,
   To buy his niece a wedding gown.

8. "Where will the wedding supper be?"
   "Way down yonder in a hollow tree."

9. "What will the wedding supper be?"
   "A fried mosquito and a roasted flea."

10. First to come in were two little ants,
    Fixing around to have a dance.

11. Next to come in was a bumble bee,
    Bouncing a fiddle on his knee.

12. Next to come in was a fat sassy lad,
    Thinks himself as big as his dad.

13. Thinks himself a man indeed,
    Because he chews the tobacco weed.

14. And next to come in was a big tomcat,
    He swallowed the frog
    And the mouse and the rat.

15. Next to come in was a big old snake,
    He chased the party into the lake.

Go Tell Aunt Rhody

Traditional

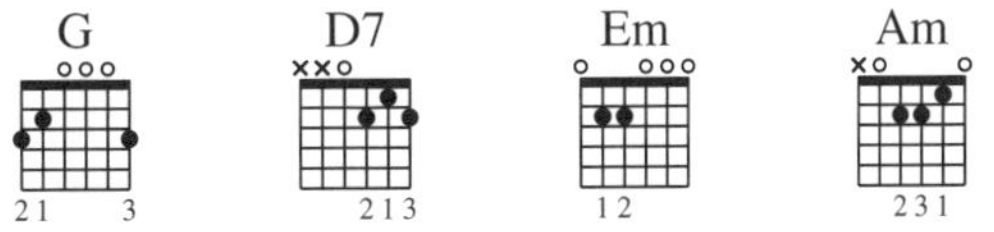

Strum Pattern: 3
Pick Pattern: 3

Verse
Slowly

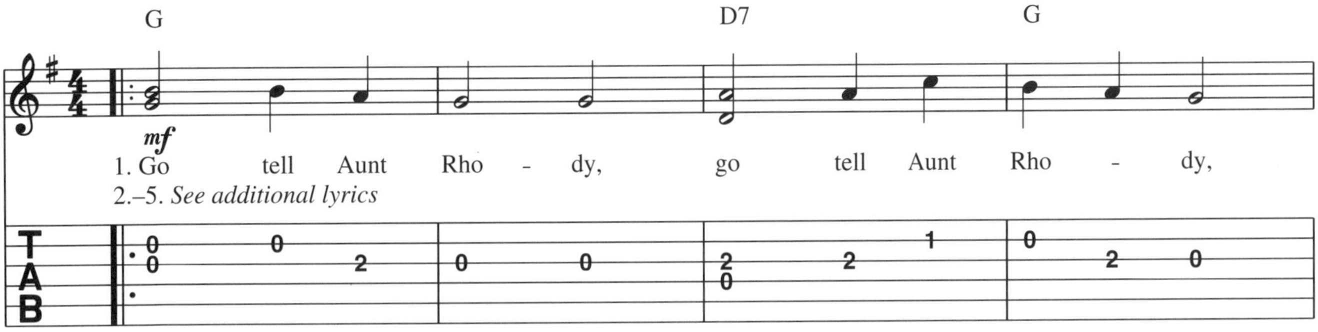

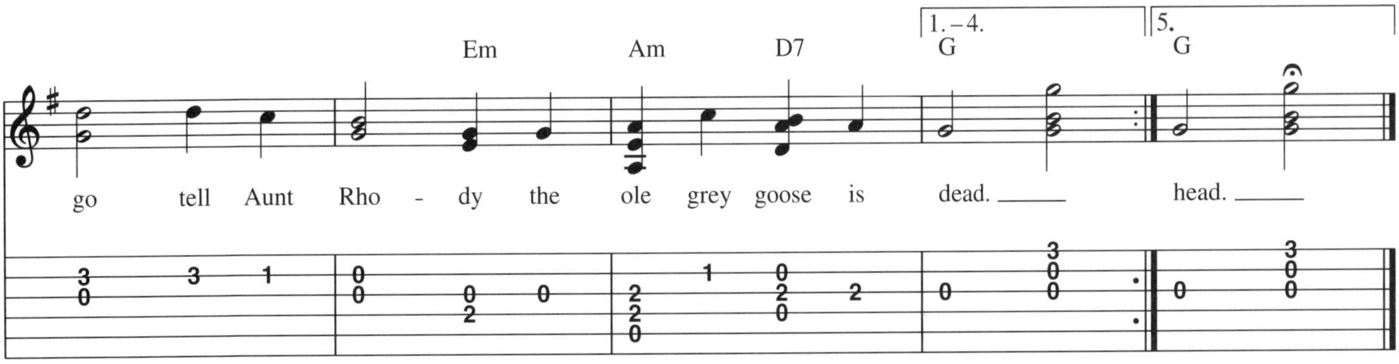

Additional Lyrics

2. The one she was saving,
   The one she was saving,
   The one she was saving,
   To make a feather bed.

3. The gander is weeping,
   The gander is weeping,
   The gander is weeping,
   Because his wife is dead.

4. The goslings are crying,
   The goslings are crying,
   The goslings are crying,
   Because their mama's dead.

5. She died in the water,
   She died in the water,
   She died in the water,
   With her heels above her head.

Git Along, Little Dogies
Western American Cowboy Song
C F G7 C7
Strum Pattern: 7
Pick Pattern: 8
Verse
Moderately
mf
1. As I was a - walk - in' one morn - ing for pleas - ure, I
2.–7. See additional lyrics
spied a cow - punch - er a - stroll - in' a - long. His had was throwed back and his
spurs were a - jin - glin', and as he ap - proached he was sing - ing this song. Whoop-ee
Chorus
ti - yi - yo, git a - long lit - tle do - gies; it's your mis -

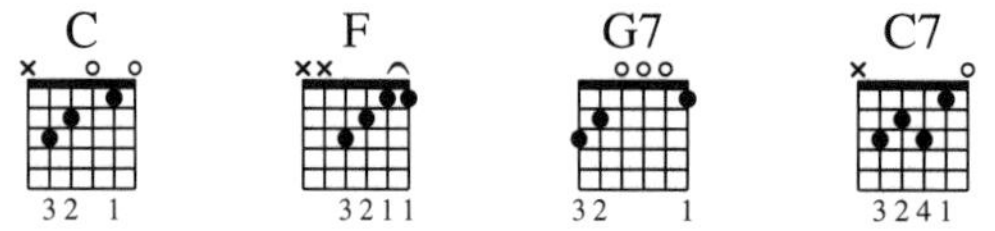

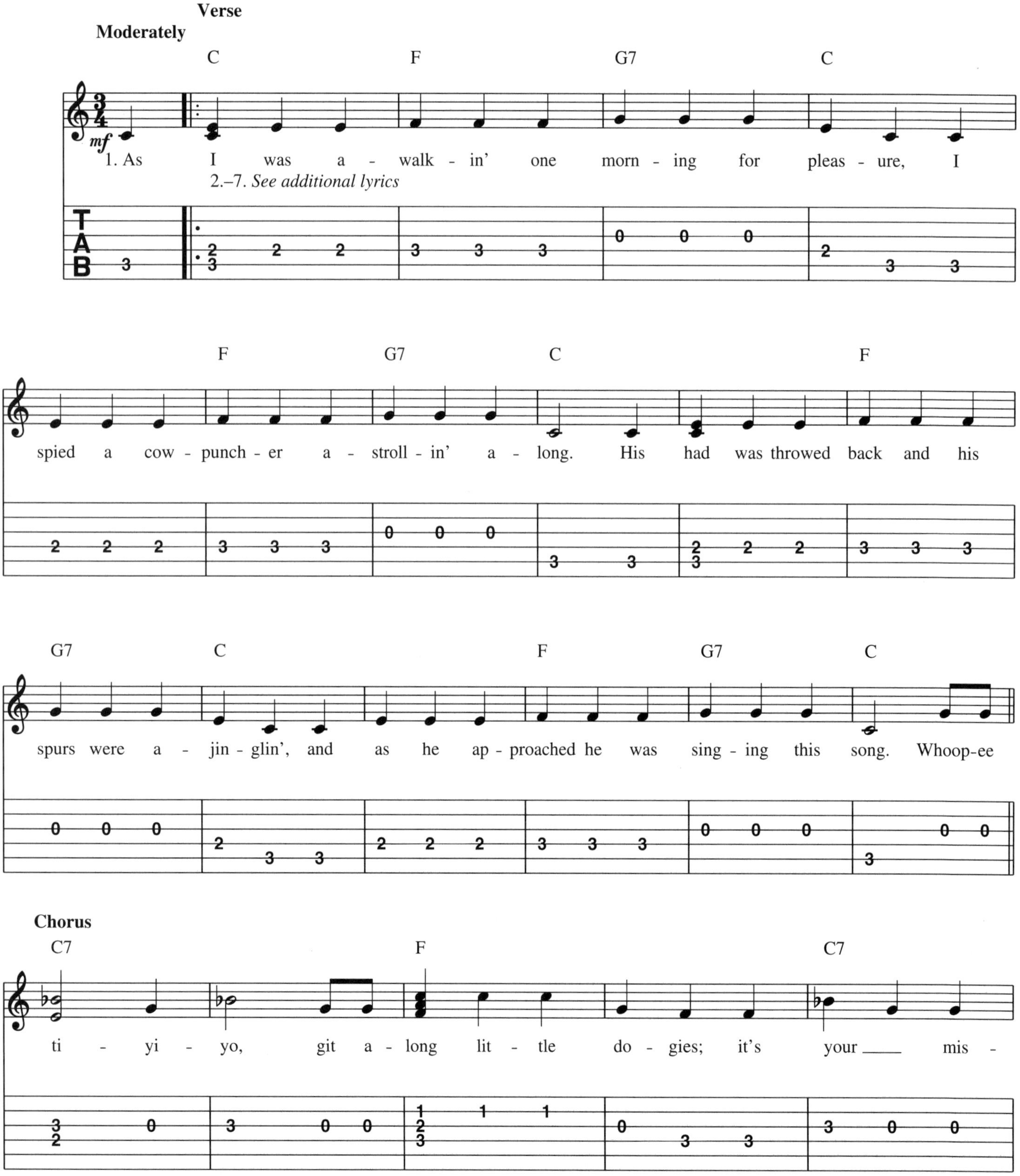

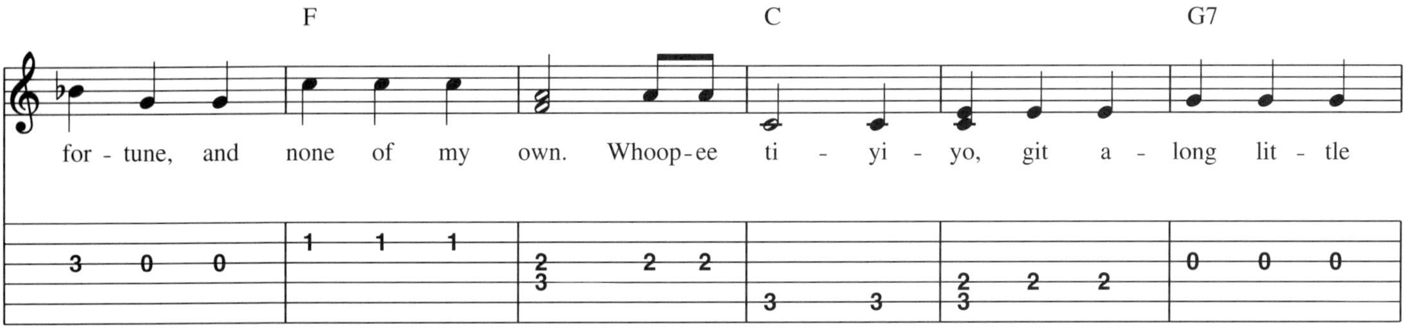

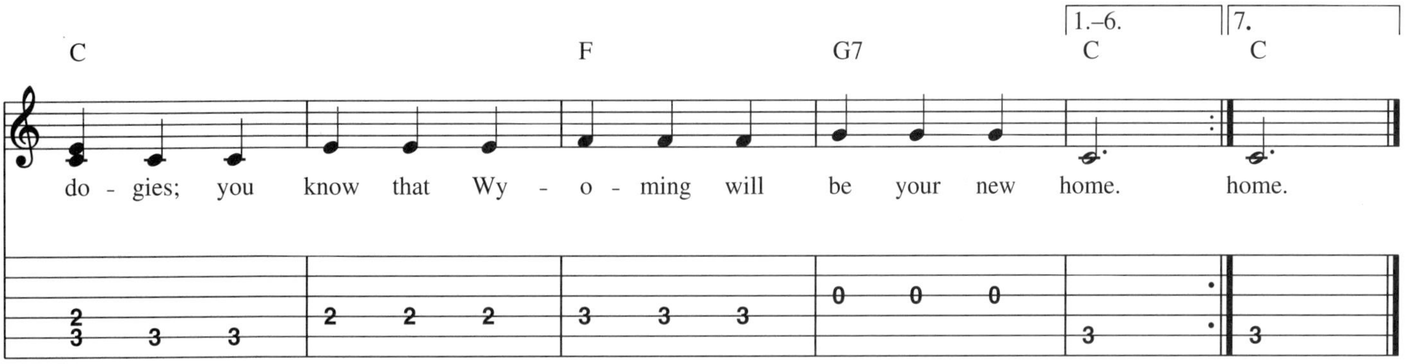

Additional Lyrics

2. Early in the springtime we'll round up the dogies,
   Slap on their brands and bob off their tails;
   Round up our horses, load up the chuck wagon,
   Then throw those dogies upon the trail.

3. It's whooping and yelling and driving the dogies,
   Oh, how I wish you would go on.
   It's whooping and punching and go on, little dogies,
   For you know Wyoming will be your new home.

4. Some of the boys goes up the trails for pleasure,
   But that's where they git it most awfully wrong;
   For you haven't any idea the trouble they give us,
   When we go driving them dogies along.

5. When the night comes on and we hold them on the bed-ground,
   These little dogies that roll on so slow;
   Roll up the herd and cut out the strays,
   And roll the little dogies that never rolled before.

6. Your mother she was raised way down in Texas,
   Where the jimson weed and sandburs grow;
   Now we'll fill you up on prickly pear and cholla,
   Till you are ready for the trail to Idaho.

7. Oh, you'll be soup for Uncle Sam's Injuns,
   "It's beef, heap beef," I hear them cry.
   Git along, git along, git along, little dogies,
   You're going to be beef steers by and by.

Goober Peas

Words by P. Pindar
Music by P. Nutt

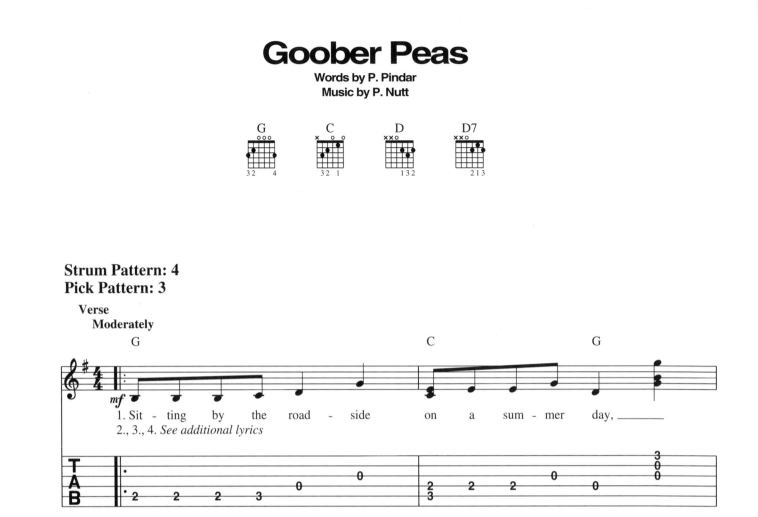

Strum Pattern: 4
Pick Pattern: 3

Verse
Moderately

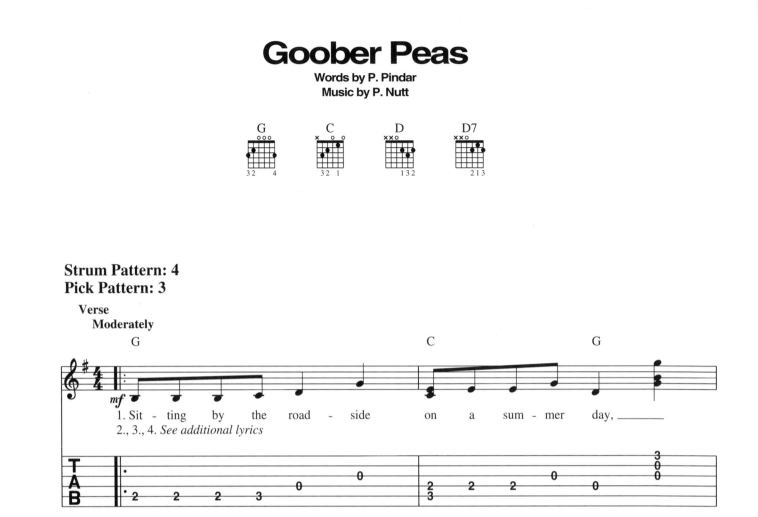

1. Sit - ting by the road - side on a sum - mer day, _____
2., 3., 4. *See additional lyrics*

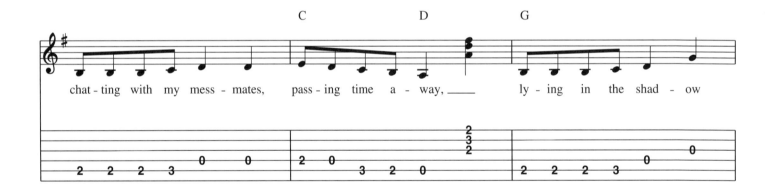

chat - ting with my mess - mates, pass - ing time a - way, _____ ly - ing in the shad - ow

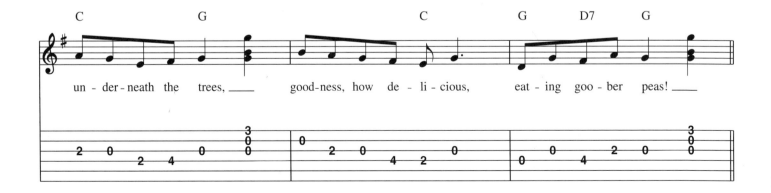

un - der - neath the trees, _____ good - ness, how de - li - cious, eat - ing goo - ber peas! _____

Chorus

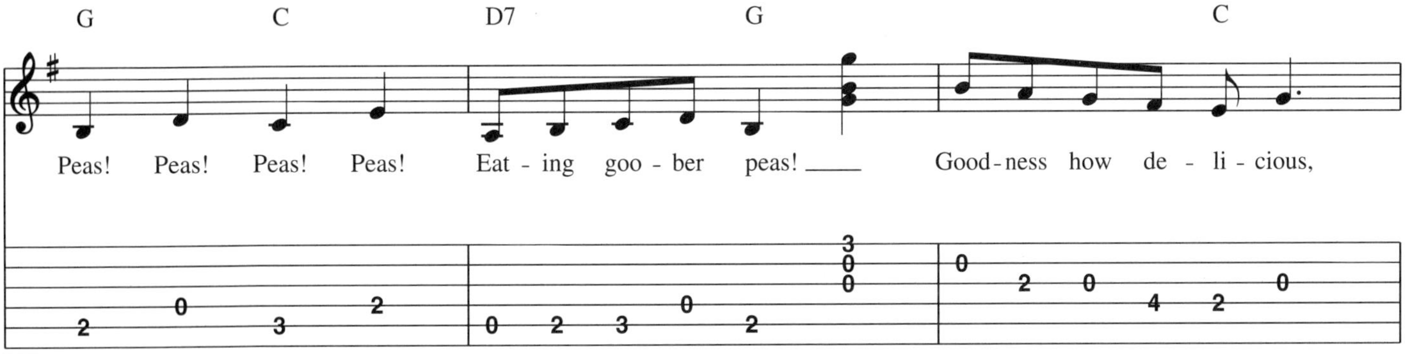

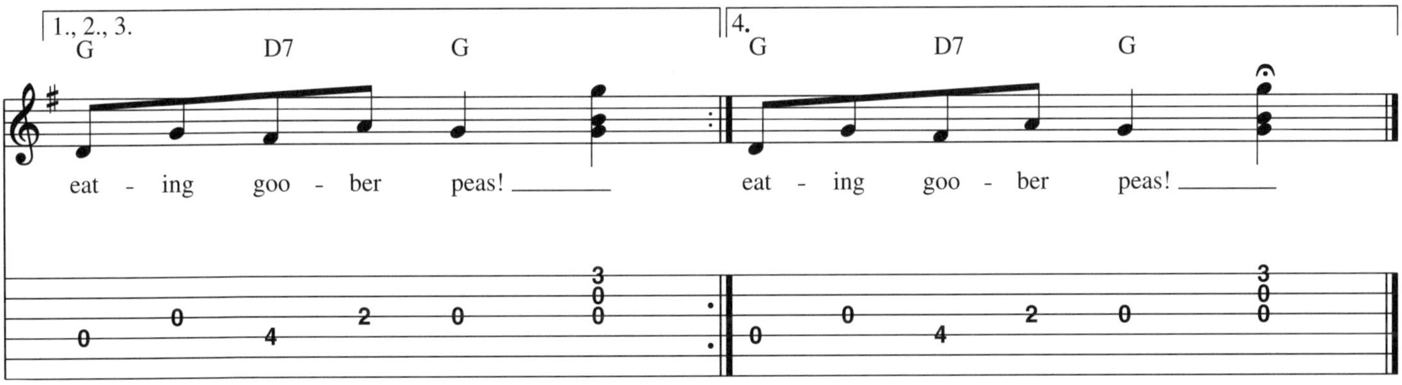

Additional Lyrics

2. When a horseman passes, the soldiers have a rule,
   To cry out at their loudest, "Mister, here's your mule!"
   But another pleasure enchantinger than these,
   Is wearing out your grinders, eating goober peas!

3. Just before the battle the Gen'ral hears a row,
   He says, "The Yanks are coming, I hear their rifles now."
   He turns around in wonder, and what do you think he sees?
   The Georgia Militia—eating goober peas!

4. I think my song has lasted almost long enough,
   The subject's interesting, but rhymes are mighty rough,
   I wish this war was over, when free from rags and fleas,
   We'd kiss our wives and sweethearts and gobble goober peas!

Goosey, Goosey Gander

Traditional

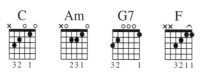

Strum Pattern: 10
Pick Pattern: 10

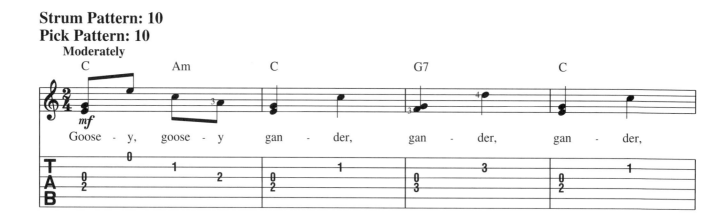

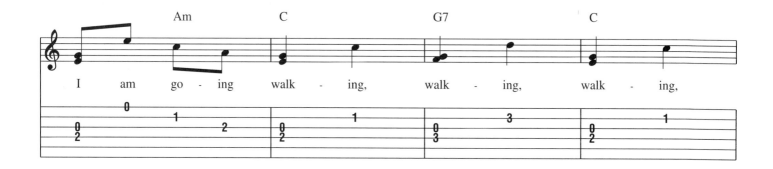

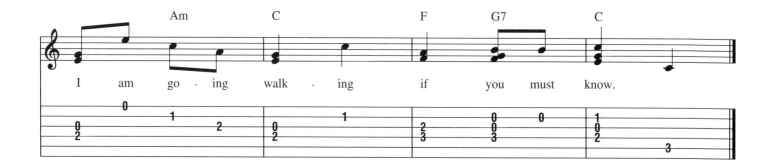

Hail, Hail, the Gang's All Here

Words by D.A. Esrom
Music by Theodore F. Morse and Arthur Sullivan

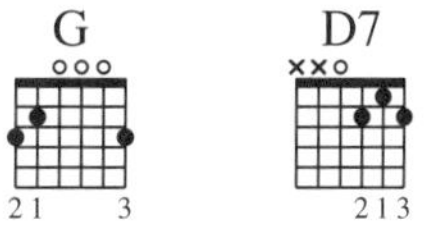

Strum Pattern: 7, 8
Pick Pattern: 7, 8

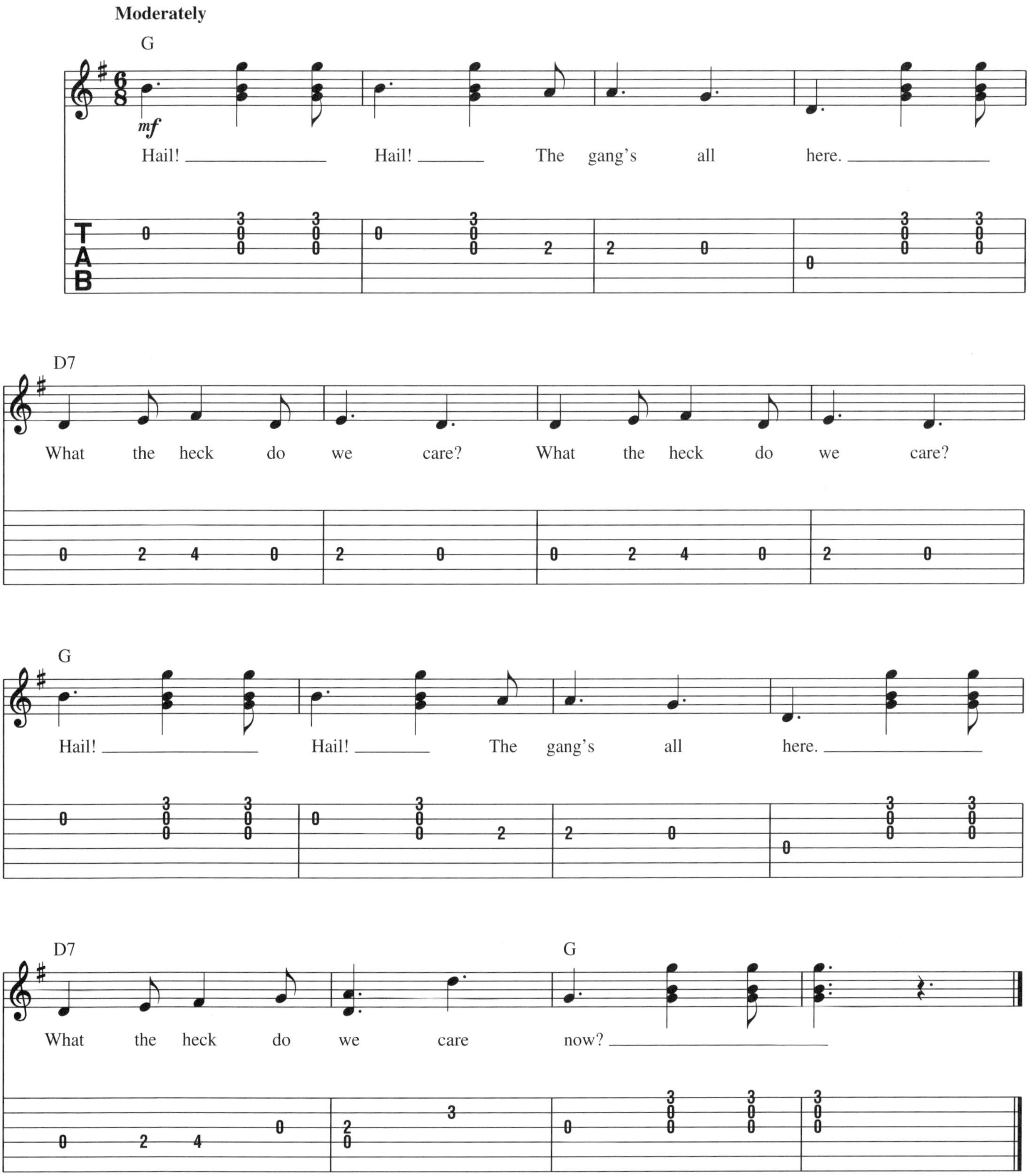

Grandfather's Clock

By Henry Clay Work

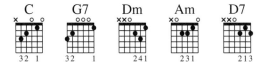

Strum Pattern: 3
Pick Pattern: 3

Verse
Moderately slow

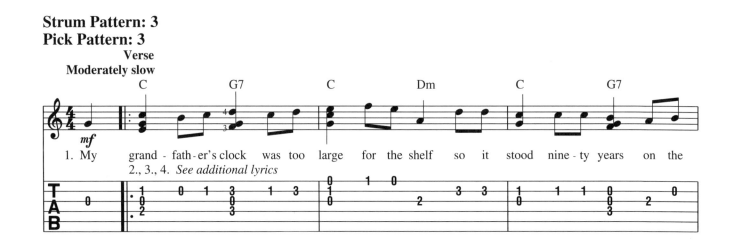

1. My grand-fath-er's clock was too large for the shelf so it stood nine-ty years on the
2., 3., 4. *See additional lyrics*

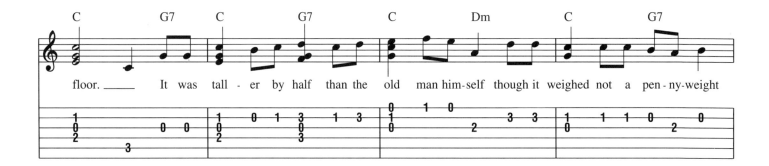

floor. ___ It was tall-er by half than the old man him-self though it weighed not a pen-ny-weight

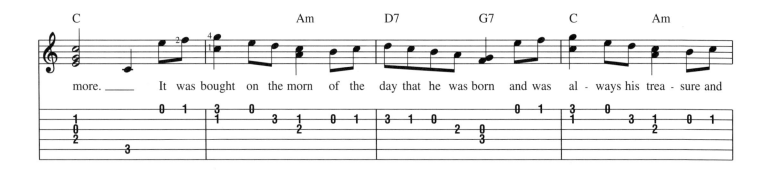

more. ___ It was bought on the morn of the day that he was born and was al-ways his trea-sure and

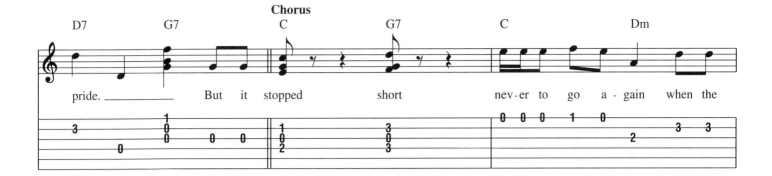

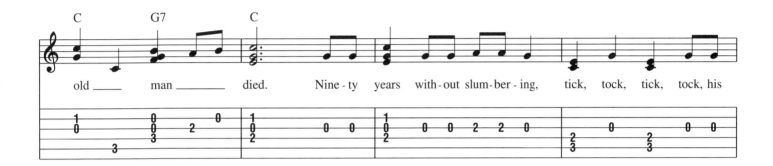

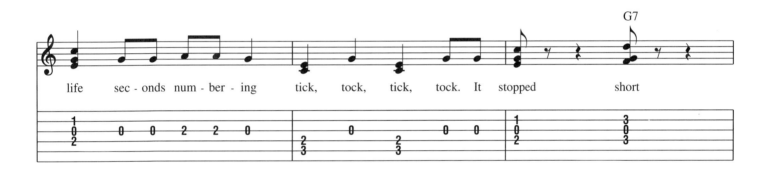

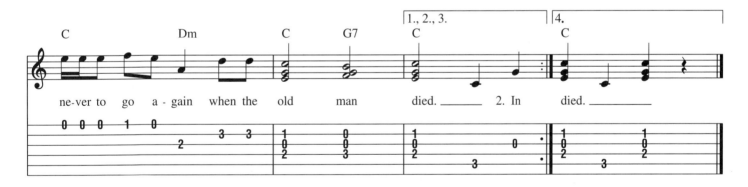

Additional Lyrics

2. In watching its pendulum swing to and fro,
   Many hours had he spent while a boy;
   And in childhood and manhood the clock seemed to know,
   And to share both his grief and his joy.
   For it struck twenty-four when he entered at the door,
   With a blooming and beautiful bride.

3. My grandfather said that of those he could hire,
   Not a servant so faithful he found;
   For it wasted no time, and had but one desire,
   At the close of each week to be wound.
   And it kept in its place, not a frown upon its face,
   And its hands never hung by its side.

4. It rang an alarm in the dead of the night,
   An alarm that for years had been dumb;
   And we knew that his spirit was pluming its flight,
   That his hour of departure had come.
   Still the clock kept the time, with a soft and muffled chime,
   As we silently stood by his side.

He's Got the Whole World in His Hands

Traditional Spiritual

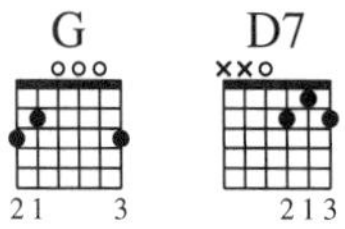

Strum Pattern: 3, 4
Pick Pattern: 1, 3

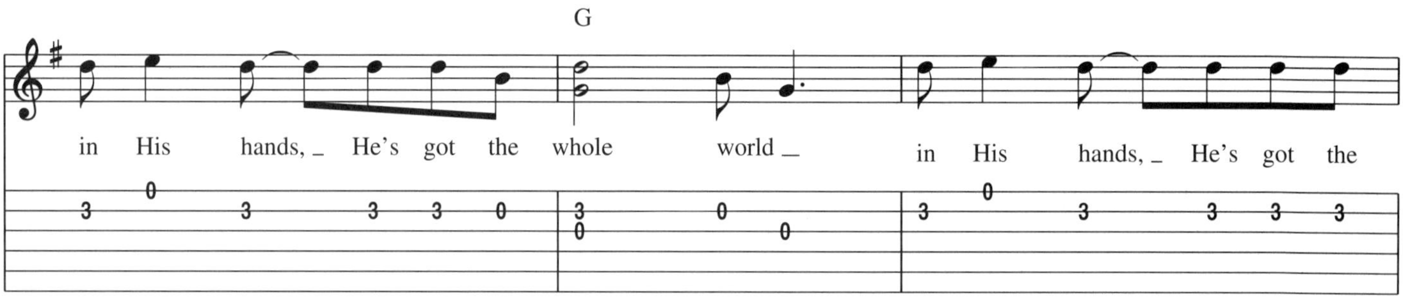

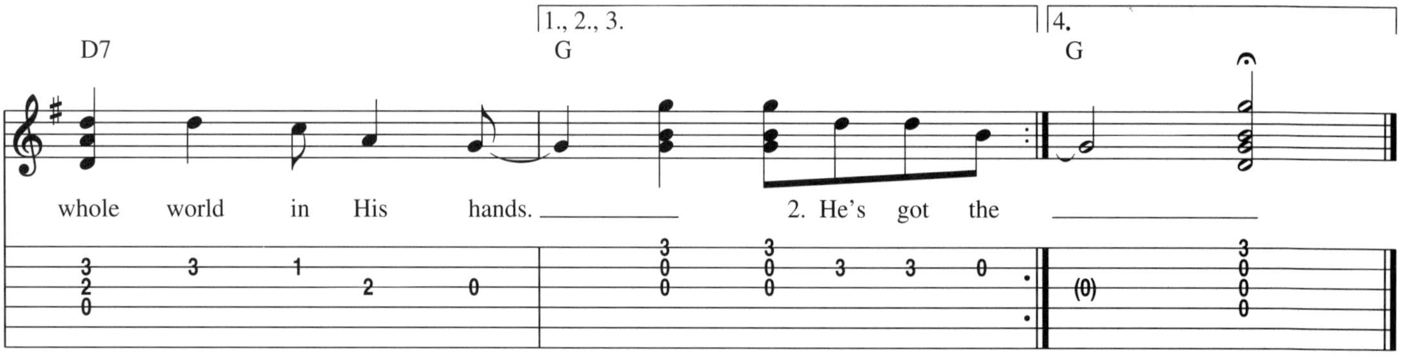

Additional Lyrics

2. He's got the wind and the rain in His hands,
He's got the wind and the rain in His hands,
He's got the wind and the rain in His hands,
He's got the whole world in His hands.

3. He's got the tiny little baby in His hands,
He's got the tiny little baby in His hands,
He's got the tiny little baby in His hands,
He's got the whole world in His hands.

4. He's got you and me, brother, in his hands,
He's got you and me, sister, in his hands,
He's got you and me, brother, in his hands,
He's got the whole world in his hands.

Hey Diddle Diddle

Traditional

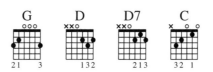

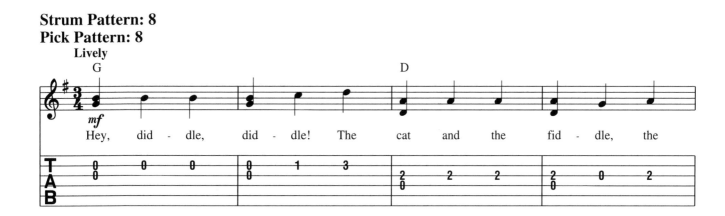

Strum Pattern: 8
Pick Pattern: 8

Lively

Hey, did - dle, did - dle! The cat and the fid - dle, the

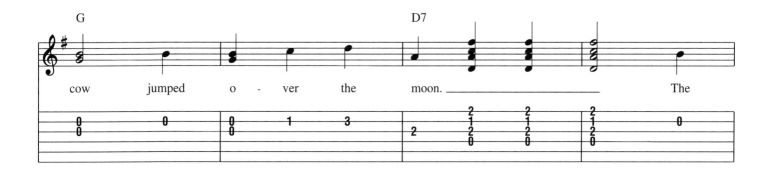

cow jumped o - ver the moon. _____ The

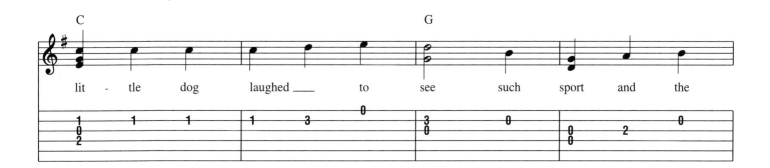

lit - tle dog laughed ____ to see such sport and the

dish ran a - way with the spoon. _____

Hey, Ho! Nobody Home

Traditional

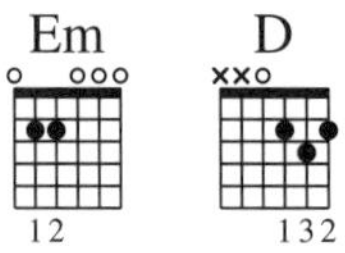

Strum Pattern: 3
Pick Pattern: 3, 4

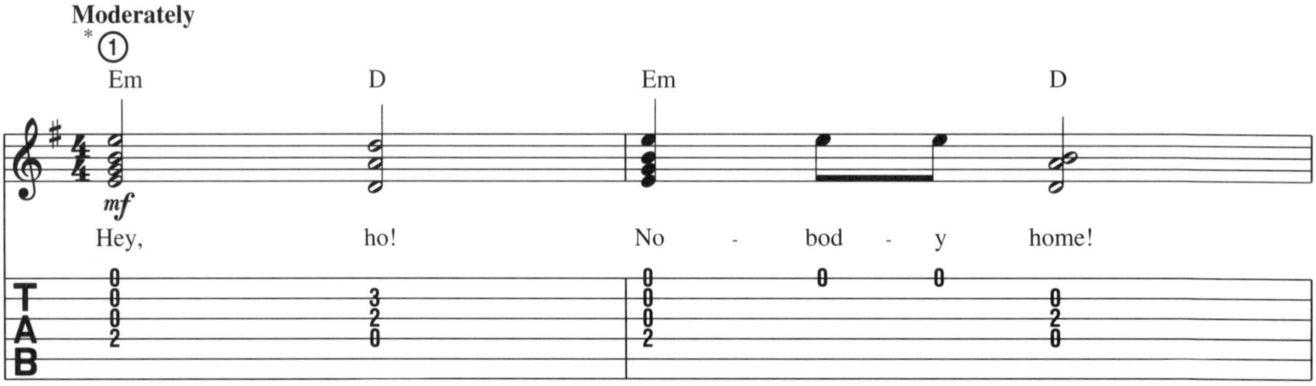

*This song may be sung as a 4-part round.

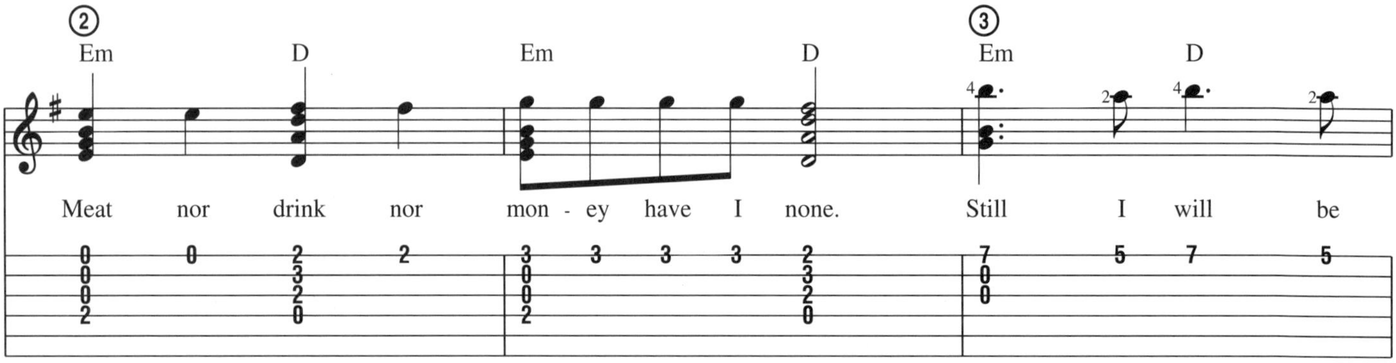

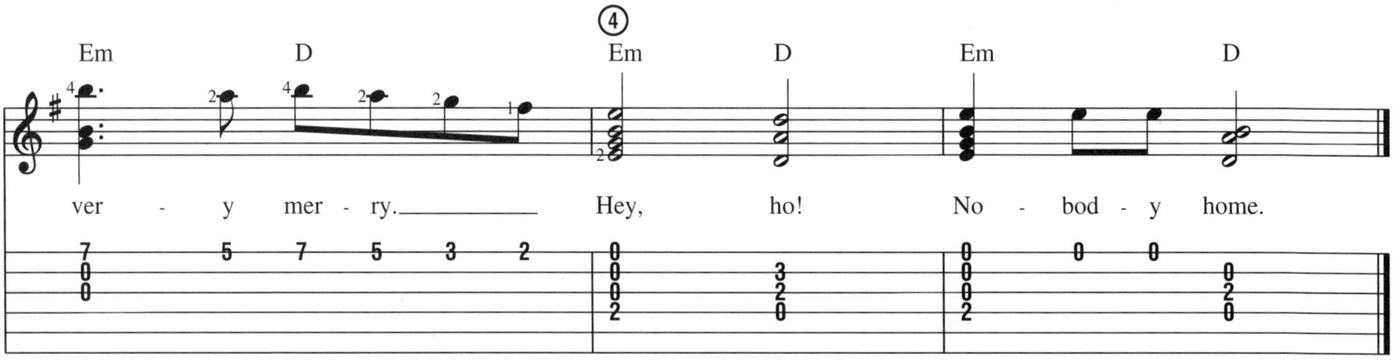

Hickory Dickory Dock

Traditional

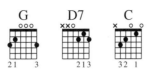

Strum Pattern: 8, 7
Pick Pattern: 8

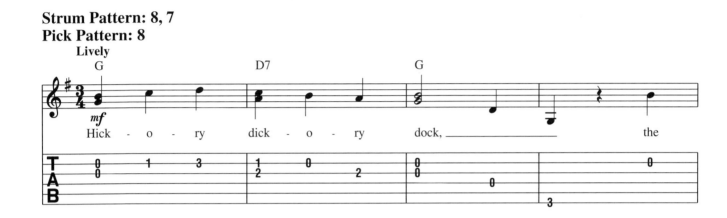

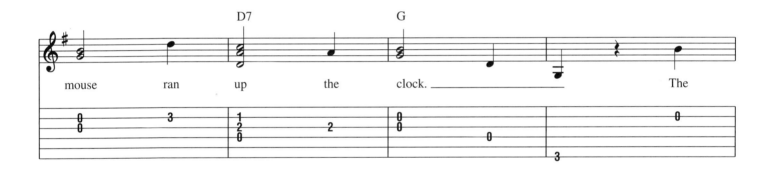

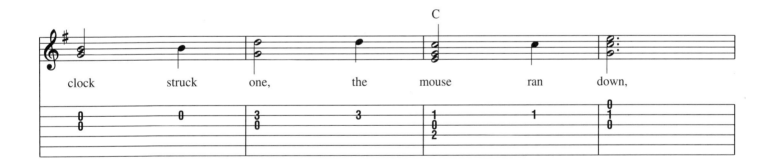

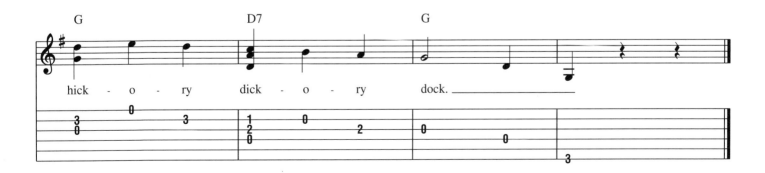

Home on the Range

Lyrics by Dr. Brewster Higley
Music by Dan Kelly

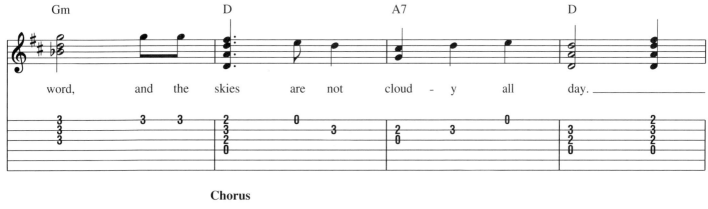

word,   and the   skies   are   not   cloud - y   all   day. ____

Chorus

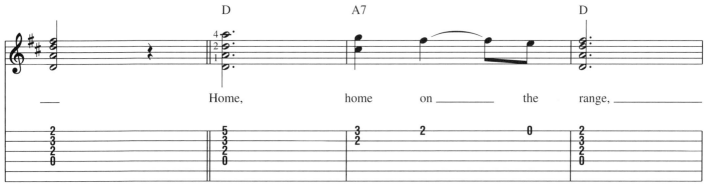

____   Home,   home   on _____   the   range, _____

____   where the   deer   and   the   an - te - lope   play. _____

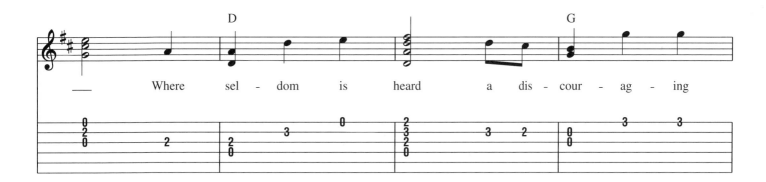

____   Where   sel - dom   is   heard   a   dis - cour - ag - ing

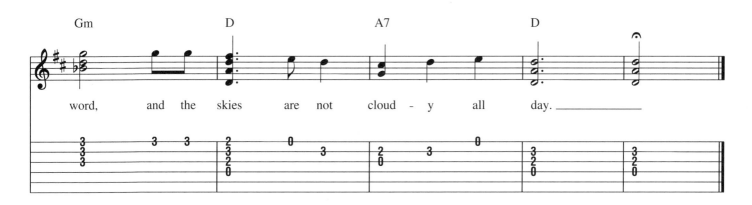

word,   and the   skies   are   not   cloud - y   all   day. _____

Hot Cross Buns

Traditional

Strum Pattern: 10
Pick Pattern: 10

Moderately

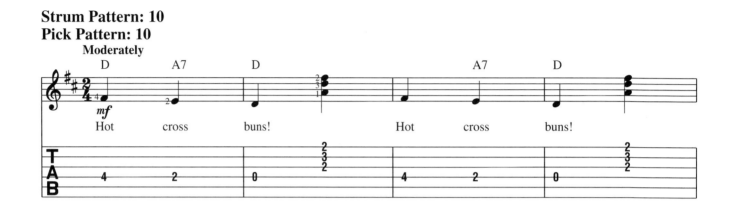

Hot cross buns! Hot cross buns!

One, a pen - ny, two, a pen - ny, hot cross buns!

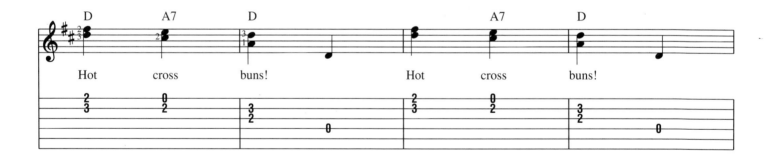

Hot cross buns! Hot cross buns!

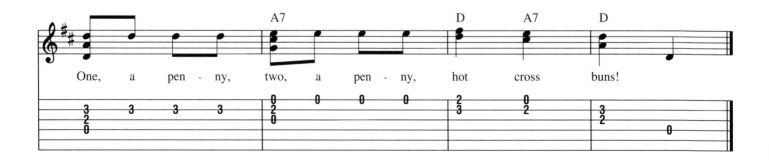

One, a pen - ny, two, a pen - ny, hot cross buns!

Humpty Dumpty

Traditional

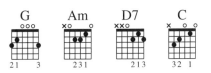

Strum Pattern: 8
Pick Pattern: 8

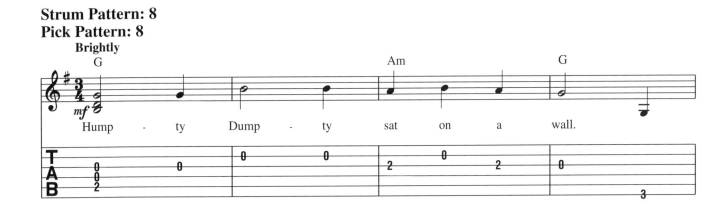

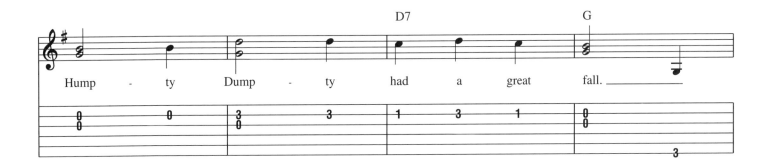

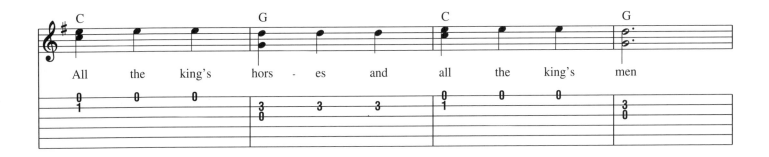

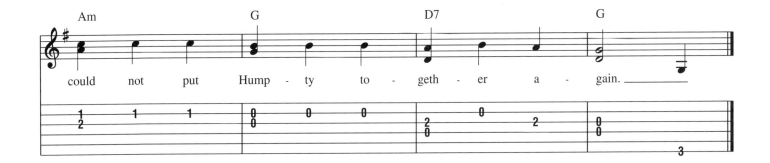

Hush, Little Baby

Carolina Folk Lullaby

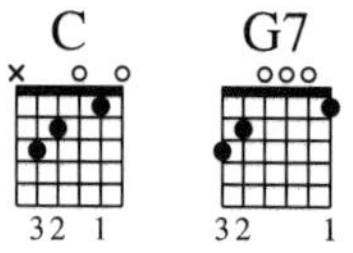

Strum Pattern: 3
Pick Pattern: 4

Verse
Moderately

1. Hush, lit - tle ba - by, don't say a word, Pa - pa's gon - na buy you a
2., 3., 4. *See additional lyrics*

mock - ing bird, and if that mock - ing bird won't sing,

Pap - pa's gon - na buy you a dia - mond ring. 2. And ba - by in town. ___

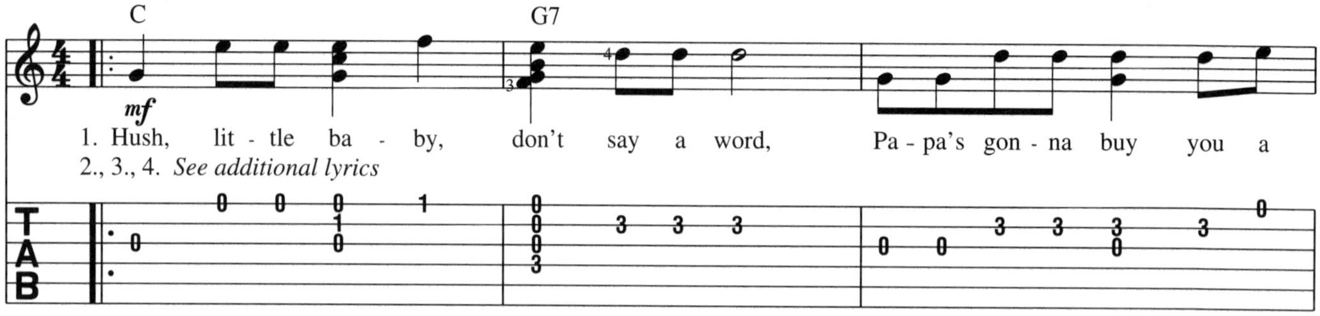

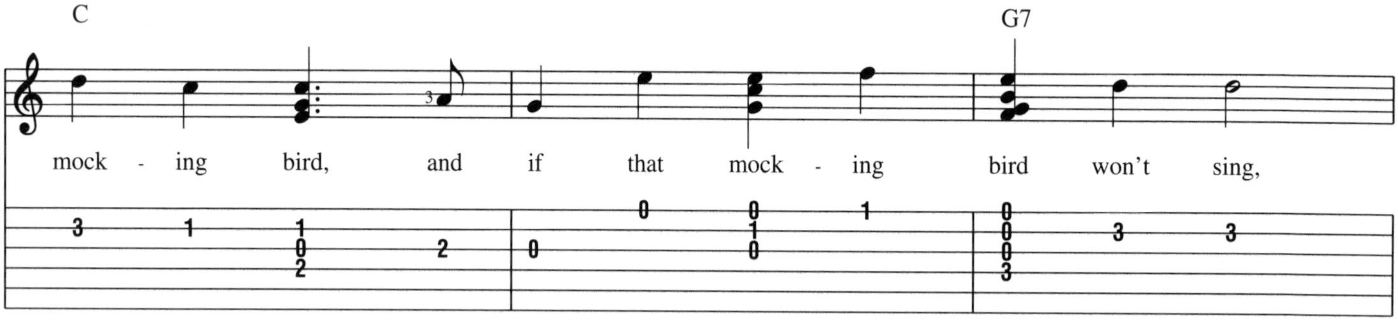

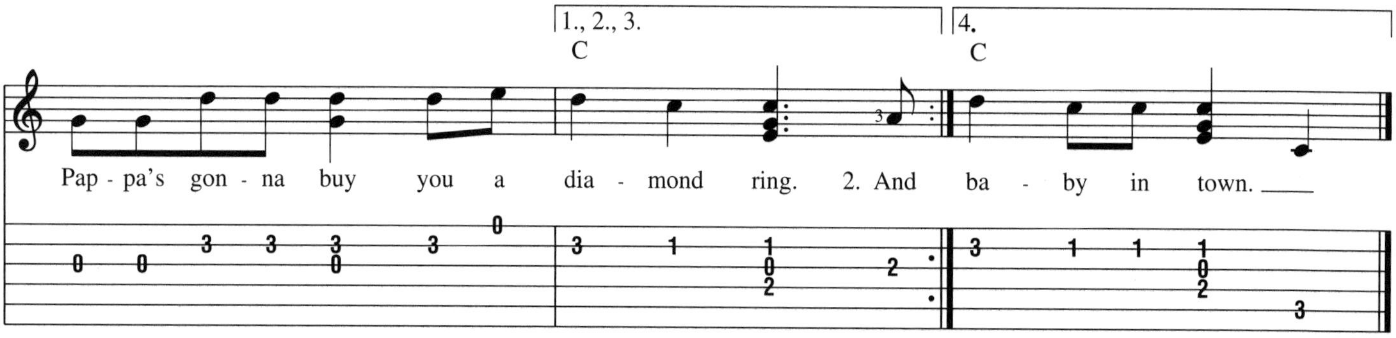

Additional Lyrics

2. And if that diamond ring is brass,
   Papa's gonna buy you a looking glass.
   And if that looking glass gets broke,
   Papa's gonna buy you a billy goat.

3. And if that billy goat don't pull,
   Papa's gonna buy you a cart and bull.
   And if that cart and bull turn over,
   Papa's gonna buy you a dog named Rover.

4. And if that dog named Rover don't bark,
   Papa's gonna buy you a horse and cart.
   And if that horse and cart fall down,
   You'll still be the sweetest little baby in town.

If You're Happy and You Know It

Words and Music by L. Smith

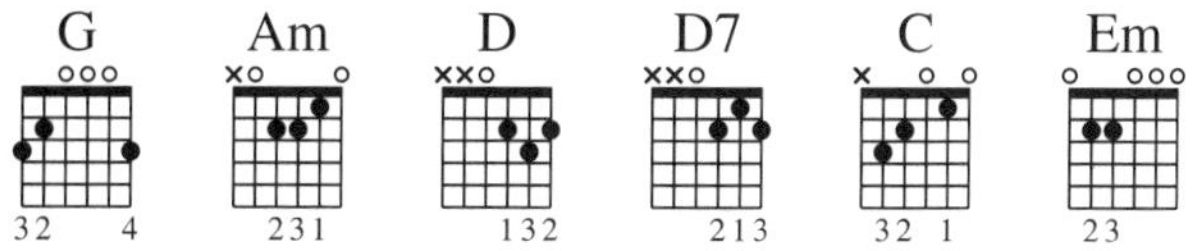

Strum Pattern: 1, 4
Pick Pattern: 2, 5

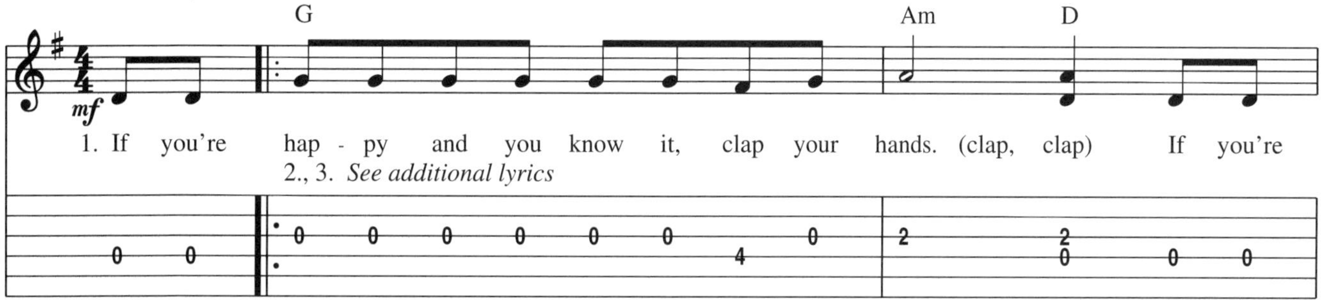

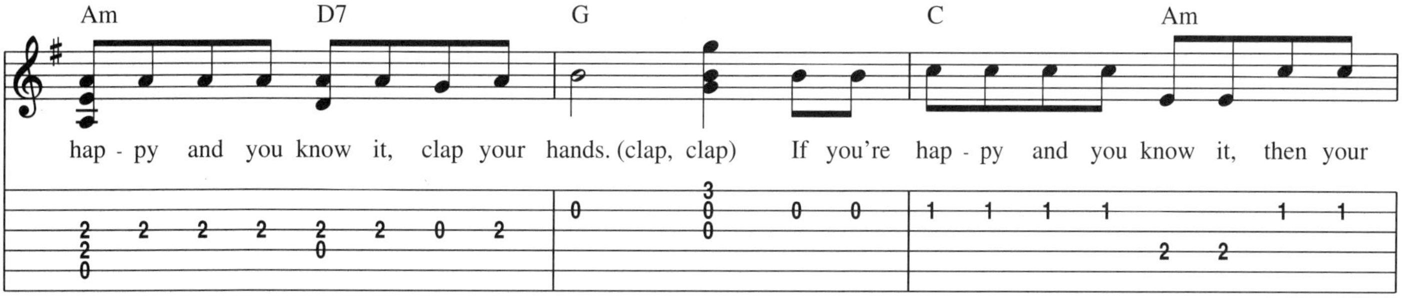

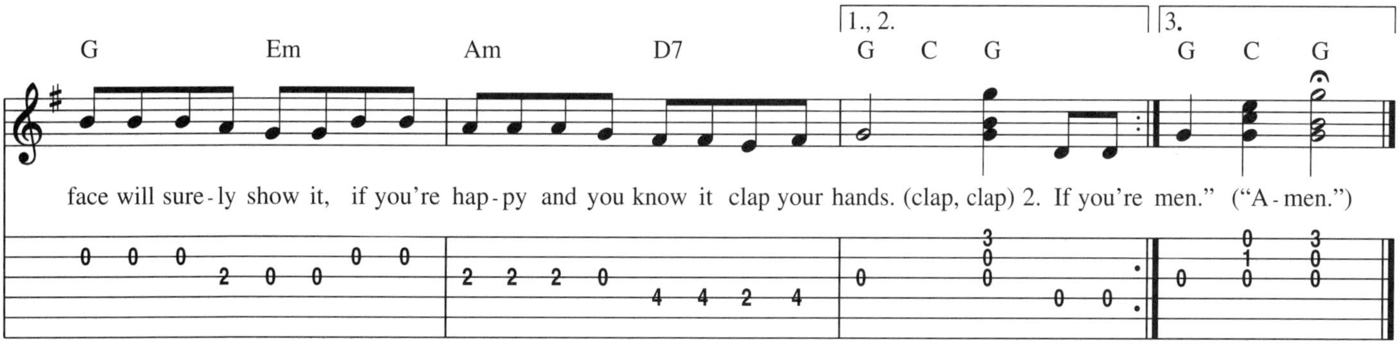

Additional Lyrics

2. If you're happy and you know it, stomp your feet. (stomp, stomp)
   If you're happy and you know it, stomp your feet. (stomp, stomp)
   If you're happy and you know it, then your face will surely show it.
   If you're happy and you know it, stomp your feet. (stomp, stomp)

3. If you're happy and you know it, say "Amen." ("Amen.")
   If you're happy and you know it, say "Amen." ("Amen.")
   If you're happy and you know it, then your face will surely show it.
   If you're happy and you know it, say "Amen." ("Amen.")

I've Been Working on the Railroad

American Folksong

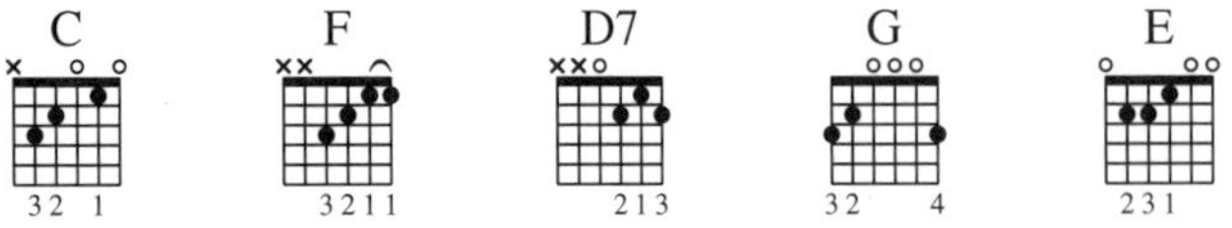

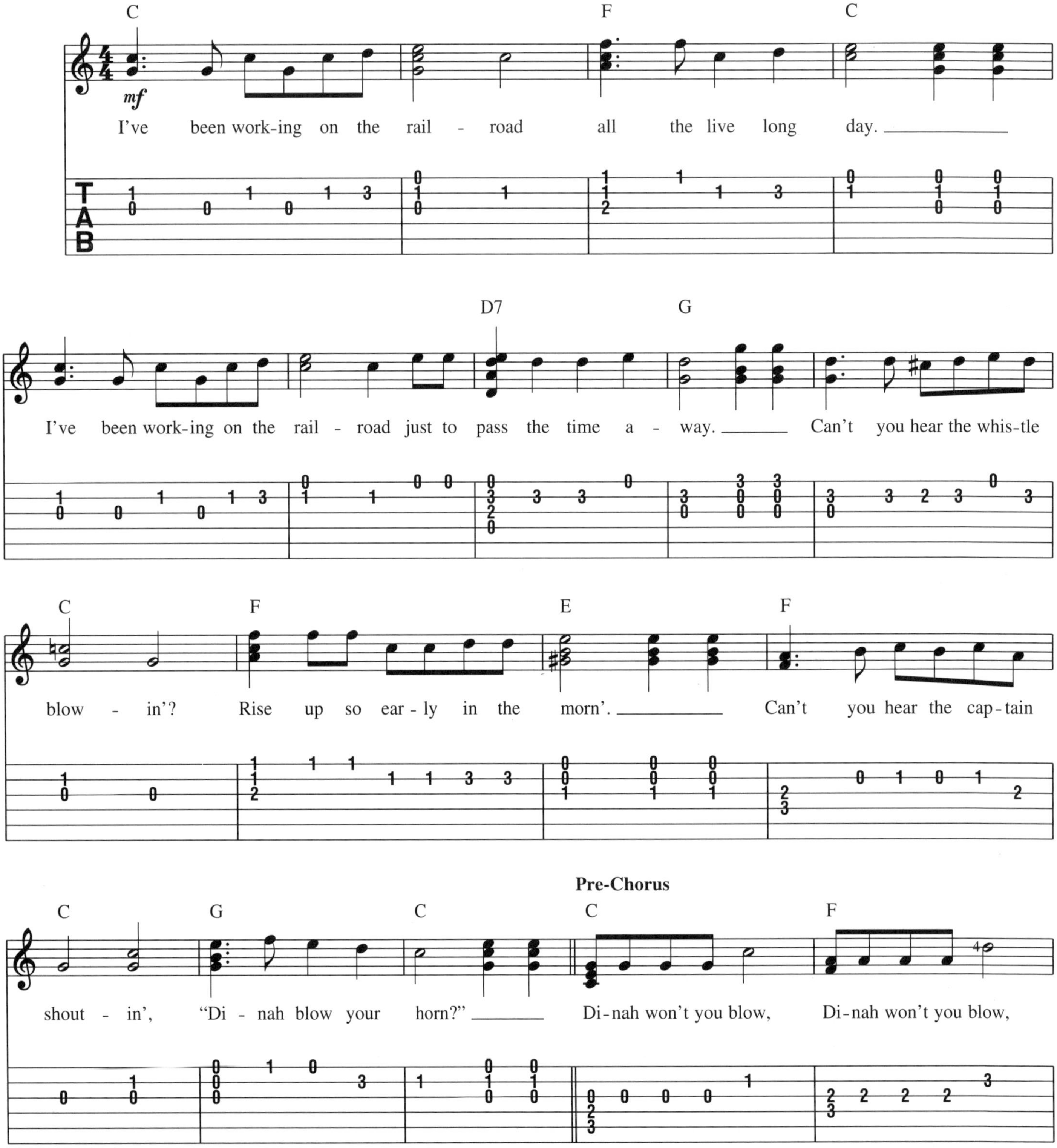

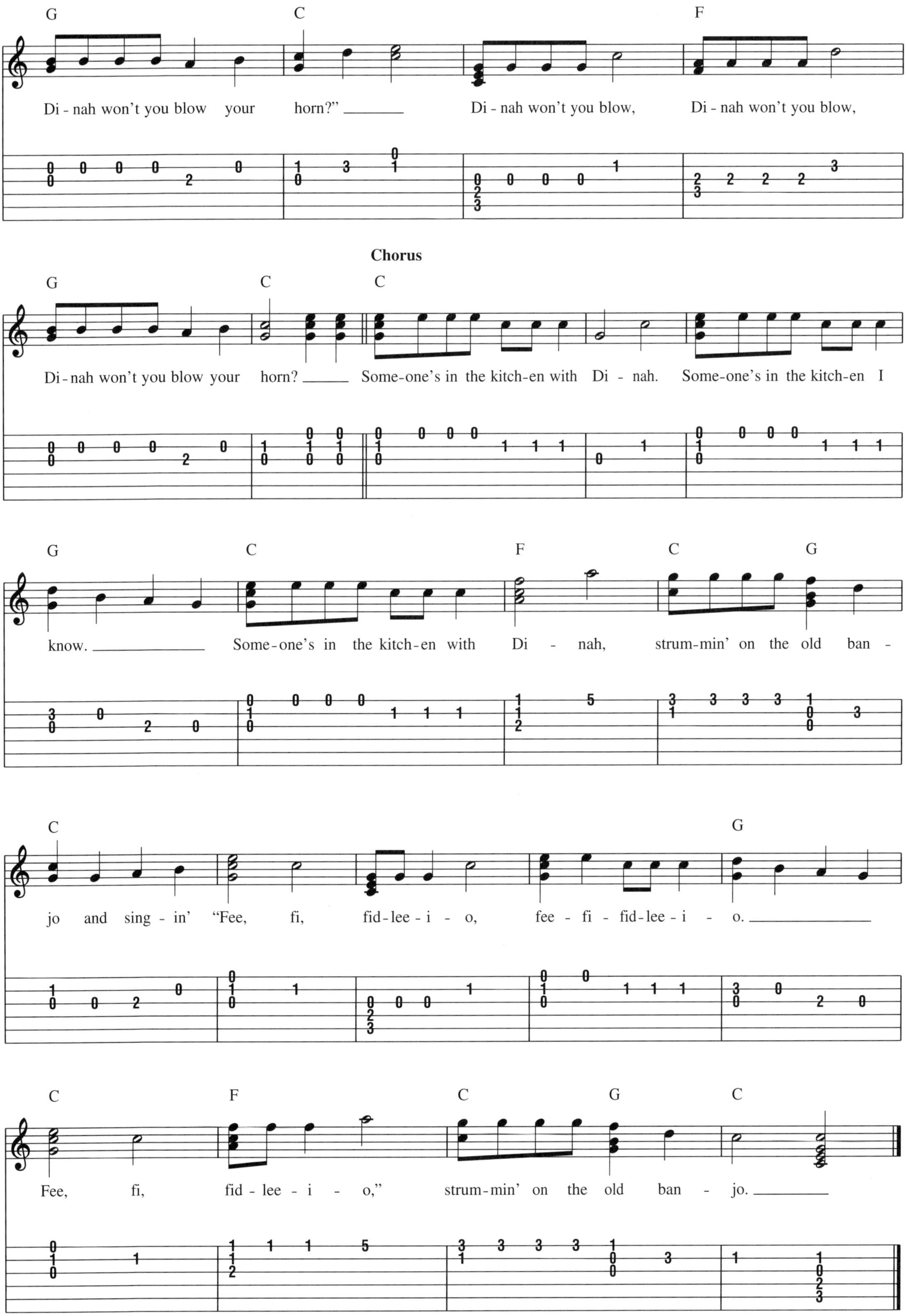
G
C
F
Di - nah won't you blow your horn?"
Di - nah won't you blow,
Di - nah won't you blow,
G
C
Chorus
C
Di - nah won't you blow your horn?
Some - one's in the kitch - en with Di - nah.
Some - one's in the kitch - en I
G
C
F
C
G
know.
Some - one's in the kitch - en with Di - nah,
strum - min' on the old ban -
C
G
jo and sing - in' "Fee, fi, fid - lee - i - o,
fee - fi - fid - lee - i - o.
C
F
C
G
C
Fee, fi, fid - lee - i - o,"
strum - min' on the old ban - jo.

It's Raining, It's Pouring

Traditional

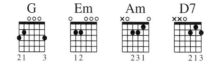

Strum Pattern: 8
Pick Pattern: 8

Moderately fast

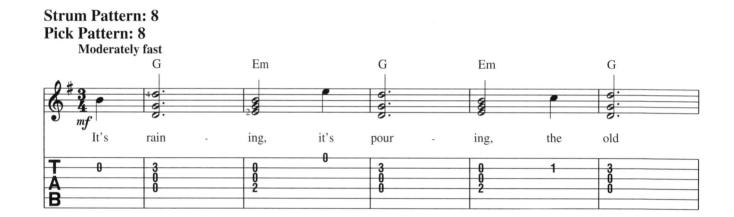

It's rain - ing, it's pour - ing, the old

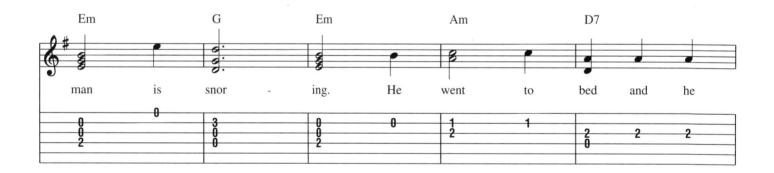

man is snor - ing. He went to bed and he

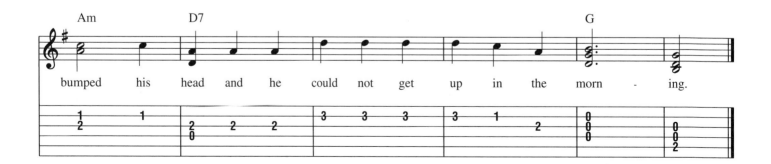

bumped his head and he could not get up in the morn - ing.

Jack and Jill

Traditional

Strum Pattern: 8
Pick Pattern: 8

Verse
Moderately fast

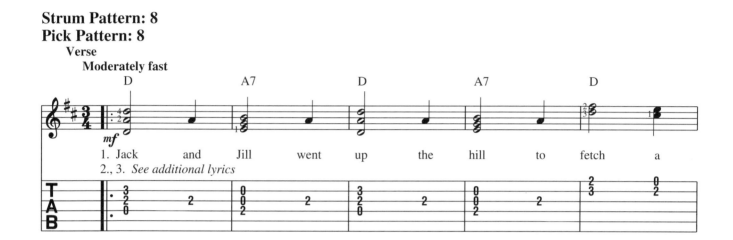

1. Jack and Jill went up the hill to fetch a
2., 3. *See additional lyrics*

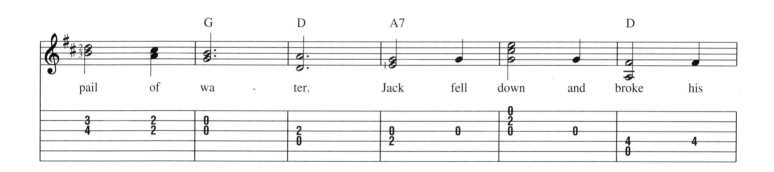

pail of wa - ter. Jack fell down and broke his

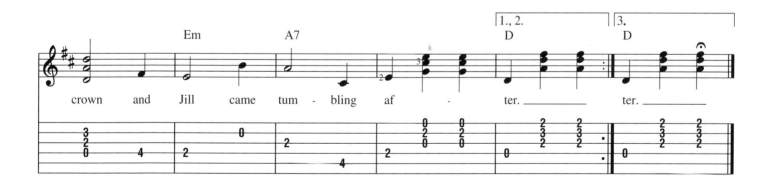

crown and Jill came tum - bling af - ter. _____ ter. _____

Additional Lyrics

2. Up Jack got and home did trot,
   As fast as he could caper.
   Went to bed to mend his head
   With vinegar and brown paper.

3. Jill came in and she did grin
   To see his paper plaster.
   Mother vexed, did whip her next
   For causing Jack's disaster.

Jesus Loves Me

Words by Anna B. Warner
Music By William B. Bradbury

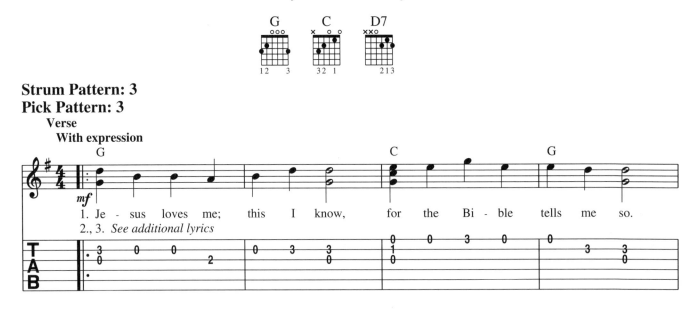

Strum Pattern: 3
Pick Pattern: 3

Verse
With expression

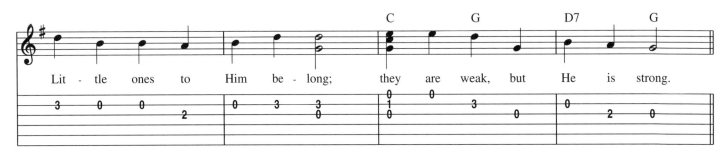

1. Je - sus loves me; this I know, for the Bi - ble tells me so.
2., 3. *See additional lyrics*

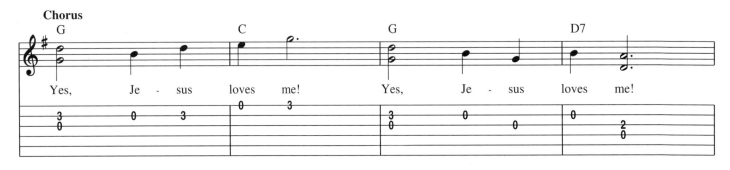

Lit - tle ones to Him be - long; they are weak, but He is strong.

Chorus

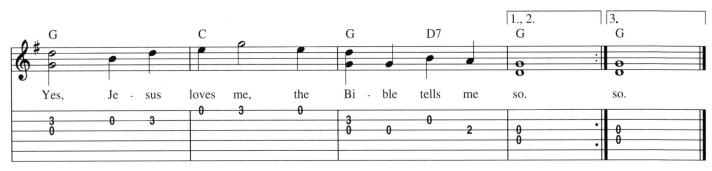

Yes, Je - sus loves me! Yes, Je - sus loves me!

Yes, Je - sus loves me, the Bi - ble tells me so. so.

Additional Lyrics

2. Jesus, take this heart of mine,
   Make it pure and wholly Thine.
   Thou hast bled and died for me,
   I will henceforth live for Thee.

3. Jesus loves me; He who died,
   Heaven's gate to open wide.
   He will wash away my sin,
   Let His little child come in.

John Jacob Jingleheimer Schmidt

Traditional

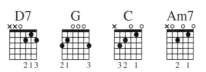

Strum Pattern: 2
Pick Pattern: 4

Intro
Briskly

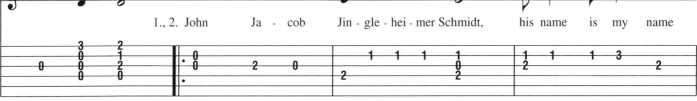

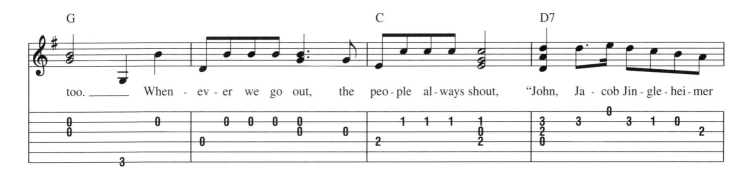

1., 2. John Ja - cob Jin - gle - hei - mer Schmidt, his name is my name

too. _____ When - ev - er we go out, the peo - ple al - ways shout, "John, Ja - cob Jin - gle - hei - mer

Schmidt." Dah, dah, dah, dah, dah, dah, dah. Schmidt." Dah, dah, dah, dah, dah, dah, dah, dah. _____

Kum Ba Yah

Traditional Spiritual

Strum Pattern: 4
Pick Pattern: 1, 2

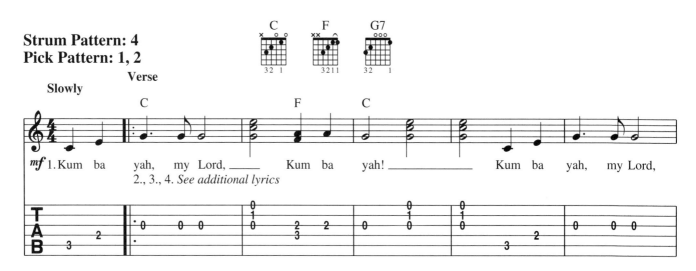

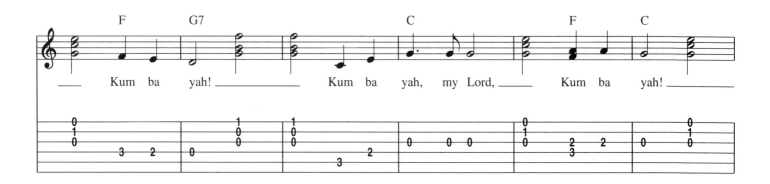

Additional Lyrics

2. Hear me crying, Lord, Kum ba yah!
Hear me crying, Lord, Kum ba yah!
Hear me crying, Lord, Kum ba yah!
Oh Lord! Kum ba yah!

3. Hear me praying, Lord, Kum ba yah!
Hear me praying, Lord, Kum ba yah!
Hear me praying, Lord, Kum ba yah!
O Lord! Kum ba yah!

4. Oh I need you, Lord, Kum ba yah!
Oh I need you, Lord, Kum ba yah!
Oh I need you, Lord, Kum ba yah!
Oh Lord! Kum ba yah!

Lavender's Blue

English Folk Song

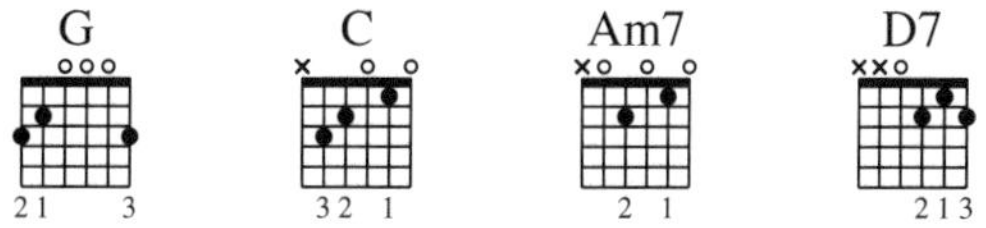

Strum Pattern: 8
Pick Pattern: 8

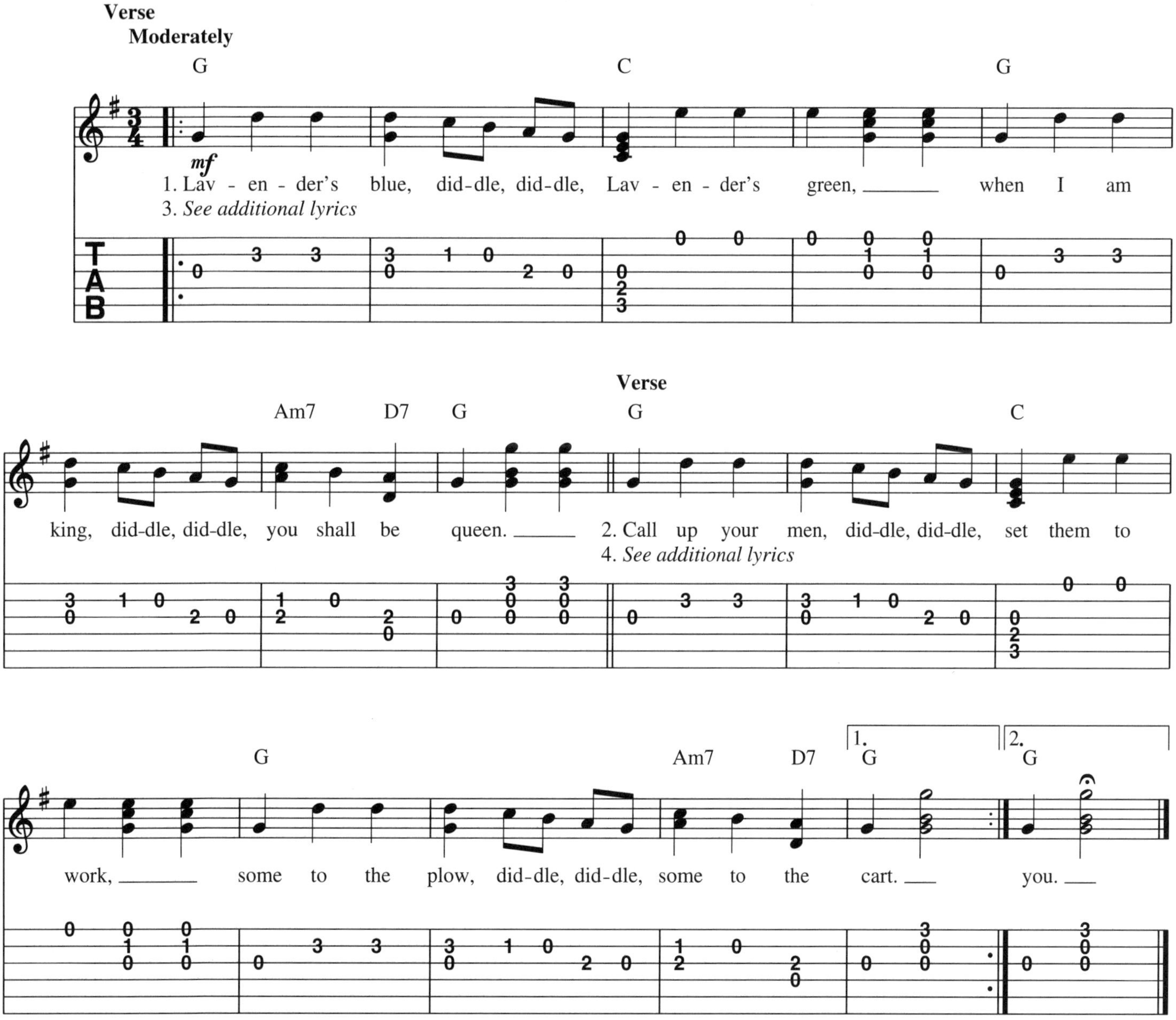

Additional Lyrics

3. Some to make hay, diddle, diddle,
   Some to cut corn,
   While you and I, diddle, diddle,
   Keep ourselves warm.

4. Lavender's green, diddle, diddle,
   Lavender's blue,
   If you love me, diddle, diddle,
   I will love you.

Lazy Mary, Will You Get Up?

Traditional

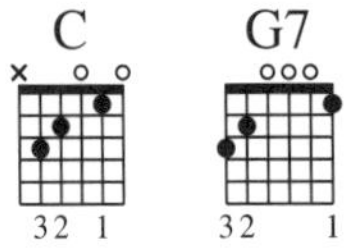

*Strum Pattern: 10
*Pick Pattern: 10

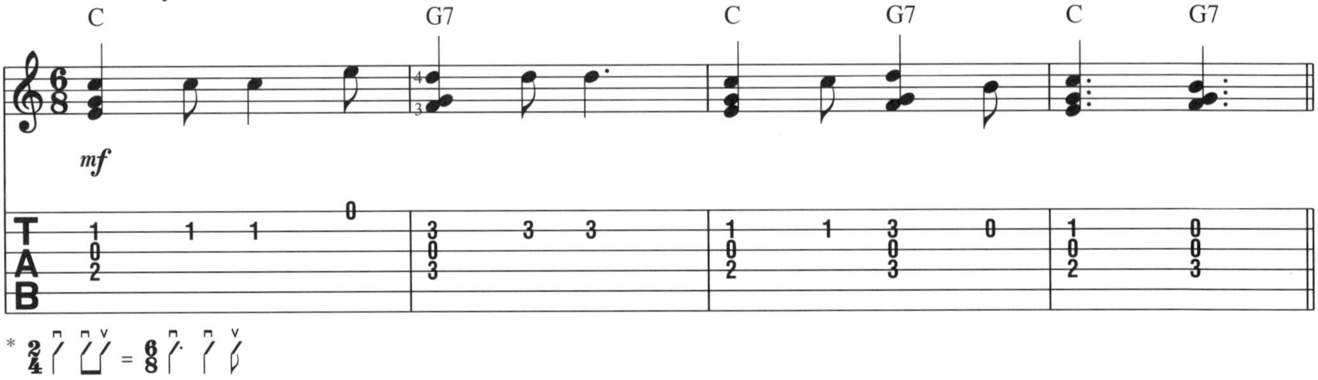

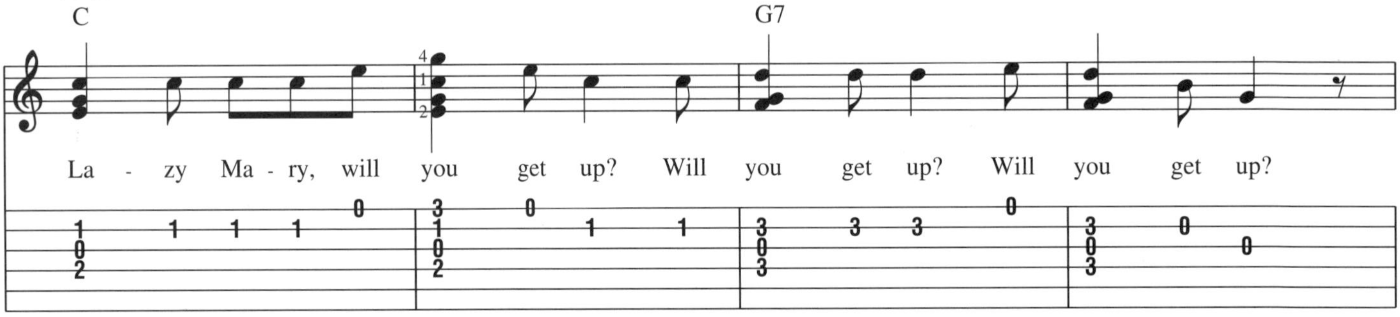

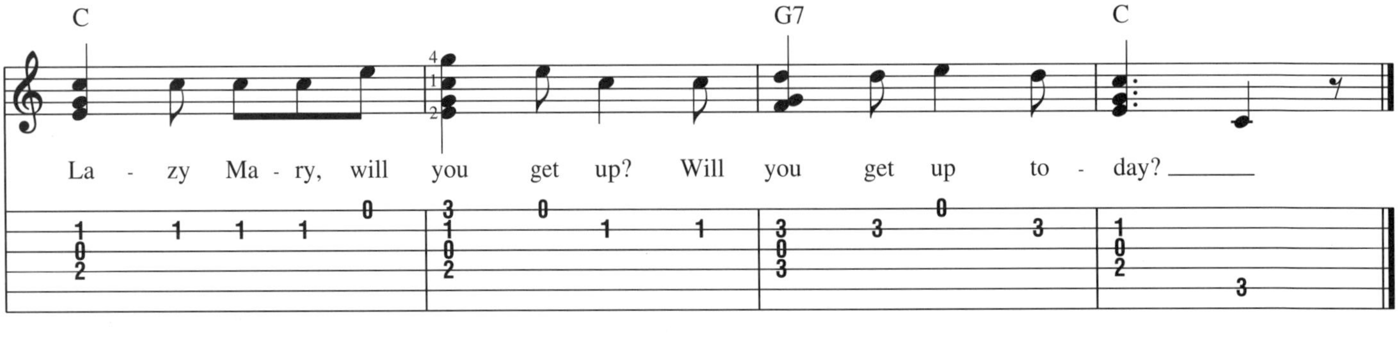

Little Bo-Peep

Traditional

*Strum Pattern: 10
*Pick Pattern: 10

Verse
Moderately

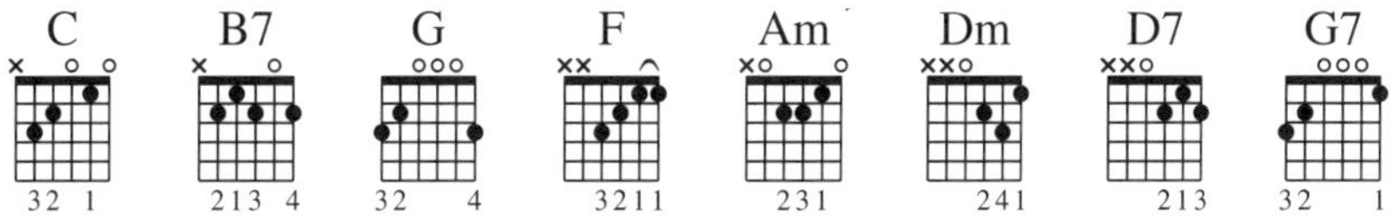

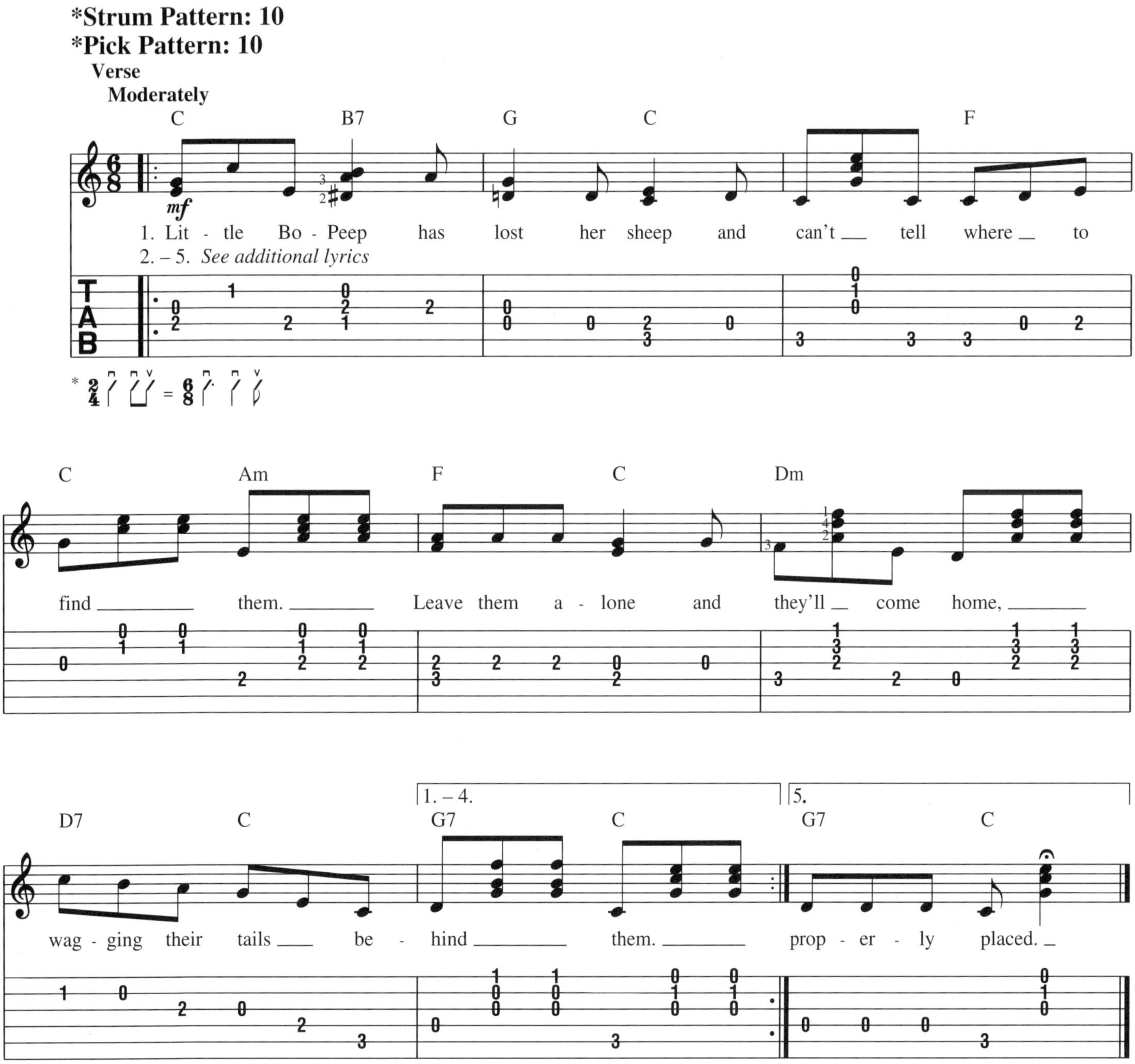

Additional Lyrics

2. Little Bo Peep fell fast asleep,
   And dreamt she heard them bleating.
   But when she awoke, she found it a joke,
   For still they all were fleeting.

3. Then up she took her little crook,
   Determined for to find them.
   She found them indeed, but it made her heart bleed,
   For they'd left all their tails behind them!

4. It happened one day, as Bo Peep did stray
   Unto a meadow hard by.
   There she espied their tails, side by side,
   All hung on a tree to dry.

5. She heaved a sigh and wiped her eye,
   And over the hillocks she raced.
   And tried what she could, as a shepherdess should,
   That each tail should be properly placed.

Little Boy Blue

Traditional

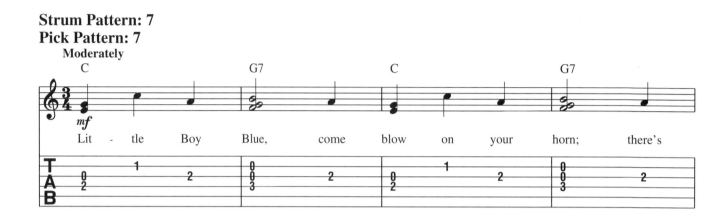

Strum Pattern: 7
Pick Pattern: 7

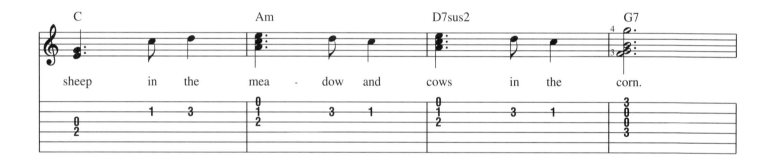

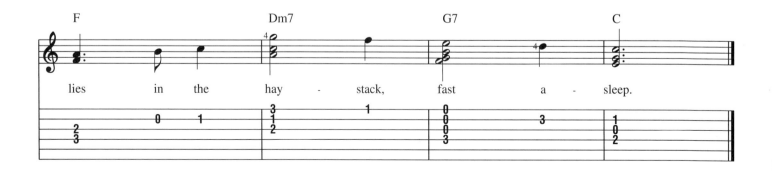

Little Jack Horner

Traditional

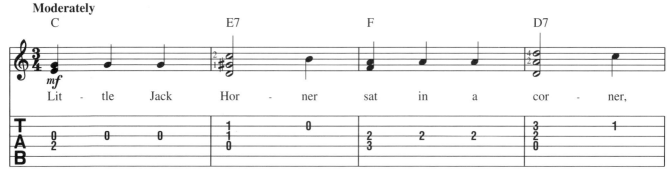

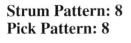

Strum Pattern: 8
Pick Pattern: 8

Moderately

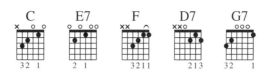

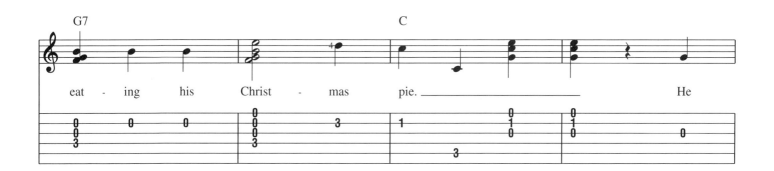

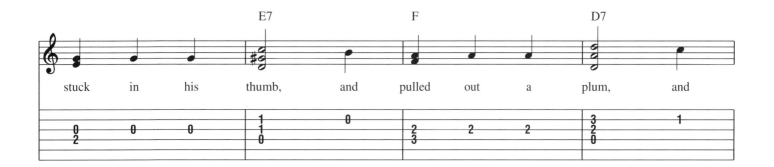

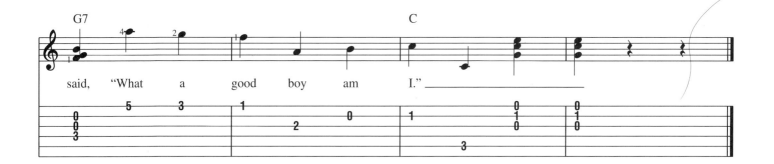

Little Miss Muffet

Traditional

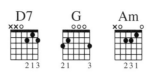

Strum Pattern: 8
Pick Pattern: 8

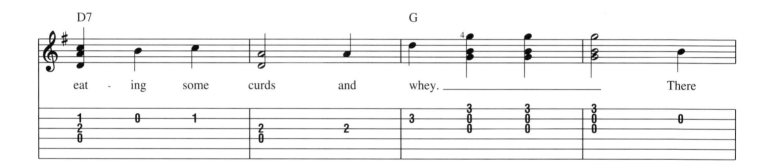

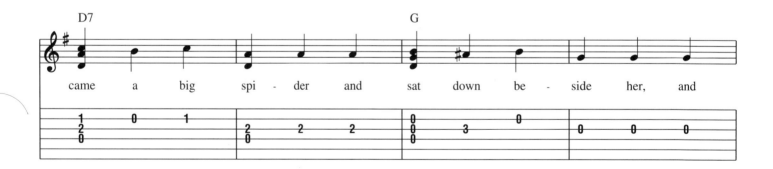

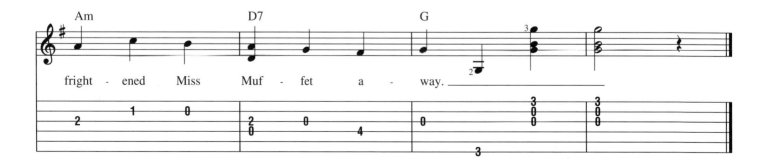

London Bridge

Traditional

Strum Pattern: 3
Pick Pattern: 3

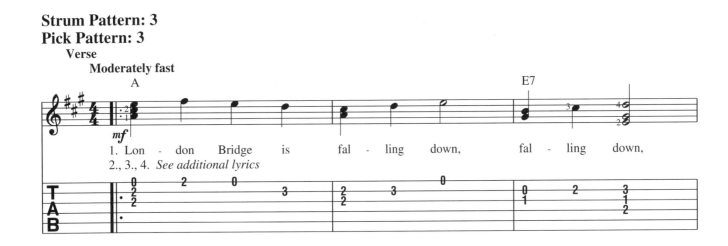

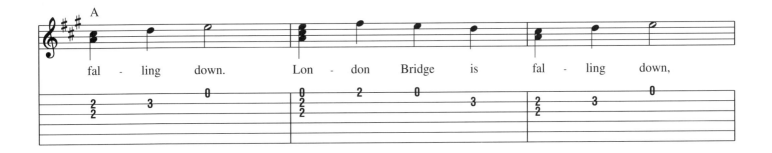

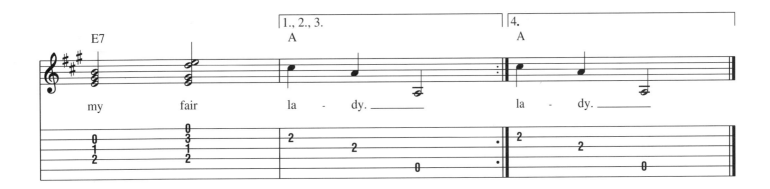

Additional Lyrics

2. Build it up with iron bars,
   Iron bars, iron bars.
   Build it up with iron bars,
   My fair lady.

3. Iron bars will bend and break,
   Bend and break, bend and break.
   Iron bars will bend and break,
   My fair lady.

4. Build it up with gold and silver,
   Gold and silver, gold and silver.
   Build it up with gold and silver,
   My fair lady.

The Man on the Flying Trapeze

Words by George Leybourne
Music by Alfred Lee

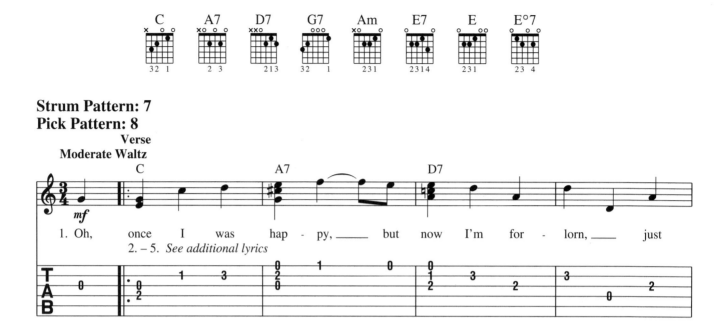

Strum Pattern: 7
Pick Pattern: 8

Verse
Moderate Waltz

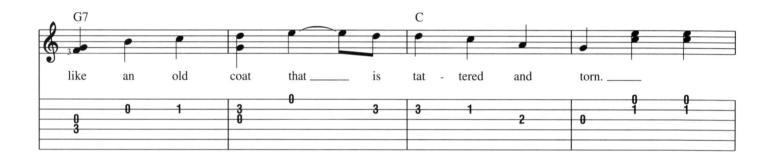

1. Oh, once I was hap - py, _____ but now I'm for - lorn, _____ just
2. – 5. *See additional lyrics*

like an old coat that _____ is tat - tered and torn. _____

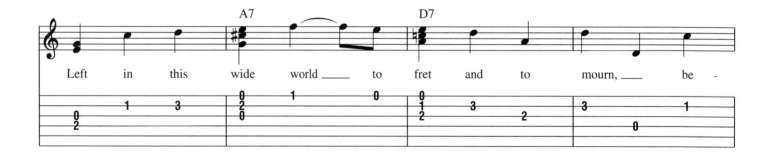

Left in this wide world _____ to fret and to mourn, _____ be -

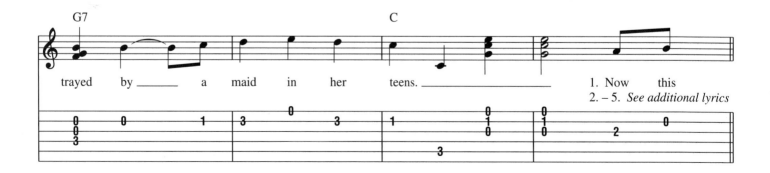

trayed by _____ a maid in her teens. _____ 1. Now this
2. – 5. *See additional lyrics*

Bridge

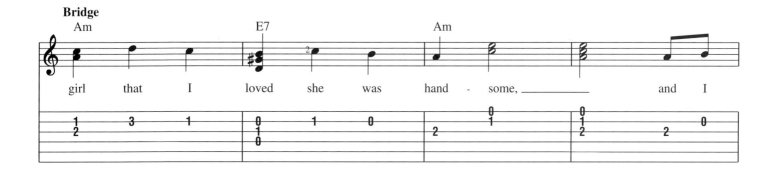

girl that I loved she was hand - some, _____ and I

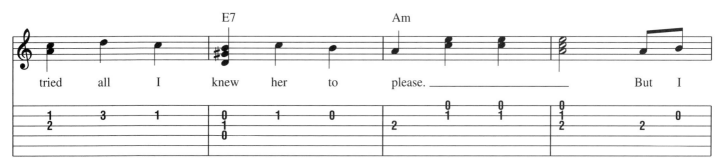

tried all I knew her to please. _____ But I

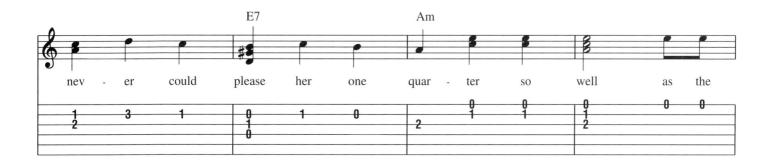

nev - er could please her one quar - ter so well as the

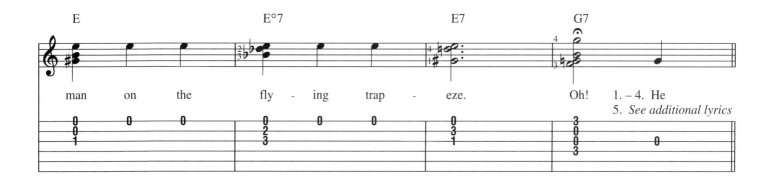

man on the fly - ing trap - eze. Oh! 1. – 4. He
5. *See additional lyrics*

Chorus

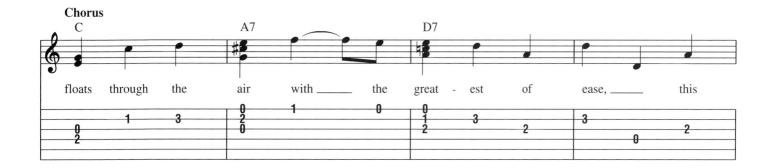

floats through the air with _____ the great - est of ease, _____ this

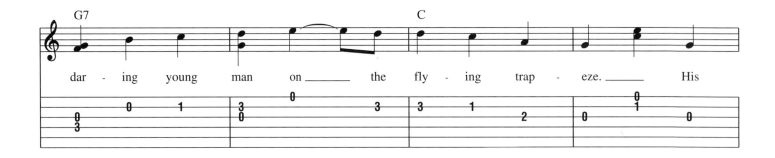

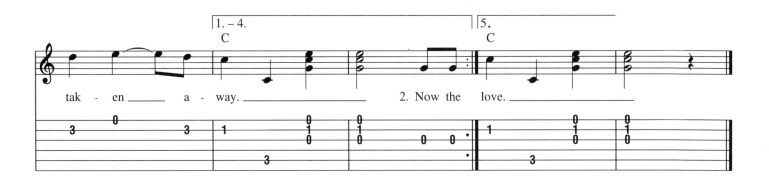

Additional Lyrics

2. Now the young man by name was Señor Boni Slang,
   Tall, big and handsome, as well made as Chang.
   Where'er he appeared, how the hall loudly rang,
   With ovations from all people there.

Bridge 2. He'd smile from the bar on the people below
   And one night he smiled on my love,
   She winked back at him, and she shouted "Bravo!"
   As he hung by his nose from above.

3. Her father and mother were both on my side
   And tried very hard to make her my bride.
   Her father, he sighed, and her mother, she cried
   To see her throw herself away.

Bridge 3. 'Twas all no avail, she went there ev'ry night
   And threw her bouquets on the stage,
   Which caused him to meet her — how he ran me down,
   To tell it would take a whole page.

4. One night I as usual went to her dear home,
   And found there her mother and father alone.
   I asked for my love, and soon 'twas made known,
   To my horror, that she'd run away.

Bridge 4. She packed up her boxes and eloped in the night,
   With him with the greatest of ease.
   From two stories high he had lowered her down
   To the ground on his flying trapeze.

5. Some months after that I went into a hall;
   To my surprise I found there on the wall
   A bill in red letters which did my heart gall,
   That she was appearing with him.

Bridge 5. He'd taught her gymnastics, and dressed her in tights
   To help him live at ease.
   He'd made her assume a masculine name,
   And now she goes on the trapeze.

Chorus 5. She floats through the air with the greatest of ease;
   You'd think her a man on the flying trapeze.
   She does all the work while he takes his ease,
   And that's what's become of my love.

Mary Had a Little Lamb

Words by Sarah Josepha Hale
Traditional Music

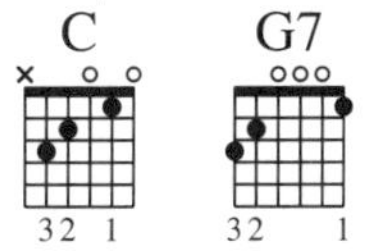

Additional Lyrics

3. He followed her to school one day,
School one day, school one day.
He followed her to school one day,
Which was against the rule.

4. It made the children laugh and play,
Laugh and play, laugh and play.
It made the children laugh and play,
To see a lamb at school.

Michael Row the Boat Ashore

Traditional Folksong

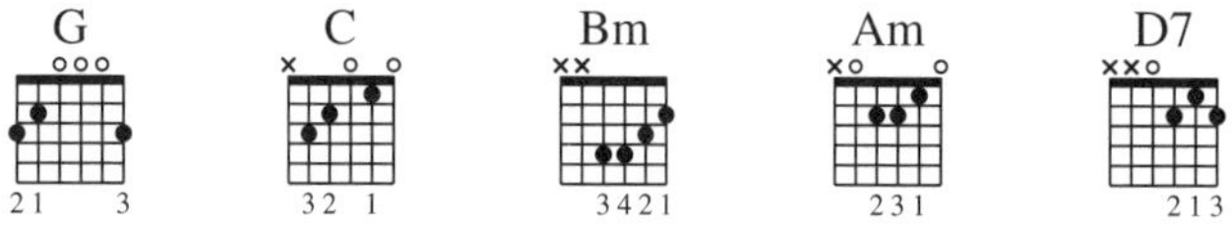

Strum Pattern: 3
Pick Pattern: 3

Chorus

Slowly

Mi-chael, row the boat a-shore, hal-le-lu - jah. Mi-chael, row the boat a-

shore, hal-le-lu - jah.

Verse

1. Sis - ter, help to trim the sail, hal-le-lu -
2., 3. See additional lyrics

jah. Sis - ter, help to trim the sail, hal-le-lu - jah. Mi-chael, jah.

1., 2. **3.**

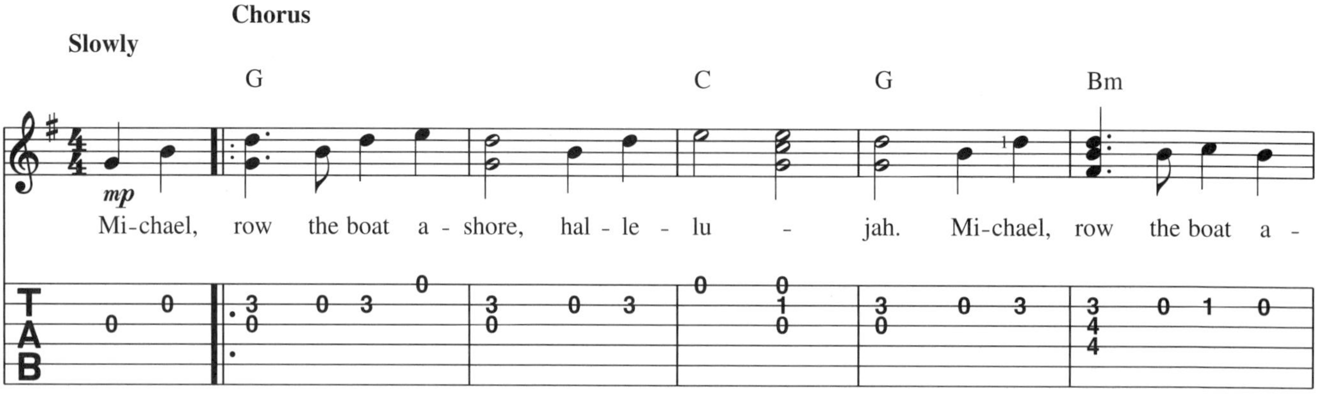

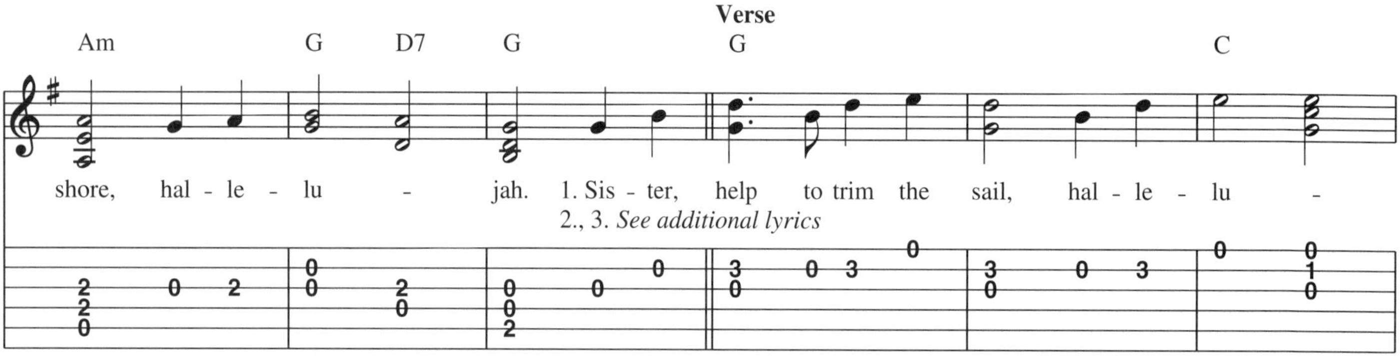

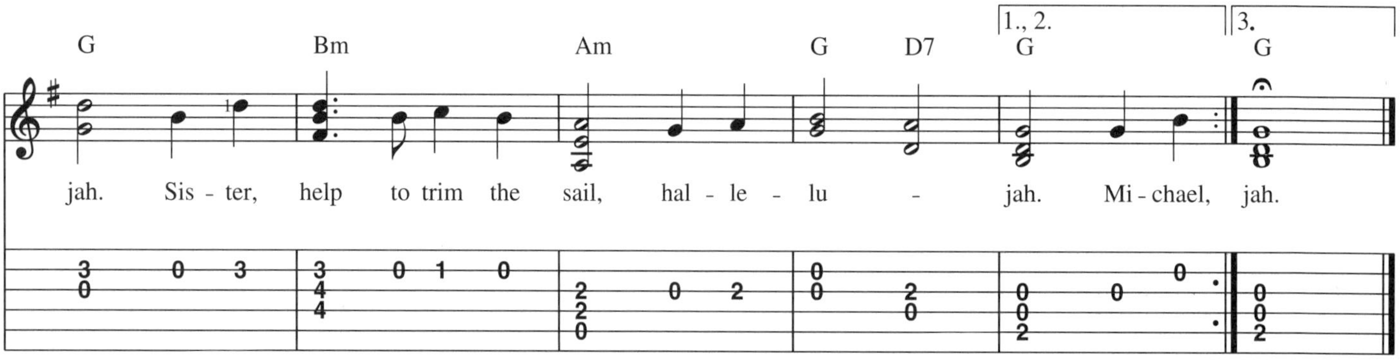

Additional Lyrics

2. Jordan River is chilly and cold, hallelujah.
   Kills the body but not the soul, halleljah.

3. Jordan River is deep and wide, hallelujah.
   Milk and honey on the other side, hallelujah.

Mister Rabbit

Traditional

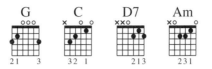

Strum Pattern: 10
Pick Pattern: 10

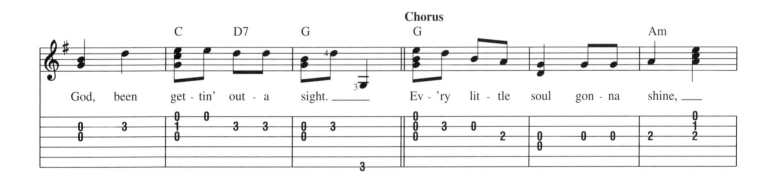

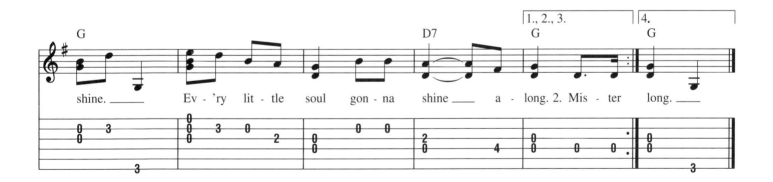

Additional Lyrics

2. Mister Rabbit, Mister Rabbit,
Your coat's mighty gray.
Yes, bless God,
Been out all day.

3. Mister Rabbit, Mister Rabbit,
Your ear's mighty long.
Yes, bless God,
Been put on wrong.

4. Mister Rabbit, Mister Rabbit,
Your ear's mighty thin.
Yes, bless God,
Been splittin' the wind.

The Monkey Song

Traditional

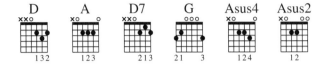

Strum Pattern: 10
Pick Pattern: 10

I _____ make mon - key mo - tions, tu - re - lu. I _____ make

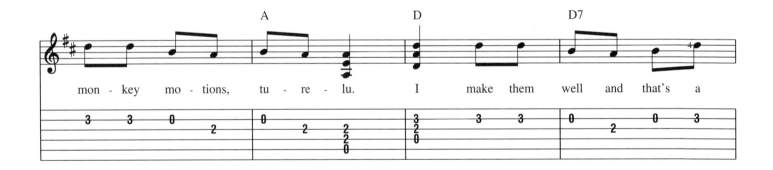

mon - key mo - tions, tu - re - lu. I make them well and that's a

fact. _____ I _____ act just like _____ those mon - keys act.

The Muffin Man

Traditional

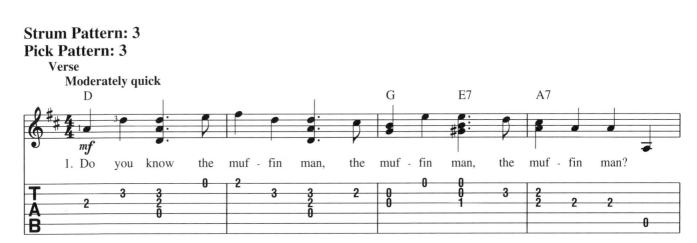

Strum Pattern: 3
Pick Pattern: 3

Verse
Moderately quick

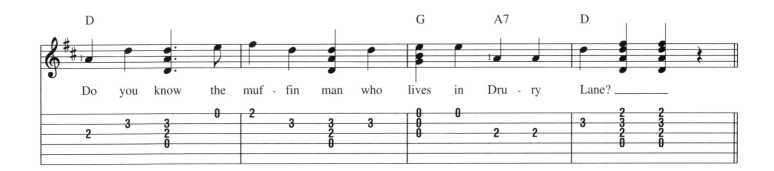

1. Do you know the muf-fin man, the muf-fin man, the muf-fin man?

Do you know the muf-fin man who lives in Dru-ry Lane?

Verse

2. Yes, we know the muf-fin man, the muf-fin man, the muf-fin man.

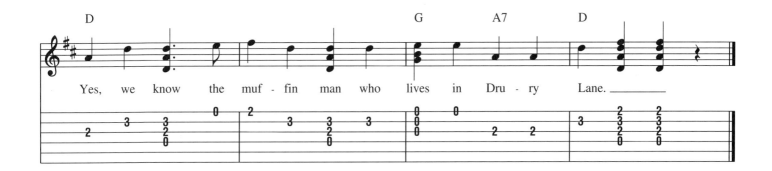

Yes, we know the muf-fin man who lives in Dru-ry Lane.

The Mulberry Bush

Traditional

Strum Pattern: 8
Pick Pattern: 8

Chorus
Lively

Here we go 'round the mul - ber - ry bush, the

mul - ber - ry bush, the mul - ber - ry bush.

Here we go 'round the mul - ber - ry bush so

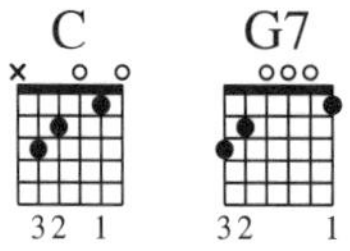

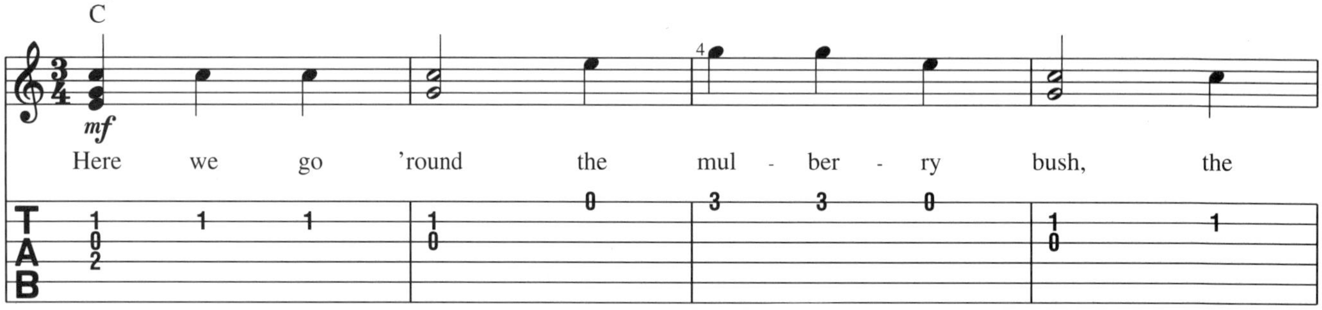

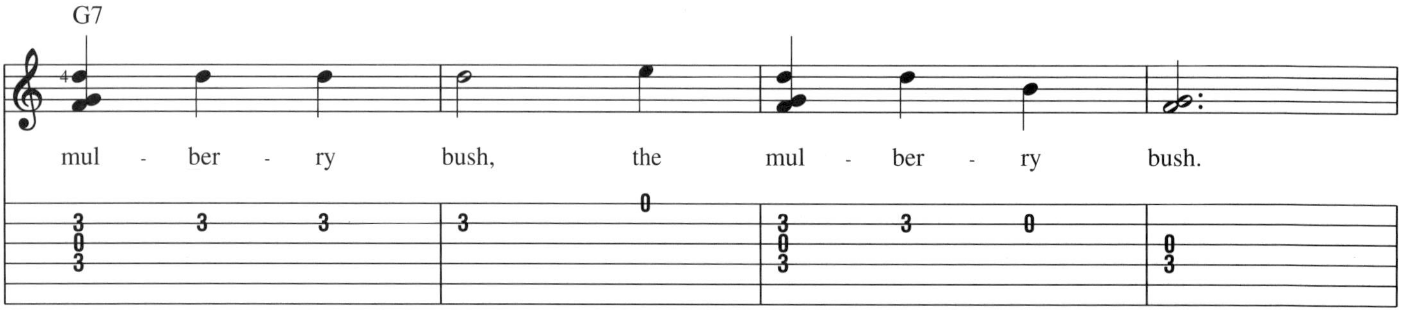

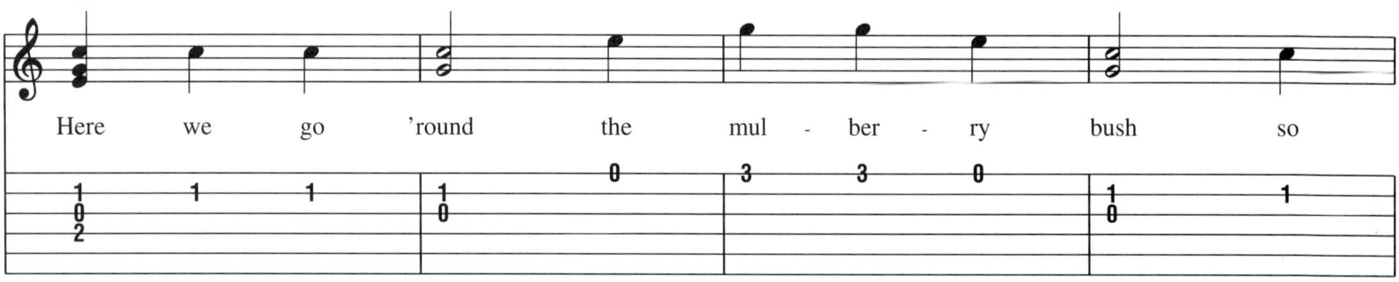

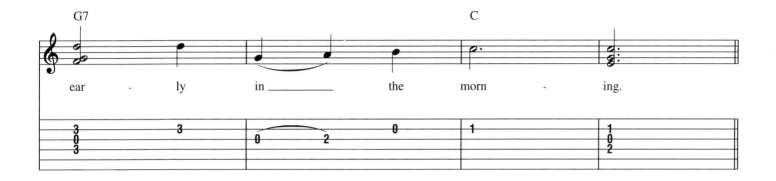

ear - ly in _____ the morn - ing.

Verse

This is the way we wash our clothes, we wash our

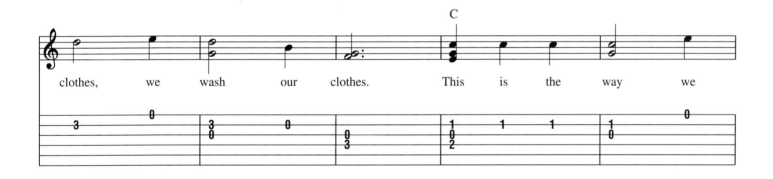

clothes, we wash our clothes. This is the way we

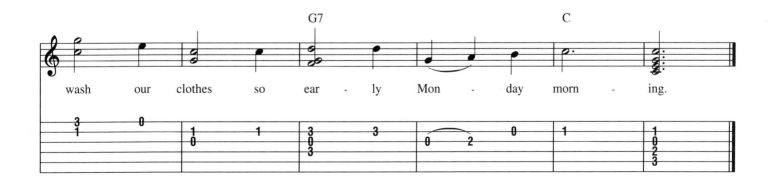

wash our clothes so ear - ly Mon - day morn - ing.

My Bonnie Lies Over the Ocean

Traditional

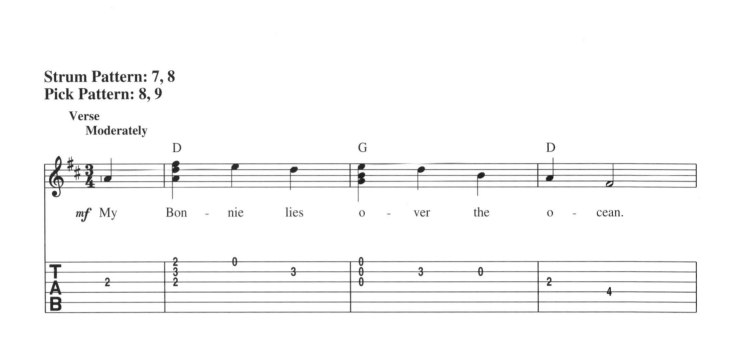

Strum Pattern: 7, 8
Pick Pattern: 8, 9

Verse
Moderately

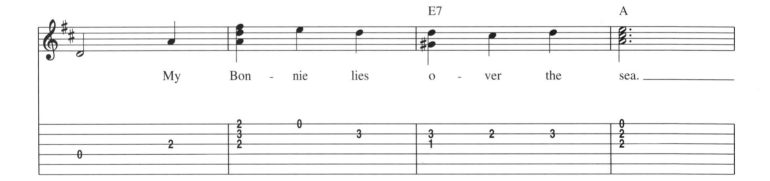

mf My Bon - nie lies o - ver the o - cean.

My Bon - nie lies o - ver the sea. _____

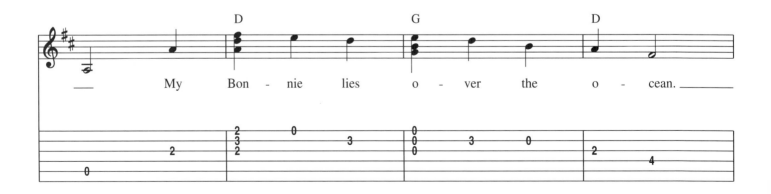

_____ My Bon - nie lies o - ver the o - cean. _____

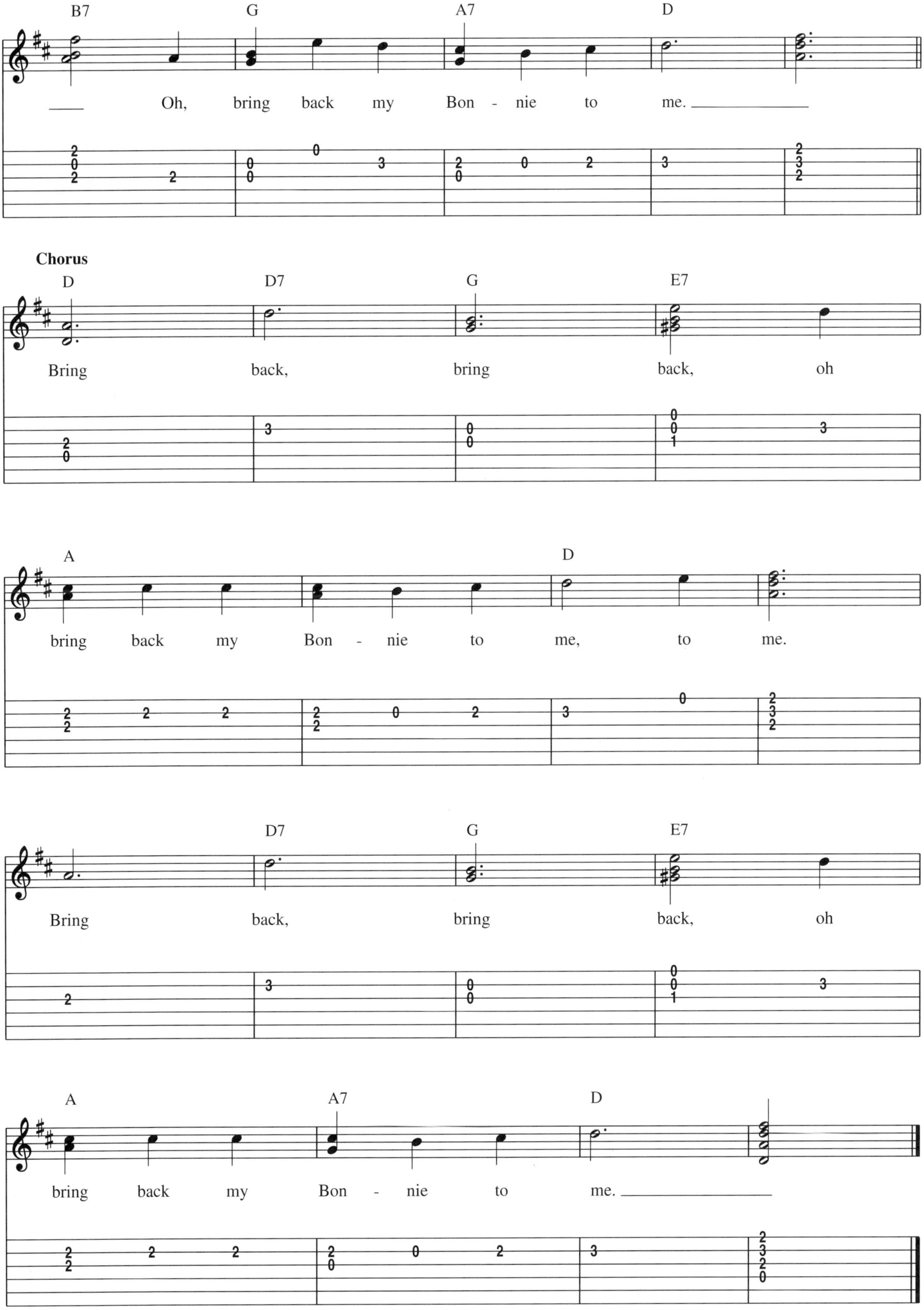
B7 G A7 D
Oh, bring back my Bon - nie to me.
Chorus
D D7 G E7
Bring back, bring back, oh
A D
bring back my Bon - nie to me, to me.
D7 G E7
Bring back, bring back, oh
A A7 D
bring back my Bon - nie to me.

My Country 'Tis of Thee
(America)

Words by Samuel Francis Smith
Music from Thesaurus Musicus

Strum Pattern: 7
Pick Pattern: 7

Verse
Moderately slow

1. My coun - try, 'tis of thee, sweet land of lib - er - ty of thee I
2., 3., 4. *See additional lyrics*

sing. _____ Land where my fa - thers died! Land of the Pil - grims' pride!

1., 2., 3 / 4.

From ev - 'ry _ mountain side, let _ free - dom ring! Great _ God, our King! _____

Additional Lyrics

2. My native country, thee,
Land of the noble free,
Thy name I love.
I love thy rocks and rills,
Thy woods and templed hills.
My heart with rapture thrills
Like that above.

3. Let music swell the breeze
And ring from all the trees
Sweet freedom's song.
Let mortal tongues awake;
Let all that breathe partake;
Let rocks their silence break,
The sound prolong.

4. Our fathers' God, to Thee
Author of liberty,
To Thee we sing.
Long may our land be bright
With freedom's holy light;
Protect us by Thy might,
Great God, our King!

Oats, Peas, Beans and Barley Grow

Traditional

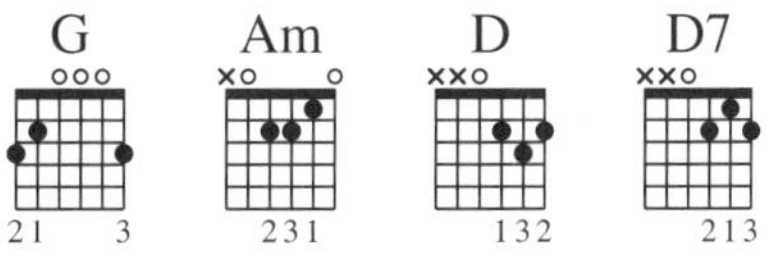

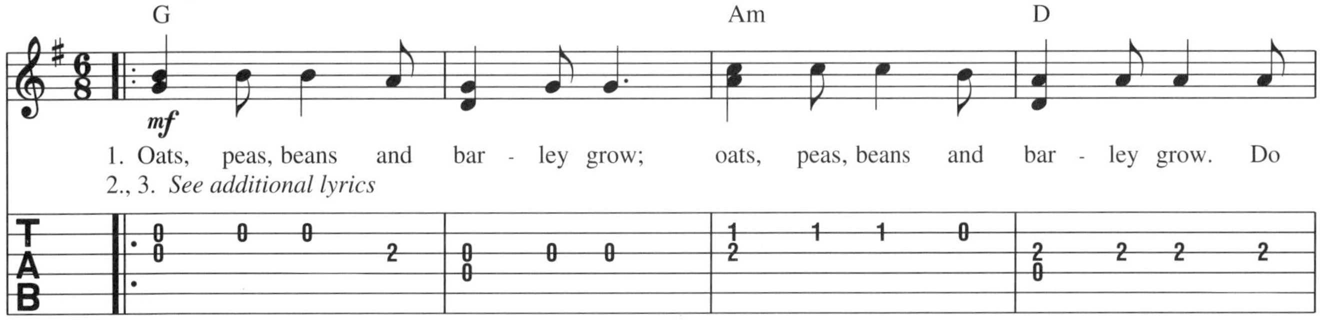

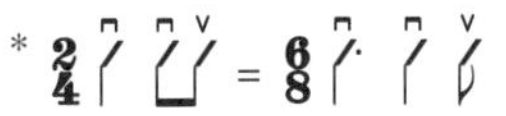

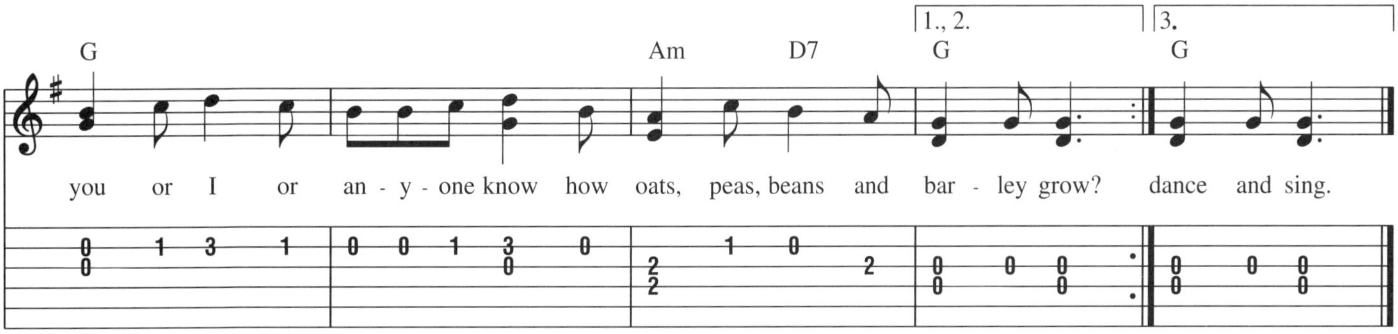

Additional Lyrics

2. First the farmer sows his seed,
   Then he stands and takes his ease;
   He stamps his foot and claps his hands,
   And turns around to view the land.

3. Waiting for a partner,
   Waiting for a partner,
   Open the ring and take one in
   While we all gaily dance and sing.

Oh! Susanna

Words and Music by Stephen C. Foster

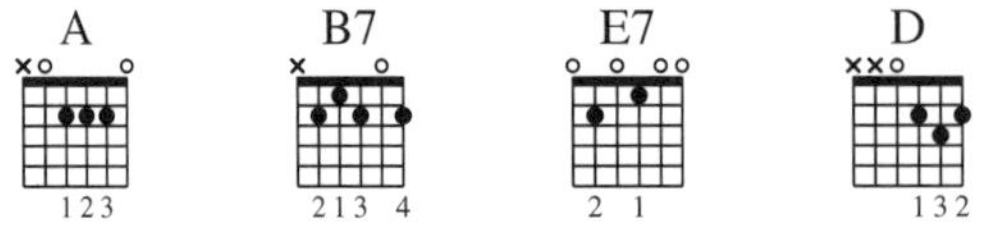

Strum Pattern: 3
Pick Pattern: 4

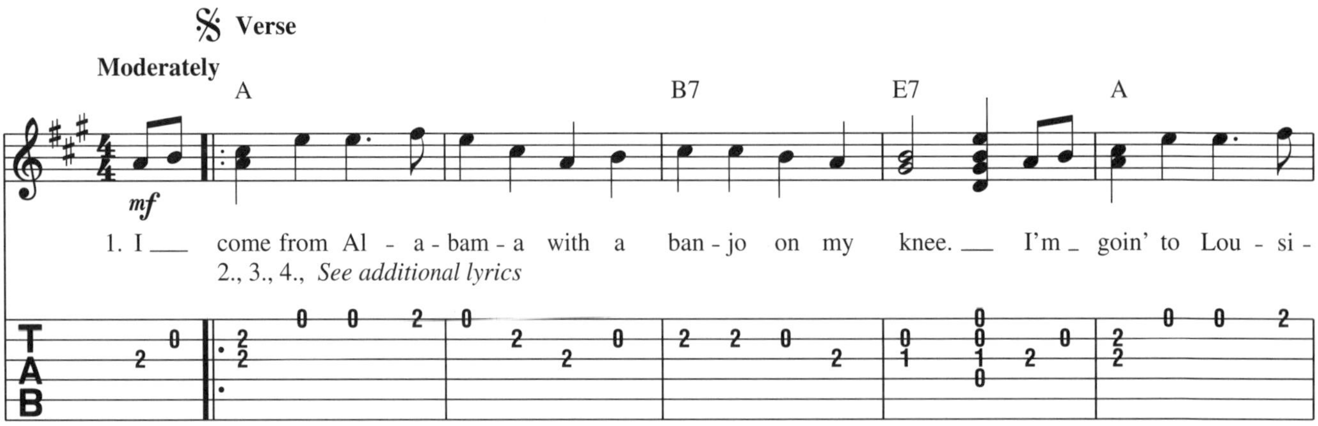

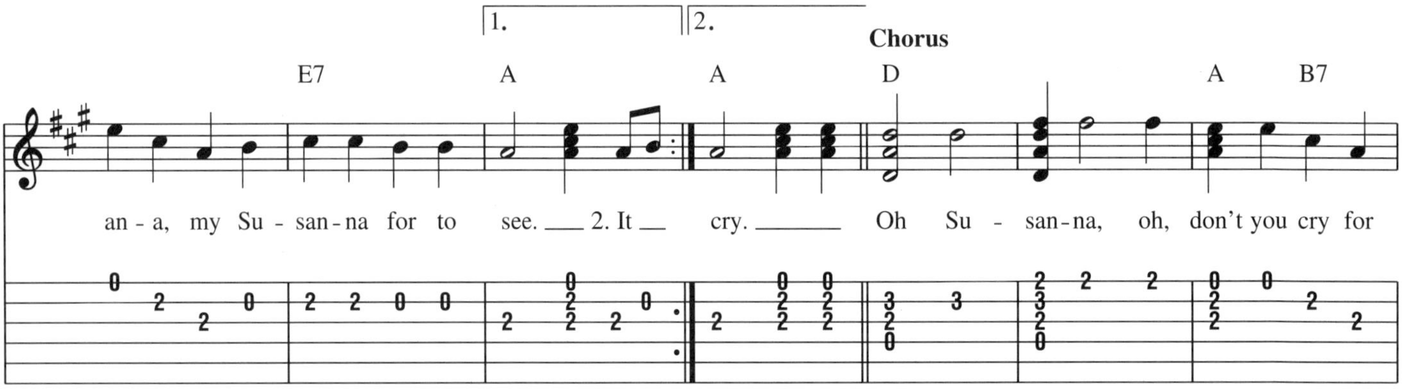

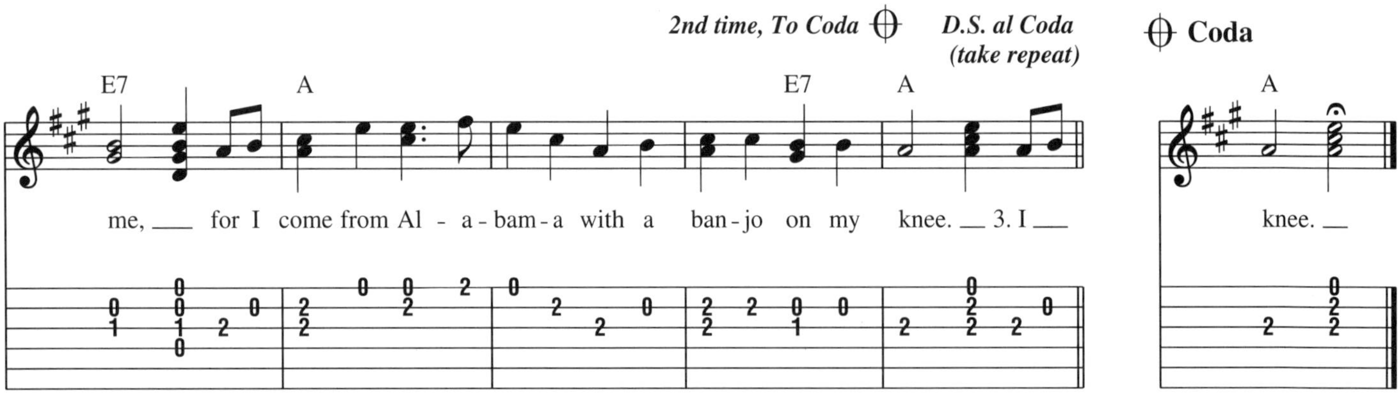

Additional Lyrics

2. It rained all night the day I left,
   The weather it was dry,
   The sun so hot I froze to death,
   Susanna don't you cry.

3. I had a dream the other night
   When everything was still,
   I thought I saw Susanna
   A-coming down the hill.

4. The buckwheat cake was in her mouth
   The tear was in her eye.
   Says I, "I'm coming from the South,
   Susanna, don't you cry."

Oh Where, Oh Where Has My Little Dog Gone

Words by Sep. Winner
Traditional Melody

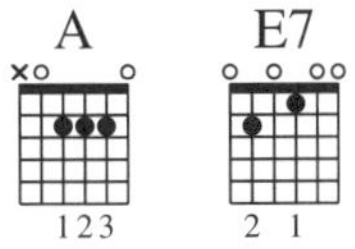

Strum Pattern: 7
Pick Pattern: 8

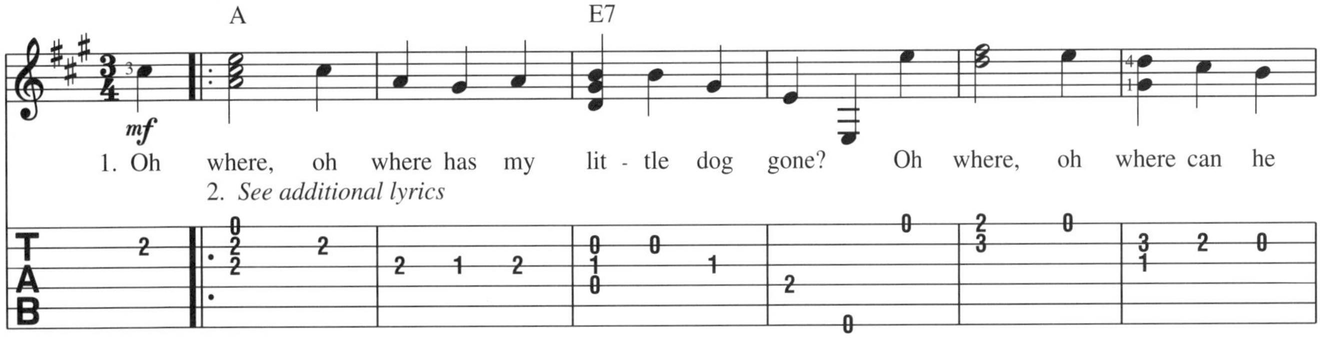

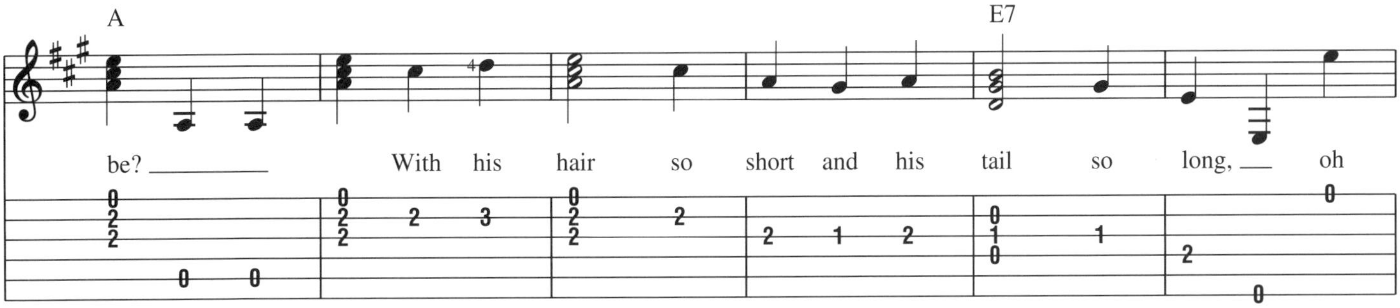

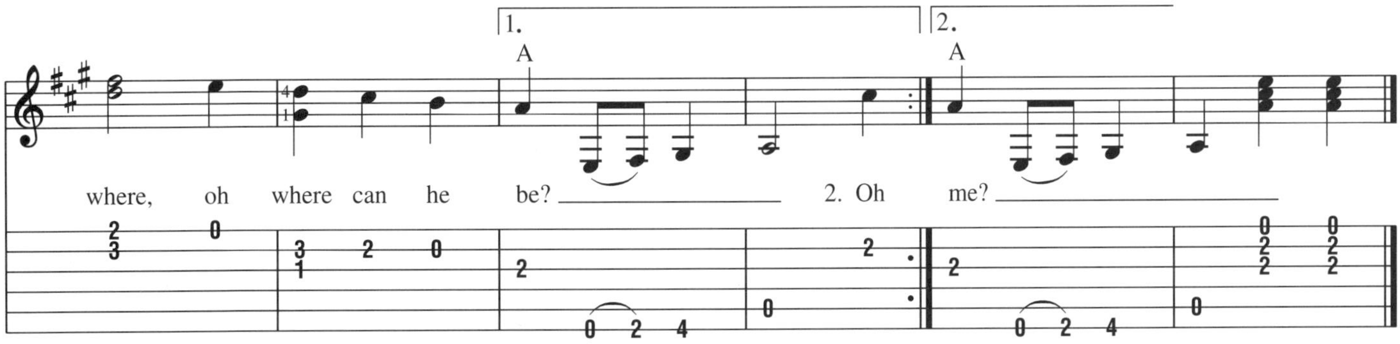

Additional Lyrics

2. Oh where, oh where has my little dog gone?
   Oh where, oh where can he be?
   If you see him anywhere, won't you please
   Bring back my doggie to me?

The Old Gray Mare

Words and Music by J. Warner

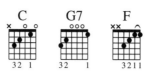

Strum Pattern: 4
Pick Pattern: 3

Moderately

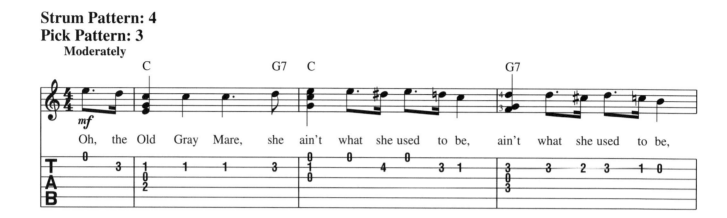

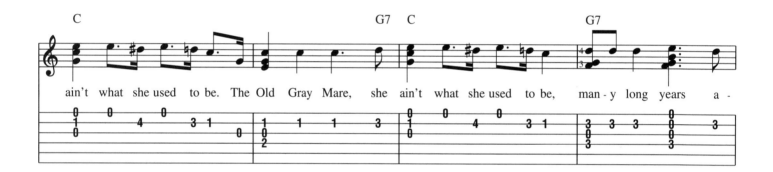

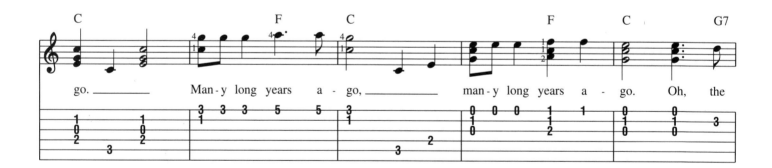

Old King Cole

Traditional

Strum Pattern: 3, 2
Pick Pattern: 3, 4

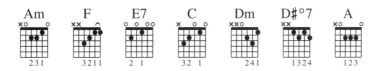

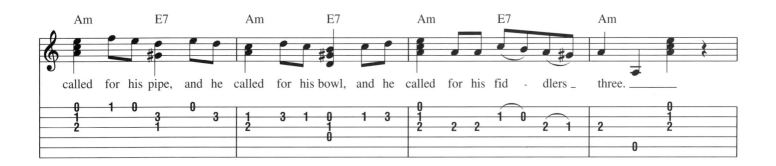

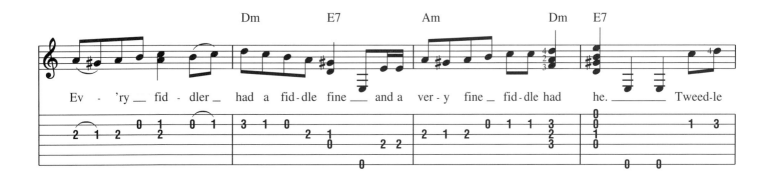

Old MacDonald

Traditional Children's Song

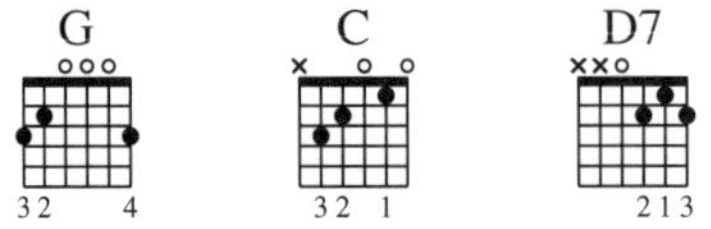

Strum Pattern: 2
Pick Pattern: 4

Verse
Lively

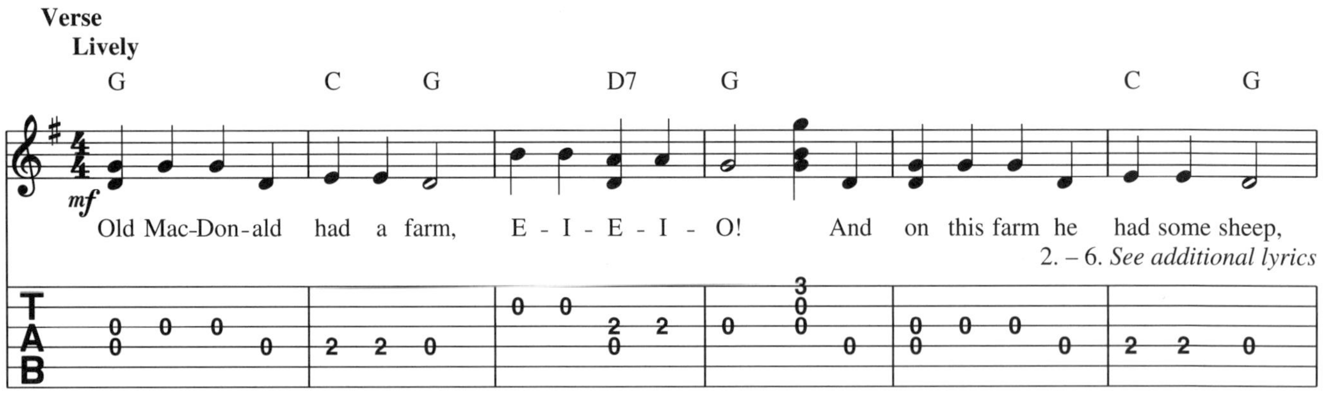

Old Mac-Don-ald had a farm, E - I - E - I - O! And on this farm he had some sheep,

2. – 6. See additional lyrics

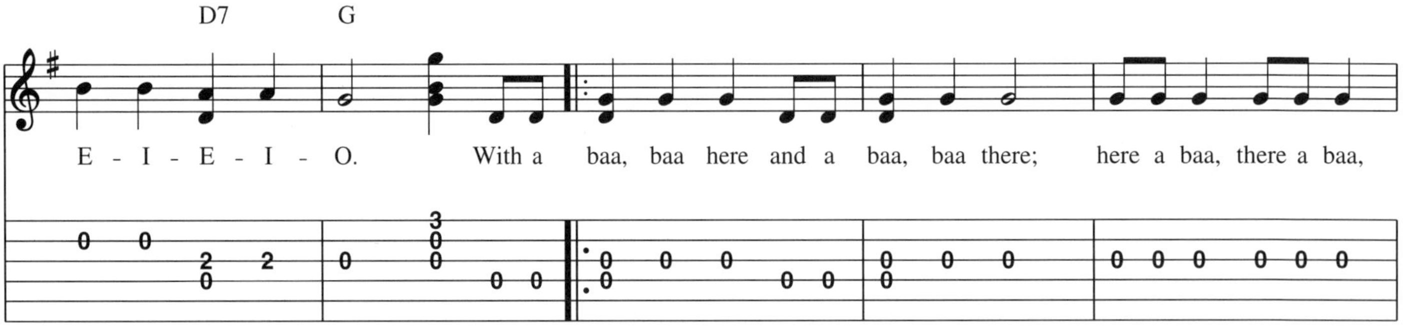

E - I - E - I - O. With a baa, baa here and a baa, baa there; here a baa, there a baa,

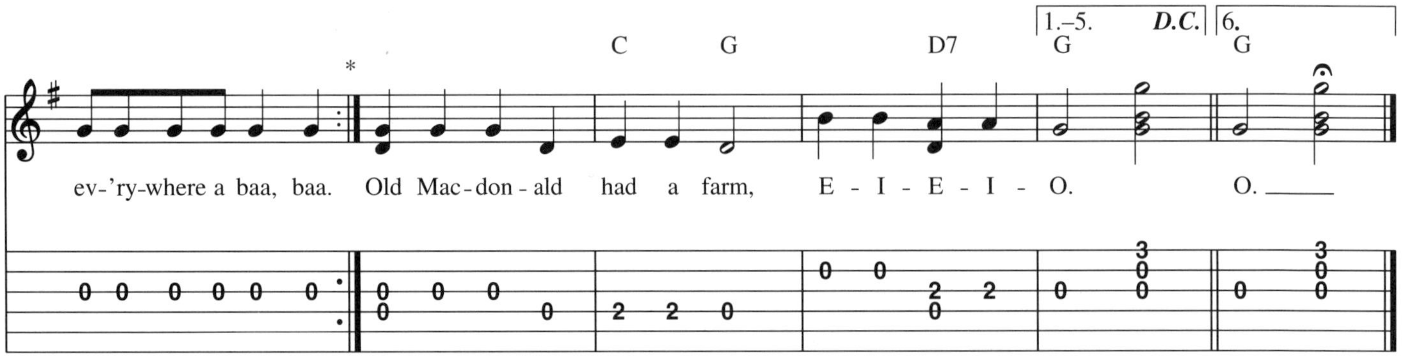

ev-'ry-where a baa, baa. Old Mac-don-ald had a farm, E - I - E - I - O. O. _____

*Repeat as needed for each animal.

Additional Lyrics

2. Cows… moo, moo.

3. Pigs… oink, oink.

4. Ducks… quack, quack.

5. Chickens… cluck, cluck.

6. Turkeys… gobble, gobble.

On Top of Old Smoky

Kentucky Mountain Folksong

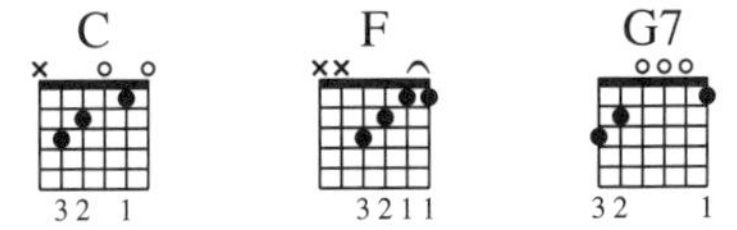

Strum Pattern: 8
Pick Pattern: 8

Verse
Moderately

1. On top of Old Smo - ky, _____ all cov - ered with snow, _____
2. - 8. *See additional lyrics*

lost my true lov - er, _____ by a-court-in' too slow. _____ 2. Well, a - ___

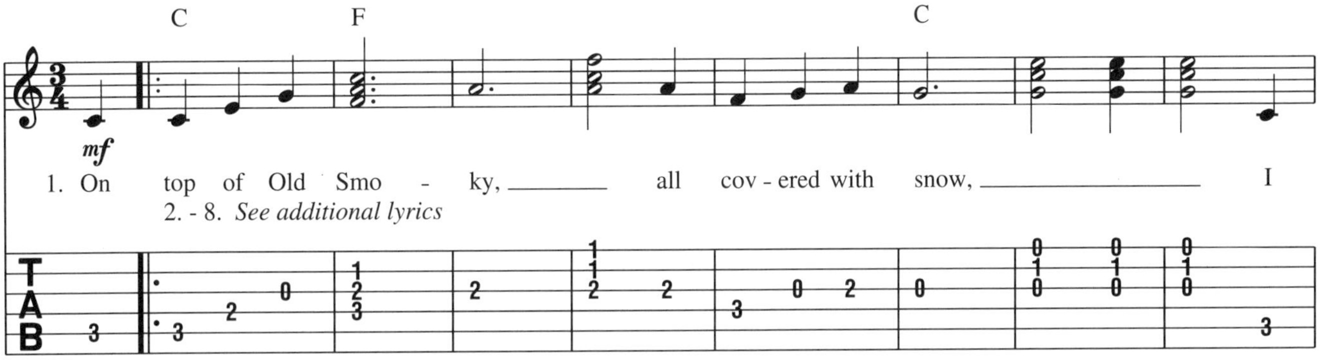

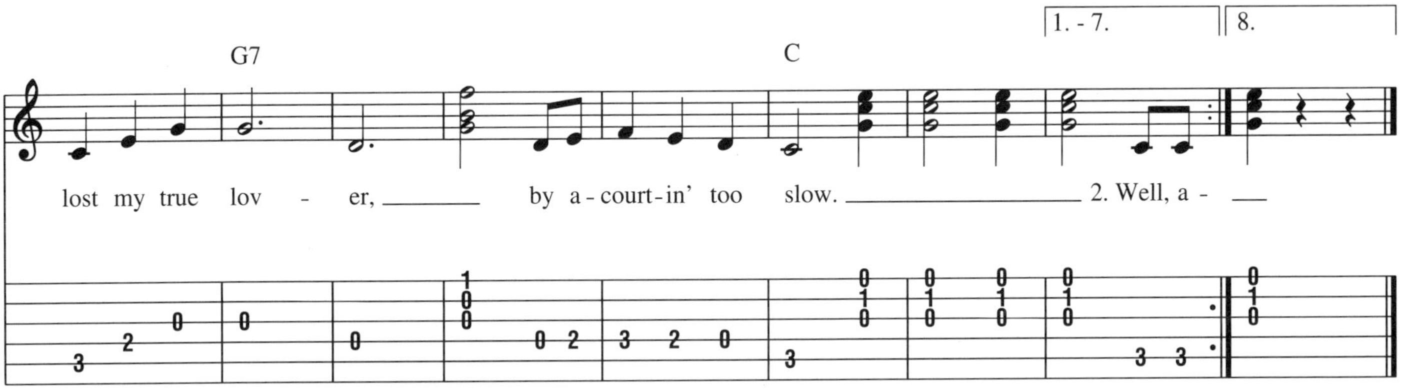

Additional Lyrics

2. Well, a-courting's a pleasure,
And parting is grief.
But a false-hearted lover
Is worse than a thief.

3. A thief he will rob you
And take all you have,
But a false-hearted lover
Will send you to your grave.

4. And the grave will decay you
And turn you to dust.
And where is the young man
A poor girl can trust?

5. They'll hug you and kiss you
And tell you more lies
Than the cross-ties on the railroad,
Or the stars in the skies.

6. They'll tell you they love you,
Just to give your heart ease.
But the minute your back's turned,
They'll court whom they please.

7. So come all you young maidens
And listen to me,
Never place your affection
On a green willow tree.

8. For the leaves they will wither
And the roots they will die.
And your true love will leave you,
And you'll never know why.

Over the River and Through the Woods

Traditional

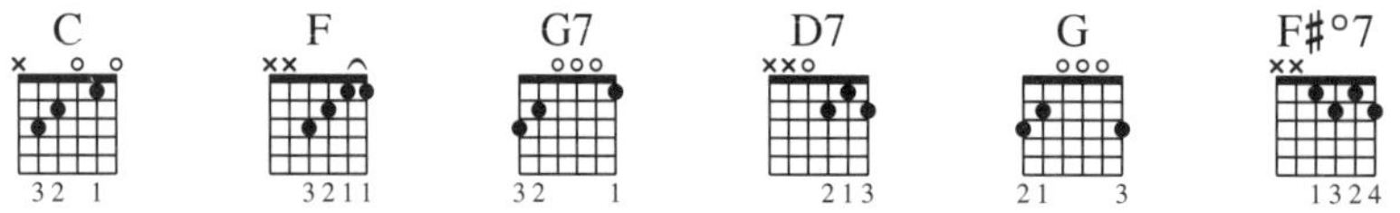

Strum Pattern: 8
Pick Pattern: 8

Verse
Briskly

1. O-ver the riv-er and through the woods, to grand-fa-ther's house we go; ___ the horse knows the way to
2., 3. See additional lyrics

car-ry the sleigh, through the white and drift-ed snow. _ O-ver the riv-er and through the words, oh how the wind does

blow! ___ It stings the toes and bites the nose as o-ver the ground we go. ___ pie!

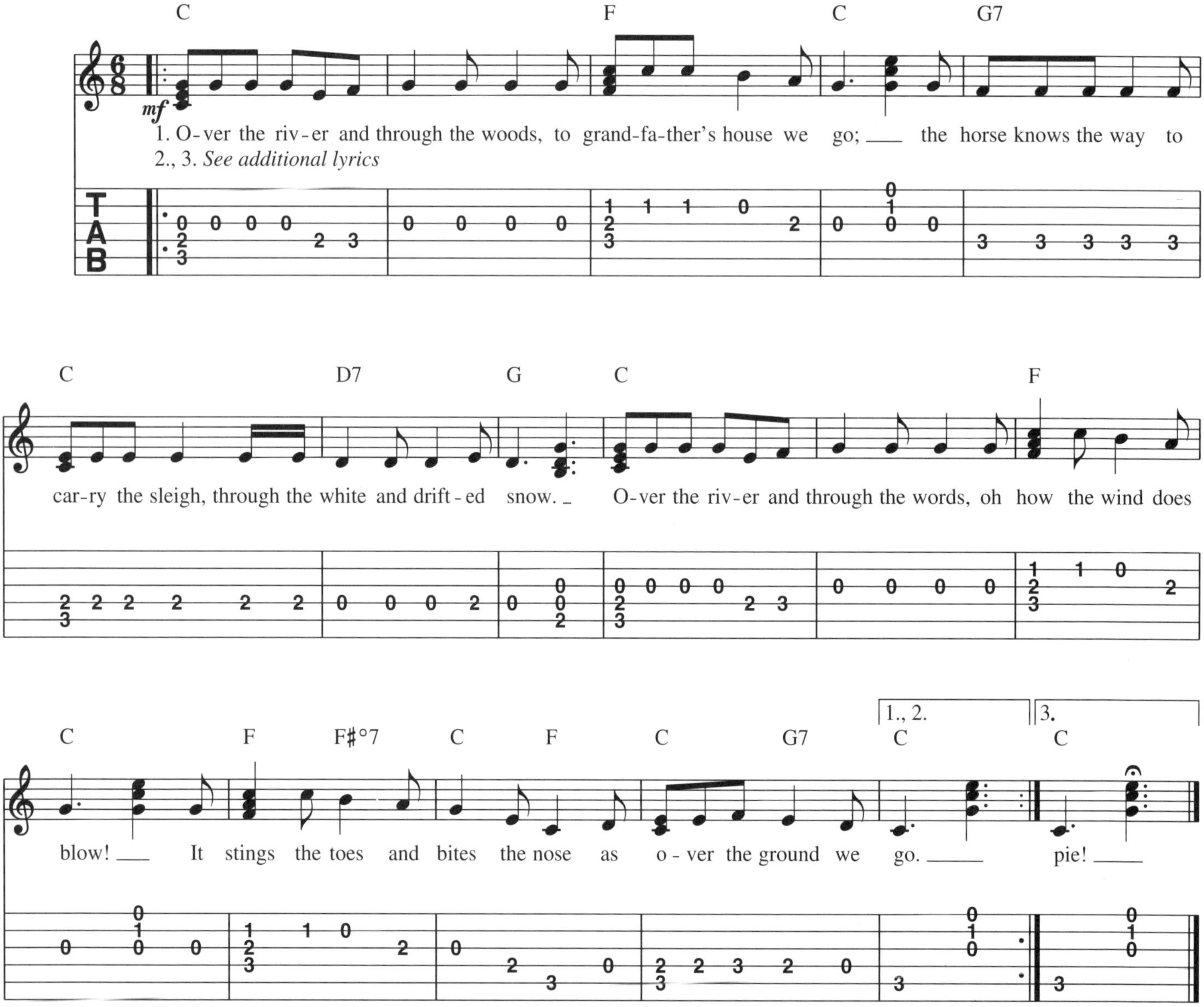

Additional Lyrics

2. Over the river and through the woods,
   To have a first-rate play;
   Oh hear the bells ring, "Ting-a-ling-ling!"
   Hurrah for Thanksgiving Day!
   Over the river and through the woods,
   Trot fast my dapple gray!
   Spring over the gound like a hunting hound!
   For this is Thanksgiving Day.

3. Over the river and through the woods,
   And straight through the barnyard gate,
   We seem to go extremely slow;
   It is so hard to wait!
   Over the river and through the woods,
   Now grandmother's cap I spy!
   Hurrah for the fun! Is the pudding done?
   Hurrah for the pumpkin pie!

The Paw Paw Patch

Traditional

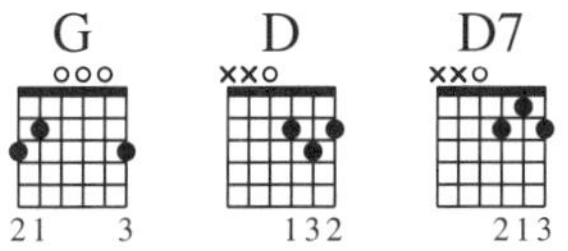

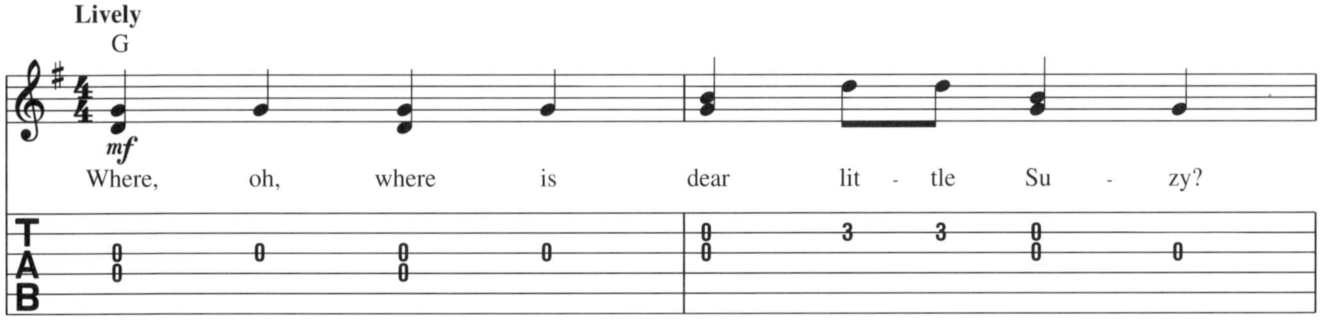

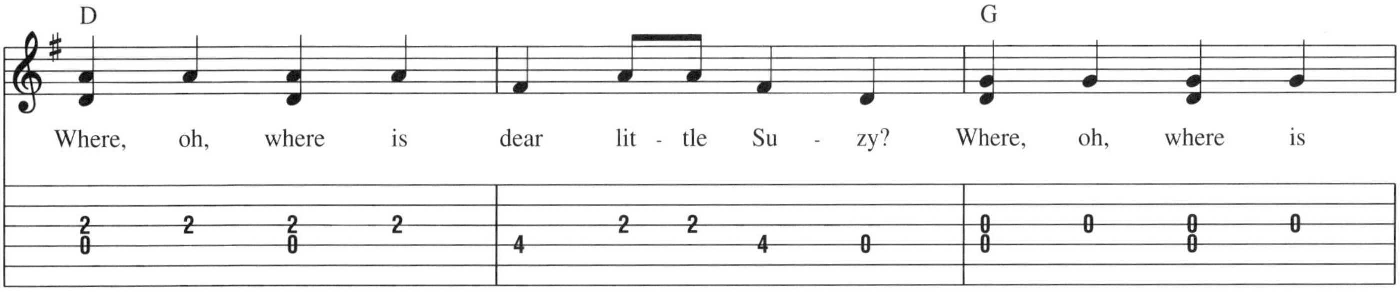

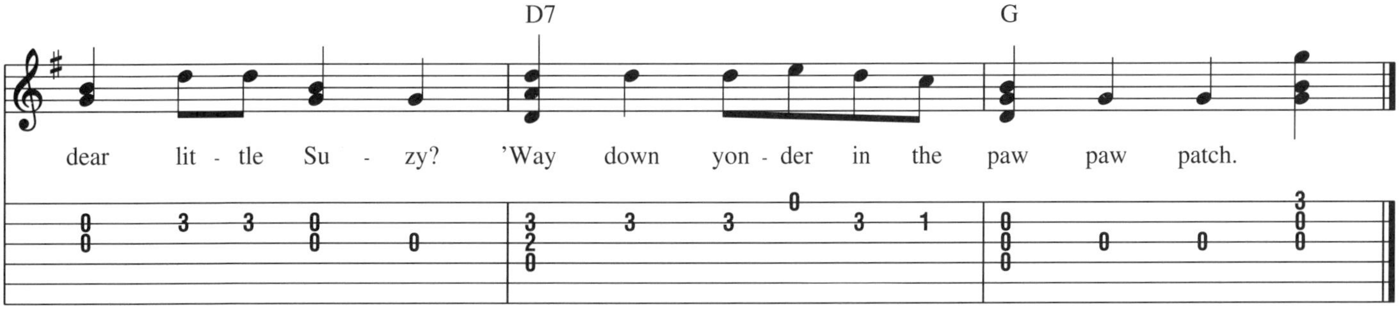

Peanut Sat on a Railroad Track

Traditional

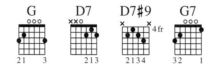

Strum Pattern: 3, 2
Pick Pattern: 3, 4

Moderately

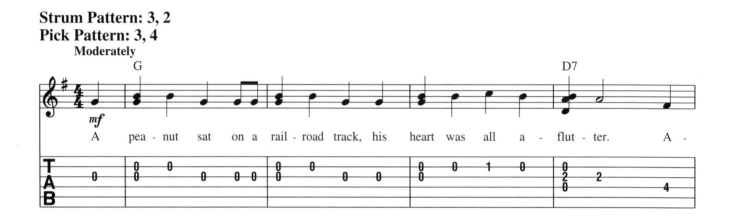

A pea - nut sat on a rail - road track, his heart was all a - flut - ter. A -

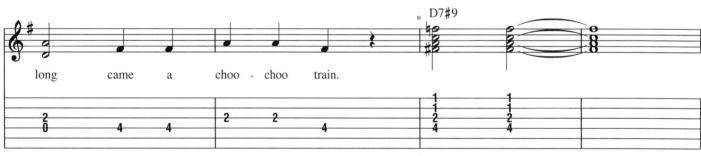

long came a choo - choo train.

*train whistle

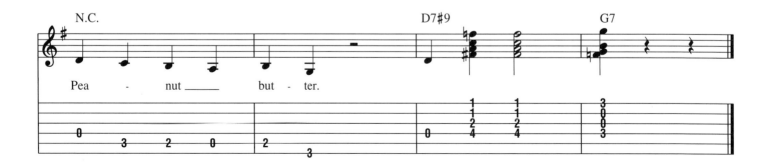

Pea - nut _____ but - ter.

Pease Porridge Hot

Traditional

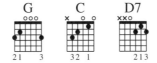

Strum Pattern: 3, 4
Pick Pattern: 3, 4

Moderately

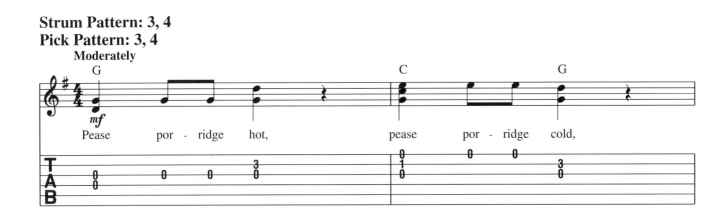

Pease por - ridge hot, pease por - ridge cold,

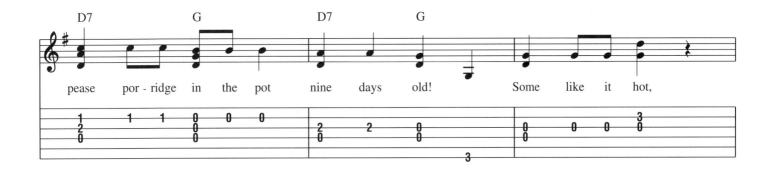

pease por - ridge in the pot nine days old! Some like it hot,

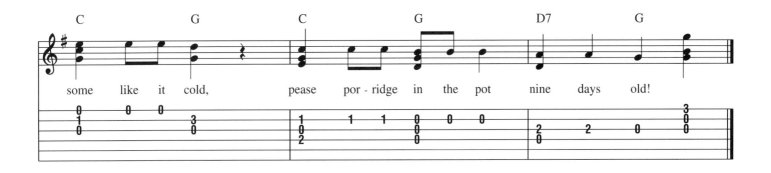

some like it cold, pease por - ridge in the pot nine days old!

Peter, Peter, Pumpkin Eater

Traditional

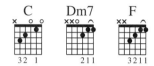

Strum Pattern: 4, 3
Pick Pattern: 3, 6

Moderately

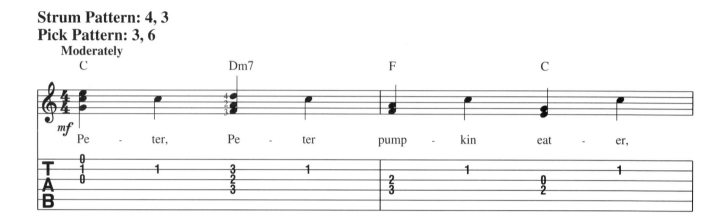

Pe - ter, Pe - ter pump - kin eat - er,

had a wife and could - n't keep her, put her in a

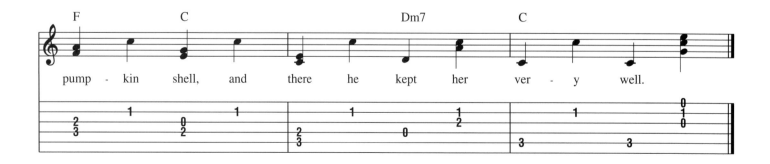

pump - kin shell, and there he kept her ver - y well.

Polly Put the Kettle On

Traditional

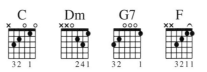

Strum Pattern: 10
Pick Pattern: 10

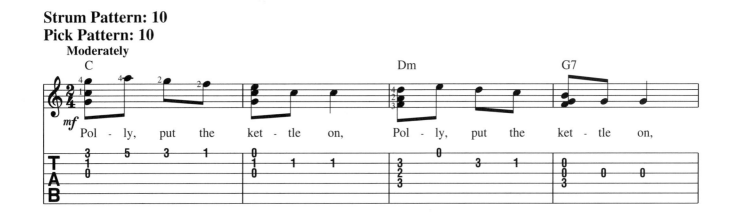

Pol - ly, put the ket - tle on, Pol - ly, put the ket - tle on,

Pol - ly, put the ket - tle on, we'll all have tea. ____

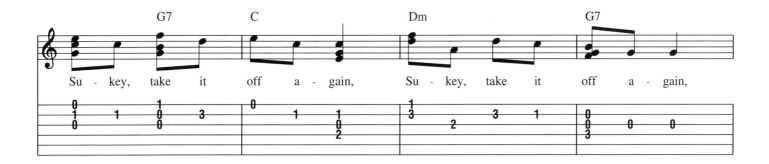

Su - key, take it off a - gain, Su - key, take it off a - gain,

Su - key, take it off a - gain, they've all gone a - way. ____

Pop Goes the Weasel

Traditional

Strum Pattern: 9
Pick Pattern: 7

Lively

Oh, all a - round the mul - ber - ry bush, the

mon - key chased the wea - sel. The mon - key thought 'twas

all ____ in fun. Pop! goes the wea - sel.

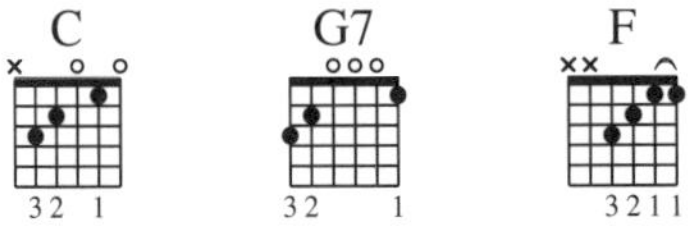

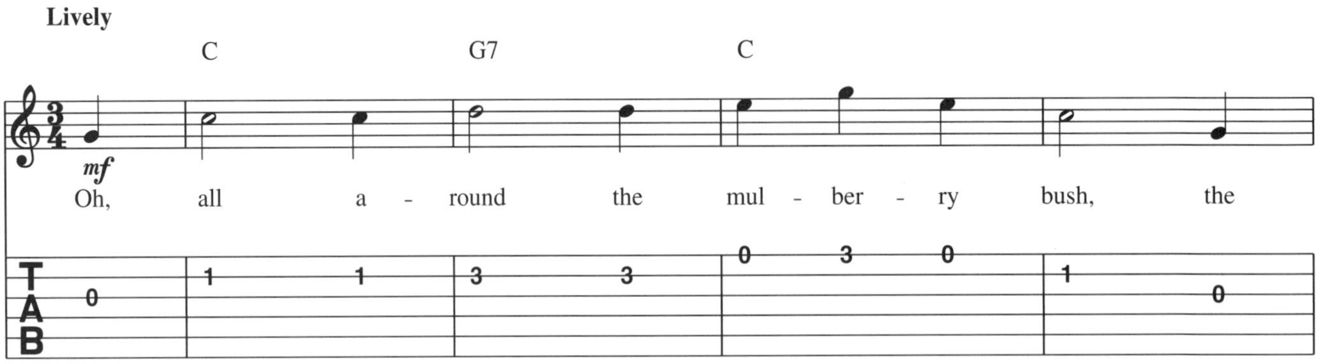

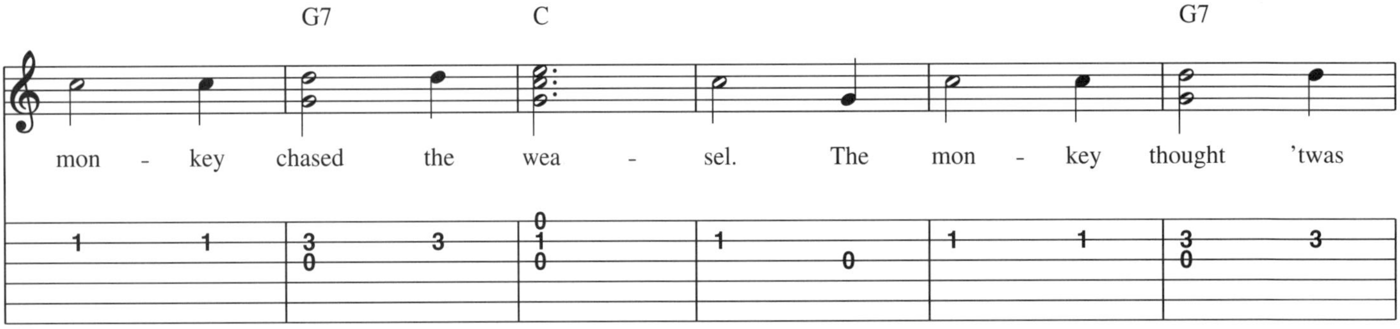

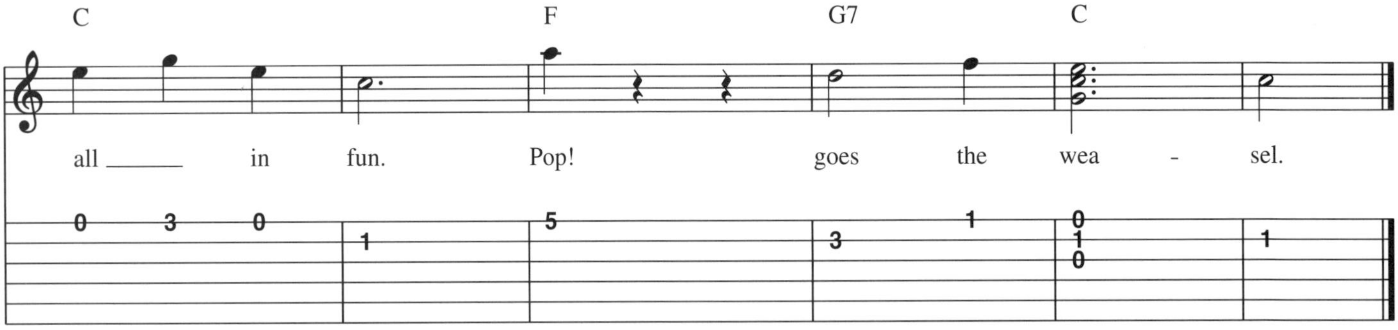

Rock-a-Bye, Baby

Traditional

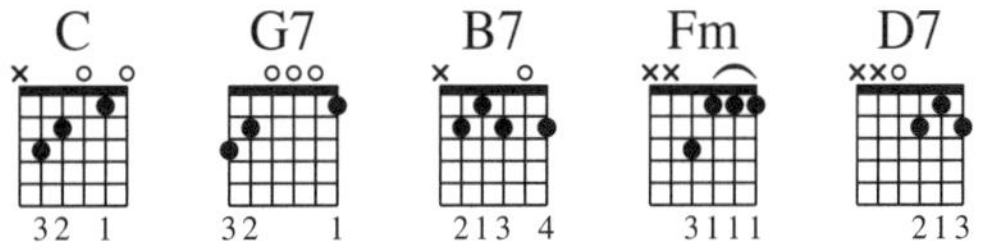

Strum Pattern: 7
Pick Pattern: 8

Moderately

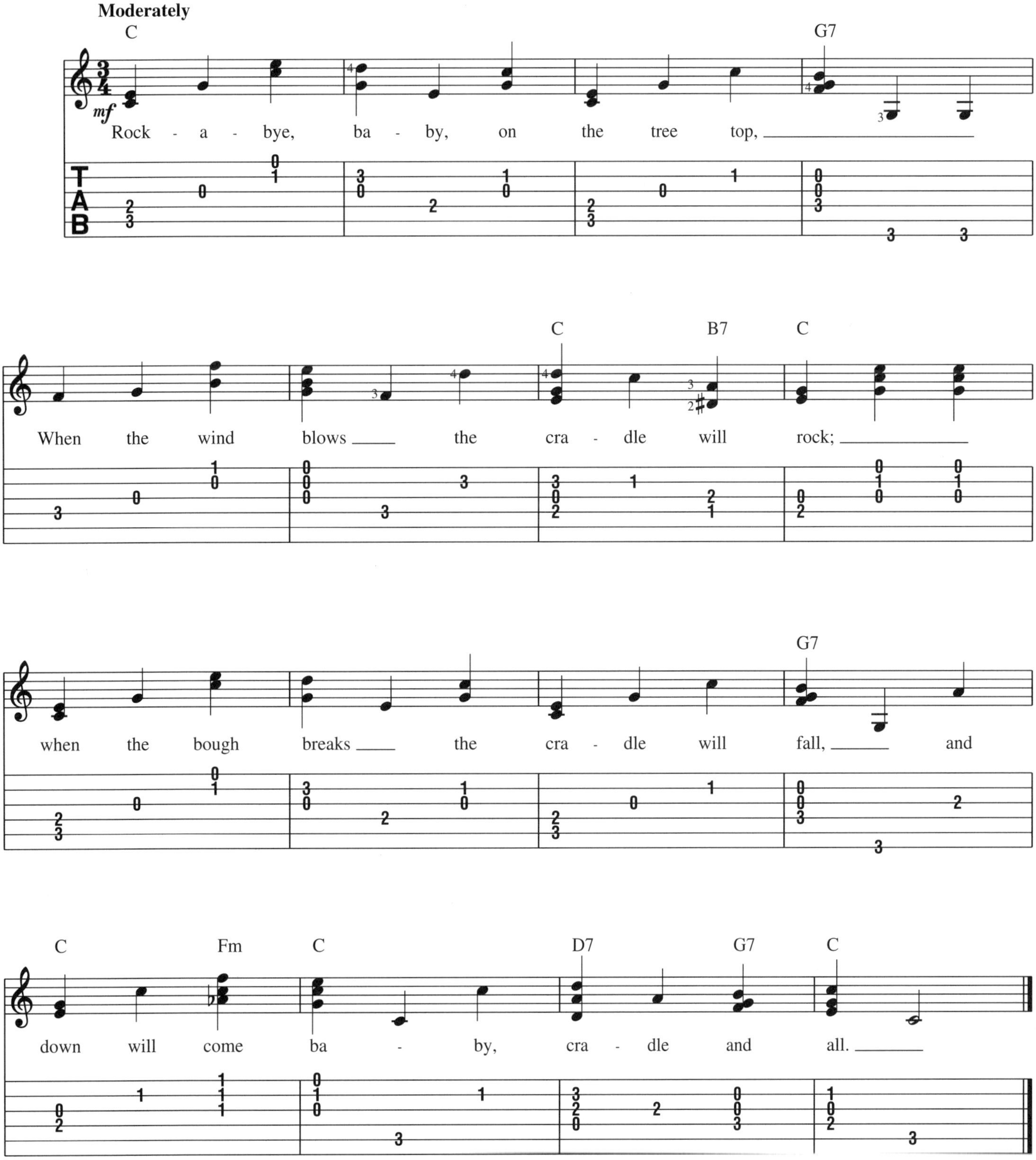

Ring Around the Rosie

Traditional

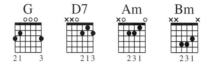

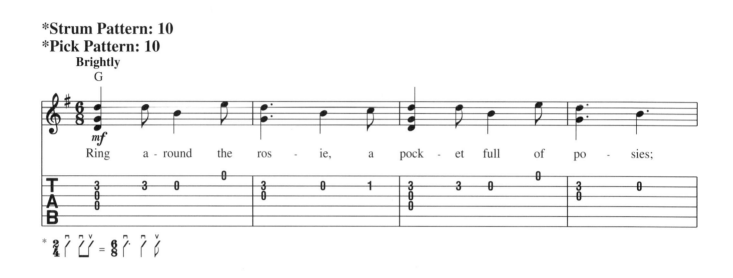

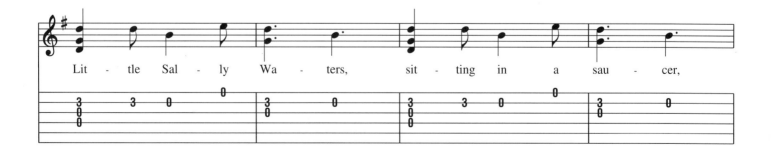

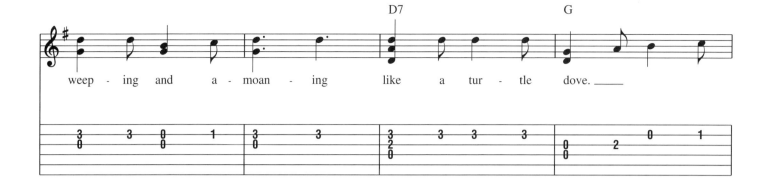

weep - ing and a - moan - ing like a tur - tle dove. _____

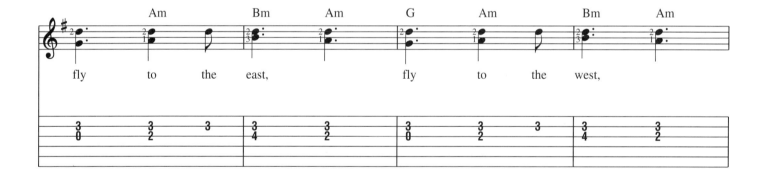

Rise, Sal - ly rise, _____ wipe your weep - ing eyes; _____

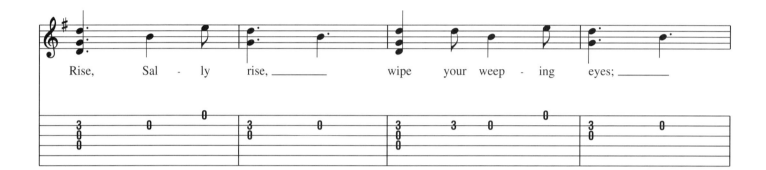

fly to the east, fly to the west,

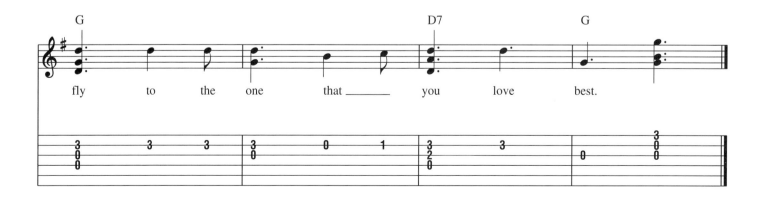

fly to the one that _____ you love best.

Row, Row, Row Your Boat

Traditional

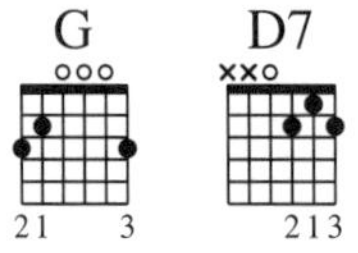

*Strum Pattern: 10
*Pick Pattern: 10

Moderately

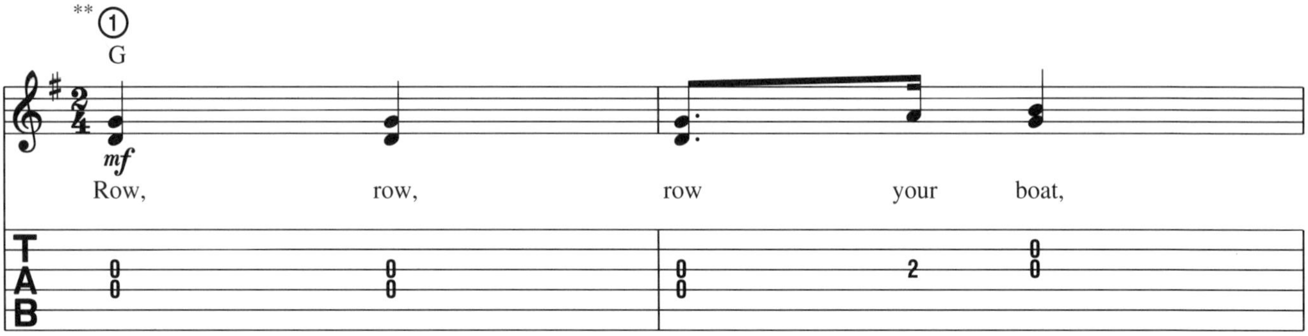

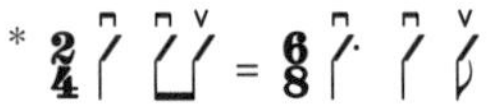

**This song can be sung as a 4-part round.

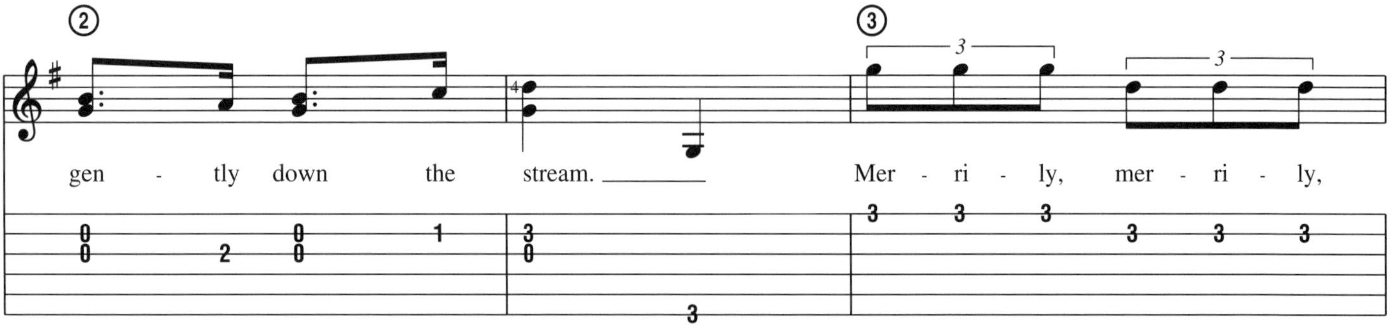

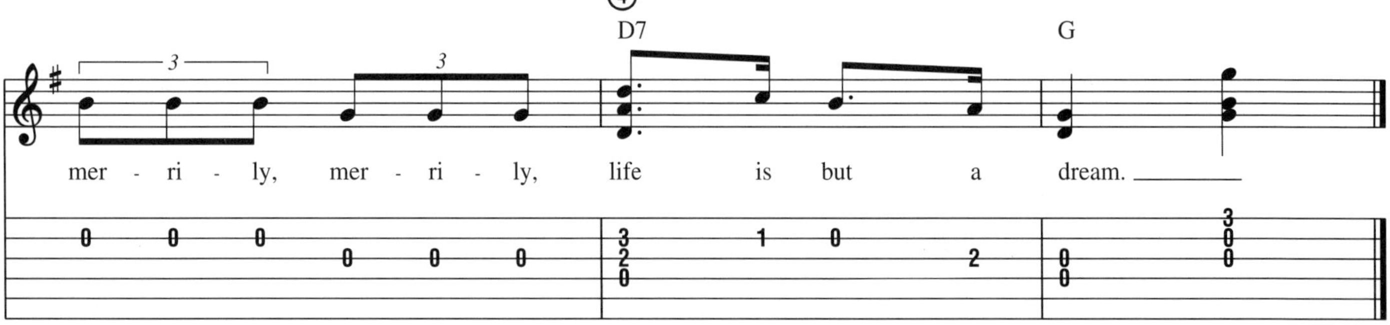

She'll Be Comin' 'Round the Mountain

Traditional

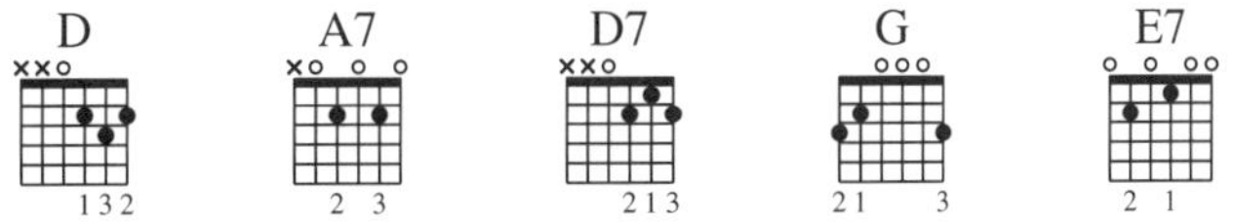

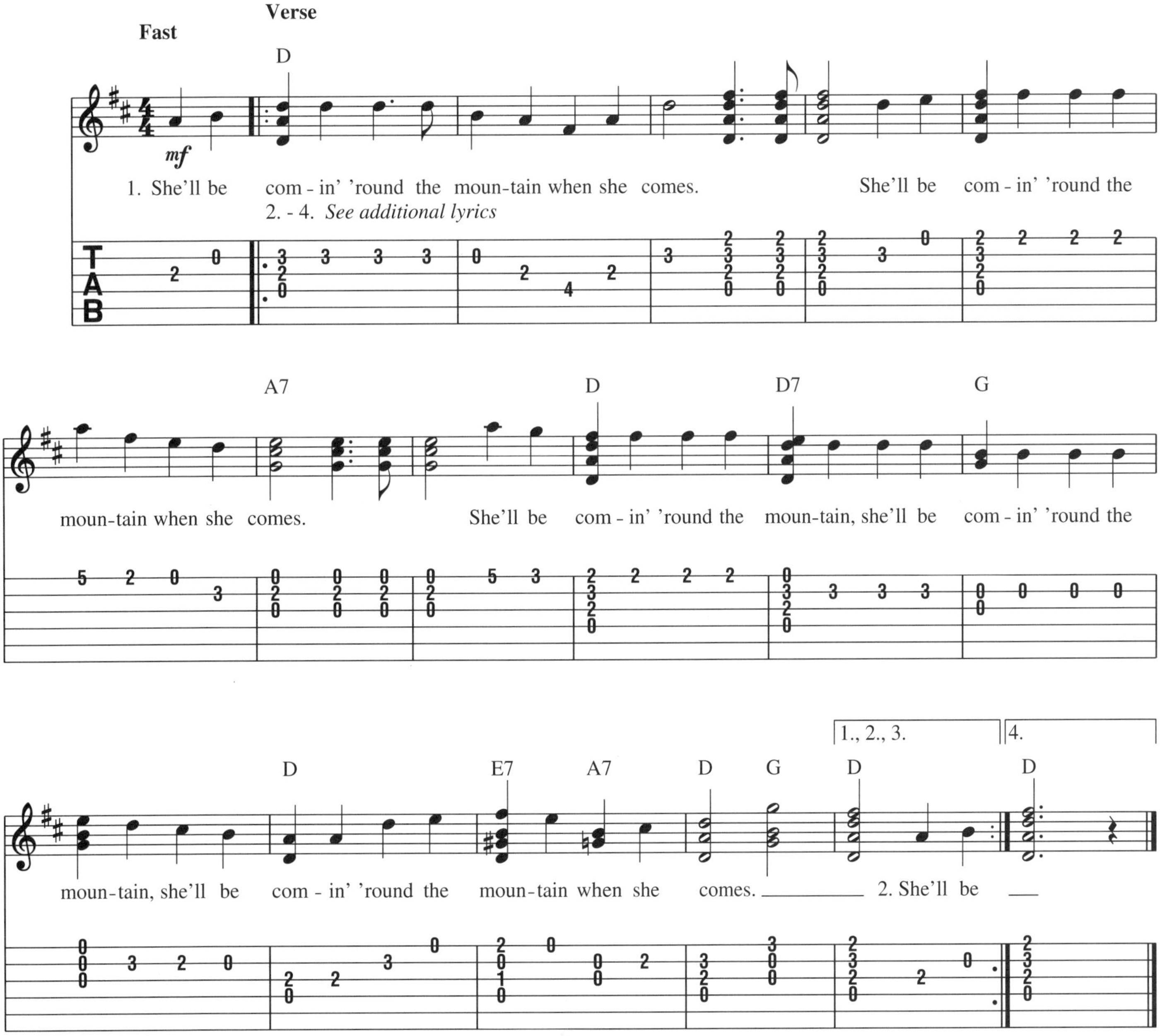

Additional Lyrics

2. She'll be drivin' six white horses when she comes.
   She'll be drivin' six white horses when she comes.
   She'll be drivin' six white horses,
   She'll be drivin' six white horses,
   She'll be drivin' six white horses when she comes.

3. Oh, we'll all go out to meet her when she comes.
   Oh, we'll all go out to meet her when she comes.
   Oh, we'll all go out to meet her,
   Oh, we'll all go out to meet her,
   Yes, we'll all go out to meet her when she comes.

4. She'll be wearin' a blue bonnet when she comes.
   She'll be wearin' a blue bonnet when she comes.
   She'll be wearin' a blue bonnet,
   She'll be wearin' a blue bonnet,
   She'll be wearin' a blue bonnet when she comes.

Shoo Fly, Don't Bother Me

Words by Billy Reeves
Music by Frank Campbell

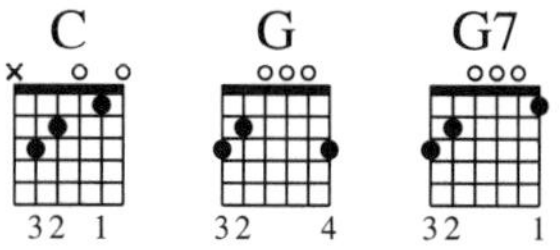

Strum Pattern: 10
Pick Pattern: 10

Chorus
Moderately

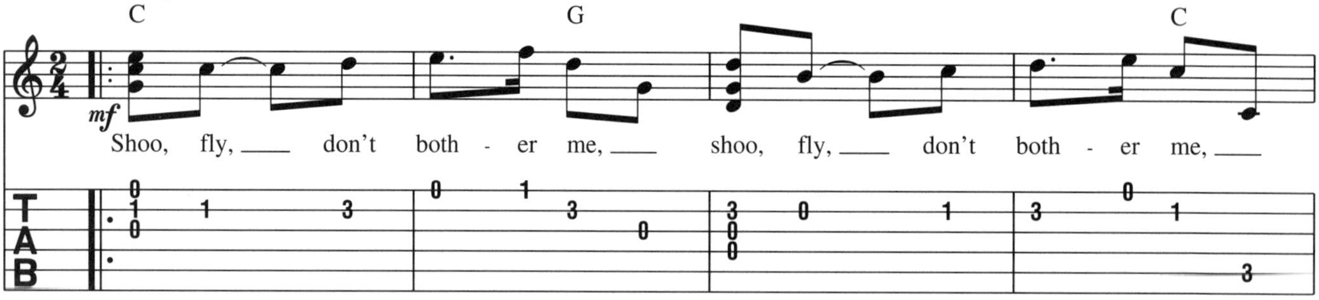

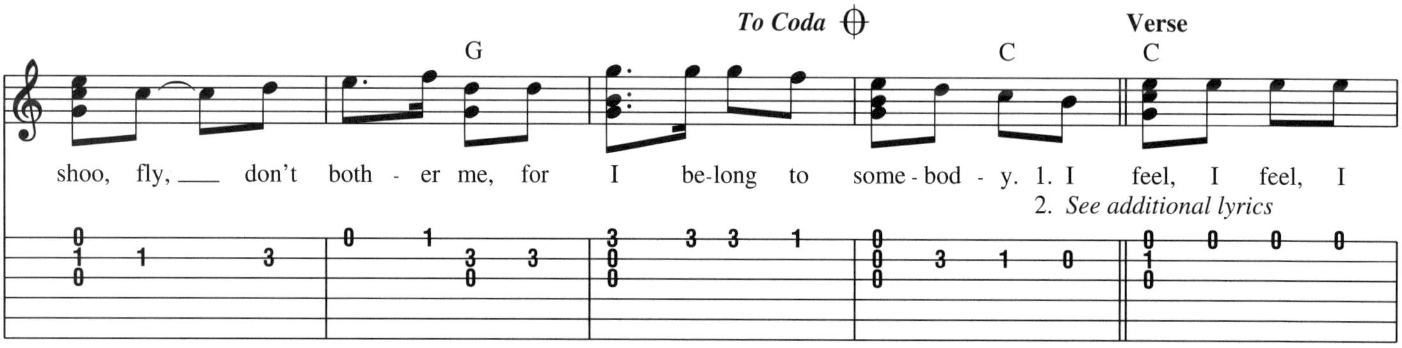

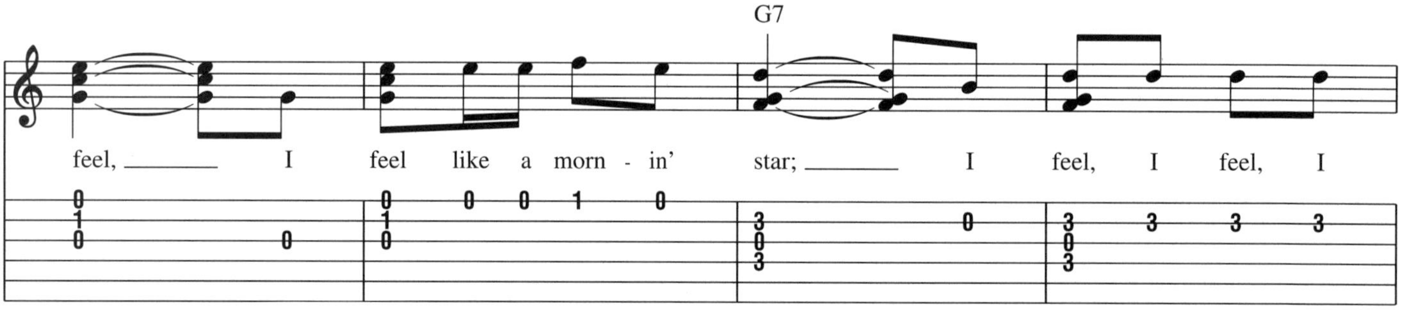

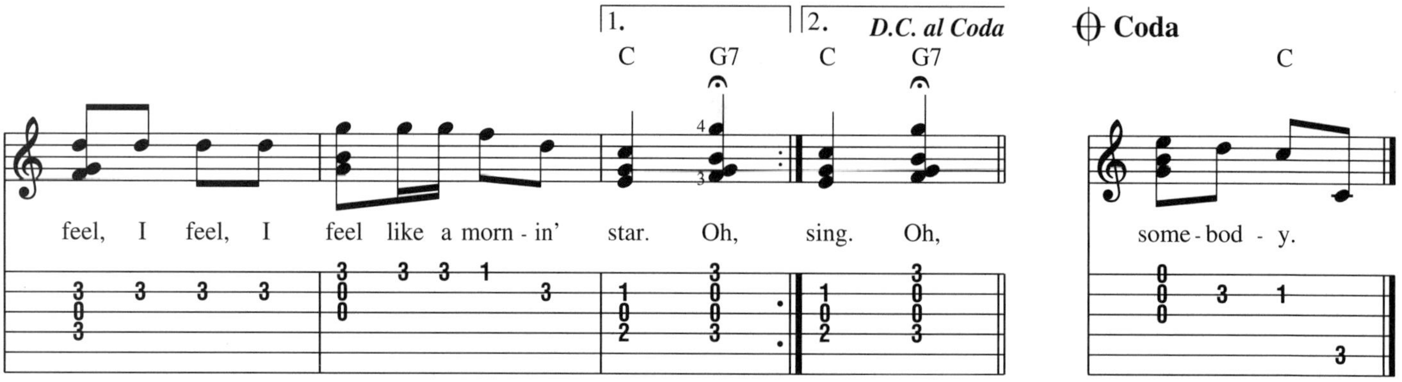

Additional Lyrics

2. I hear, I hear, I hear,
   I hear all the angels sing;
   I hear, I hear, I hear,
   I hear all the angels sing. Oh,

Simple Gifts

Traditional Shaker Hymn

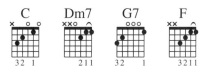

Strum Pattern: 2, 3
Pick Pattern: 2, 3

Moderately

'Tis a gift to be sim-ple, 'tis a gift to be free, 'tis a gift to come down where you ought to be. And

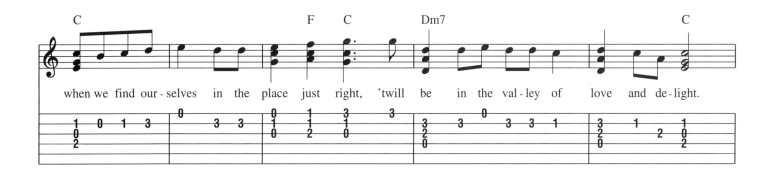

when we find our-selves in the place just right, 'twill be in the val-ley of love and de-light.

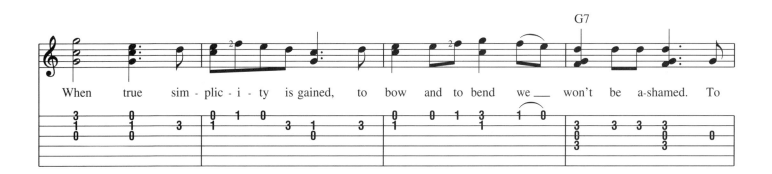

When true sim-plic-i-ty is gained, to bow and to bend we __ won't be a-shamed. To

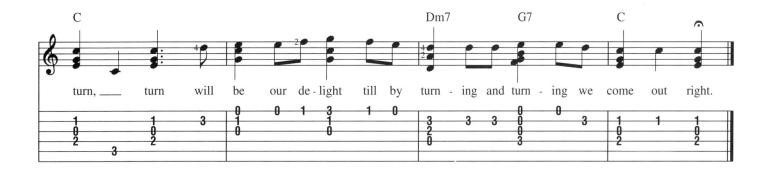

turn, __ turn will be our de-light till by turn-ing and turn-ing we come out right.

Simple Simon

Traditional

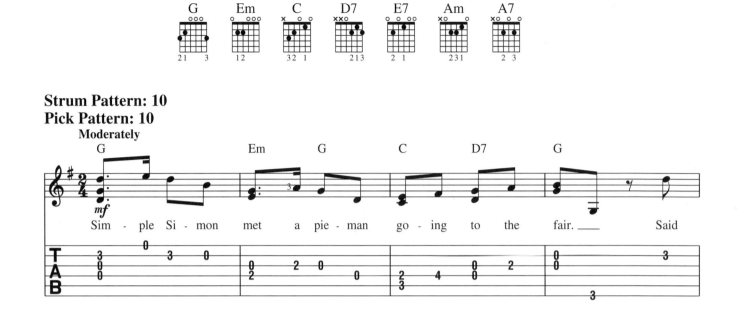

Strum Pattern: 10
Pick Pattern: 10

Moderately

Sim - ple Si - mon met a pie - man go - ing to the fair. ___ Said

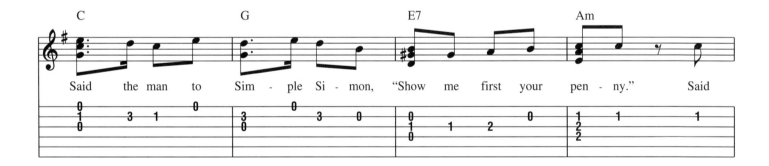

Sim - ple Si - mon to the pie - man, "Let me taste your ware." ___

Said the man to Sim - ple Si - mon, "Show me first your pen - ny." Said

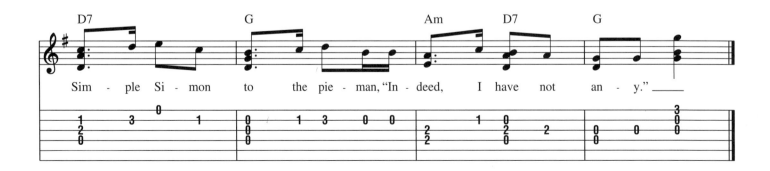

Sim - ple Si - mon to the pie - man, "In - deed, I have not an - y." ___

Skip to My Lou

Traditional

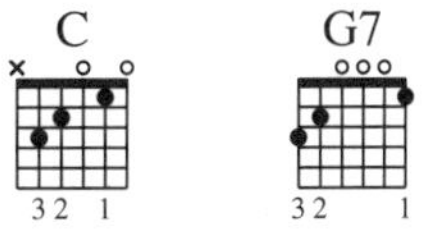

Strum Pattern: 10
Pick Pattern: 10

Chorus
Moderately fast

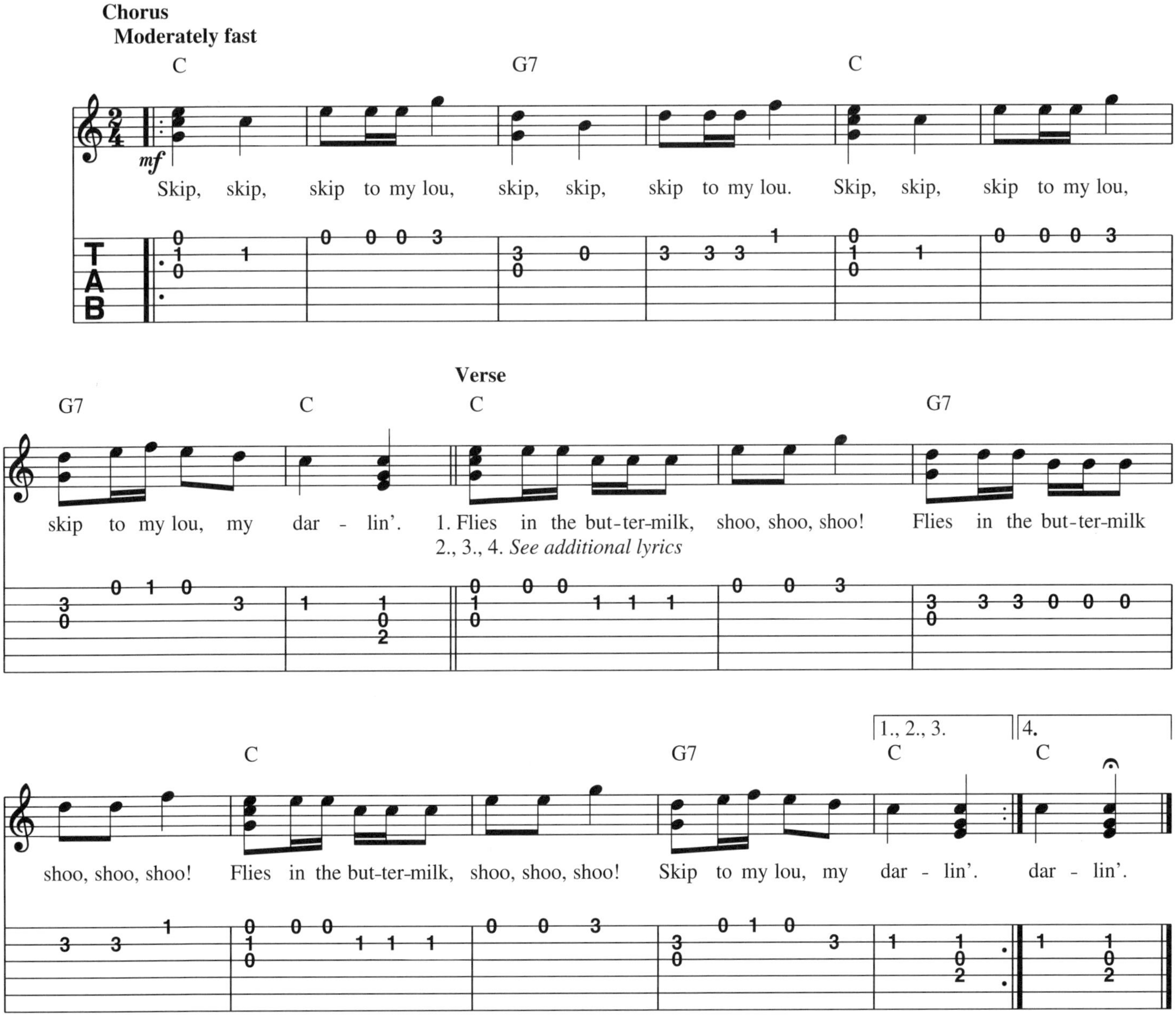

Skip, skip, skip to my lou, skip, skip, skip to my lou. Skip, skip, skip to my lou,

skip to my lou, my dar - lin'. 1. Flies in the but-ter-milk, shoo, shoo, shoo! Flies in the but-ter-milk

2., 3., 4. *See additional lyrics*

shoo, shoo, shoo! Flies in the but-ter-milk, shoo, shoo, shoo! Skip to my lou, my dar - lin'. dar - lin'.

Additional Lyrics

2. Lost my partner, what'll I do?
   Lost my partner, what'll I do?
   Lost my partner, what'll I do?
   Skip to my lou, my darlin'.

3. I'll get another one purtier than you,
   I'll get another one purtier than you,
   I'll get another one purtier than you,
   Skip to my lou, my darlin'.

4. Can't get a red bird, a blue bird'll do,
   Can't get a red bird, a blue bird'll do,
   Can't get a red bird, a blue bird'll do,
   Skip to my lou, my darlin'.

Sweet Betsy from Pike

American Folksong

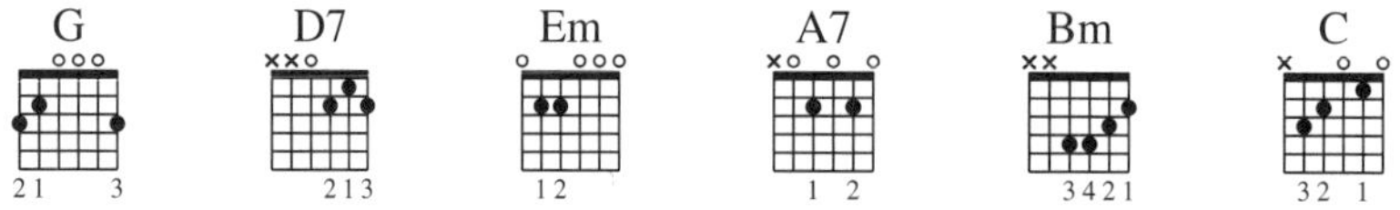

Strum Pattern: 7
Pick Pattern: 9

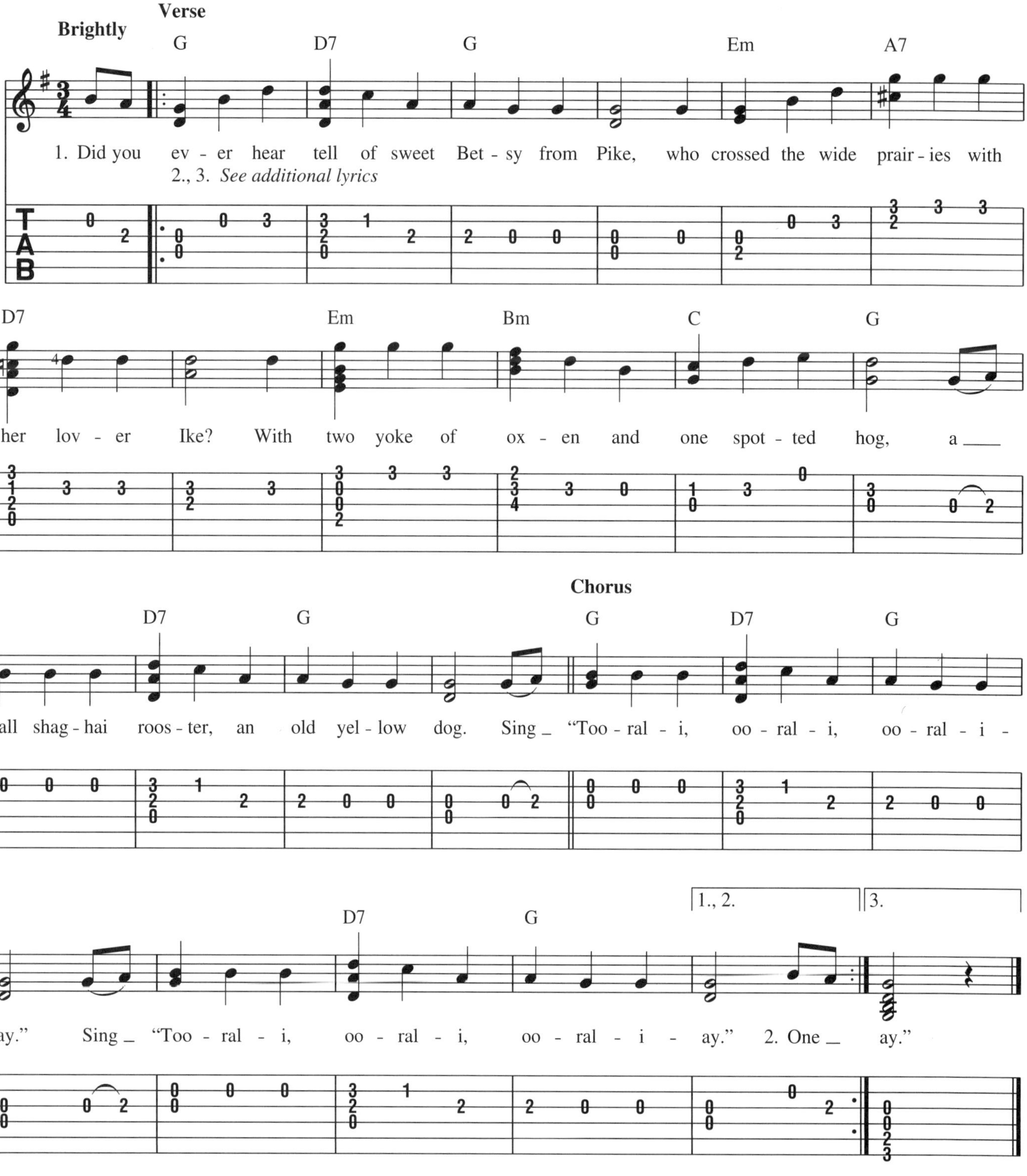

Additional Lyrics

2. One evening quite early they camped on the Platte,
    'Twas near by the road on a green shady flat
    Where Betsy, quite tired, lay down to repose
    While with wonder Ike gazed on his Pike County rose.

3. They stopped at Salt Lake to inquire the way,
    Where Brigham declared that sweet Bets' should stay.
    But Betsy got frightened and ran like a deer,
    While Brigham stood pawing the ground like a steer.

Take Me Out to the Ball Game
Words by Jack Norworth
Music by Albert von Tilzer
D A7 B7 Em E7 D7 G B♭
Strum Pattern: 8
Pick Pattern: 8
Spirited Waltz
Take me out to the ball game, take me out to the crowd.
Buy me some pea-nuts and Crack-er Jack. I don't care if I nev-er get back. Let me
root, root, root for the home team. If they don't win it's a shame. For it's
one, two, three strikes, you're out at the old ball game.

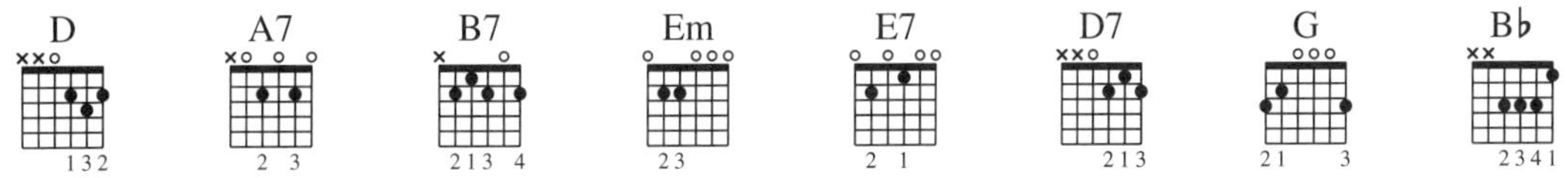

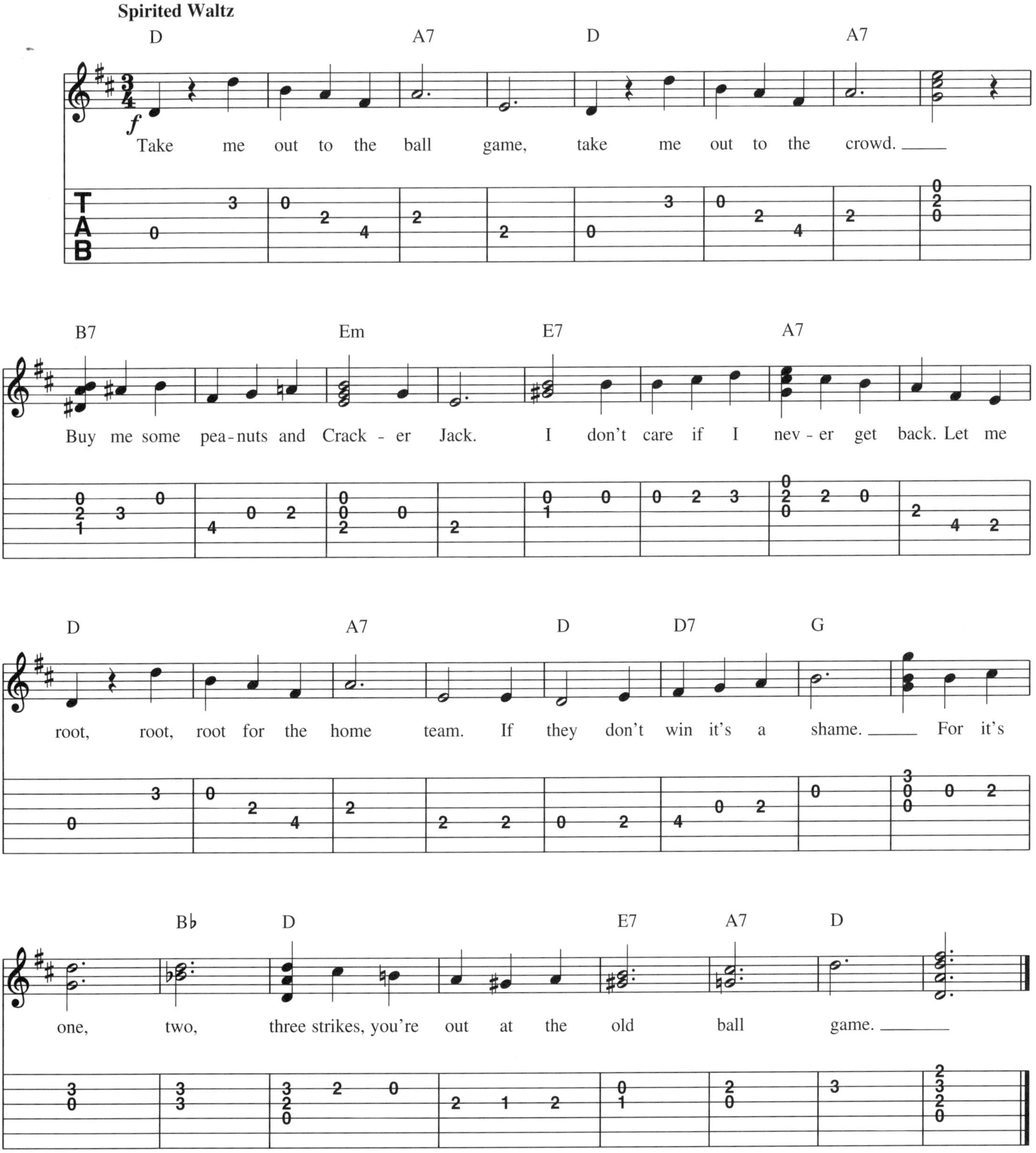

There Was an Old Woman Who Lived in a Shoe

Traditional

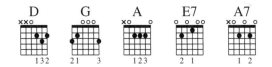

Strum Pattern: 7
Pick Pattern: 7

Moderately

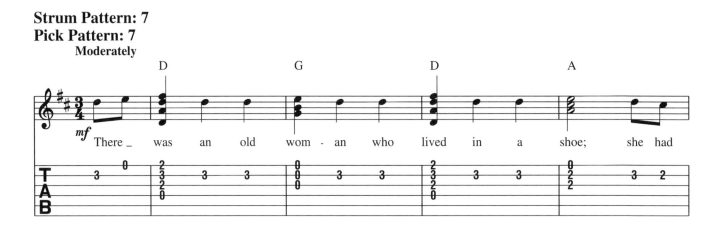

There _ was an old wom-an who lived in a shoe; she had

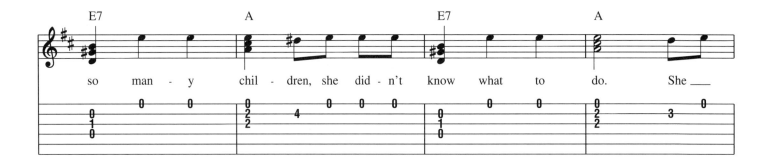

so man-y chil-dren, she did-n't know what to do. She ___

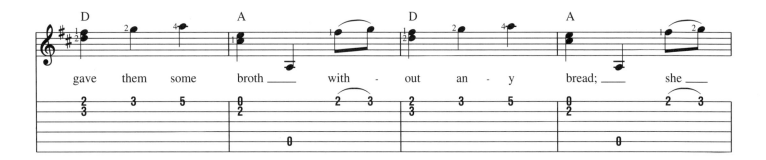

gave them some broth ___ with-out an-y bread; ___ she ___

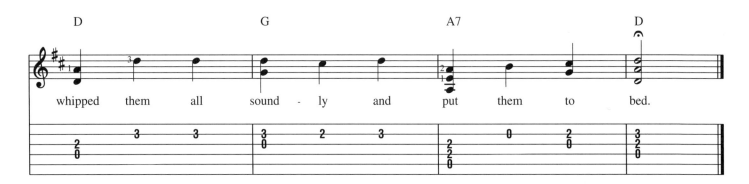

whipped them all sound-ly and put them to bed.

There's a Hole in the Bucket

Traditional

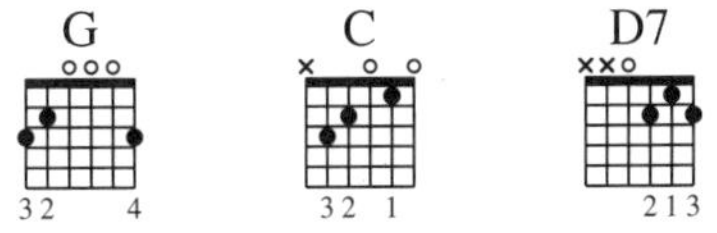

Strum Pattern: 8
Pick Pattern: 8

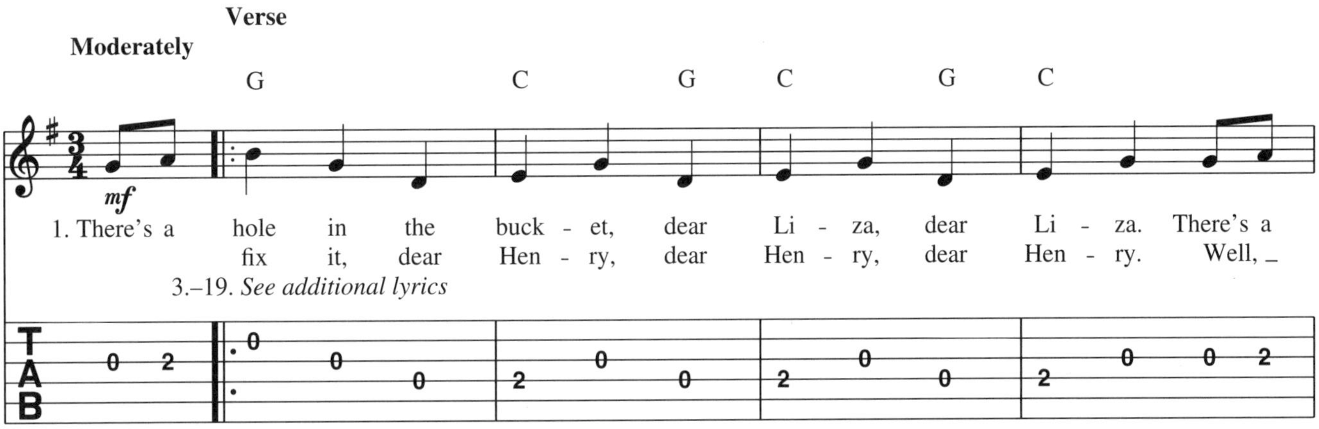

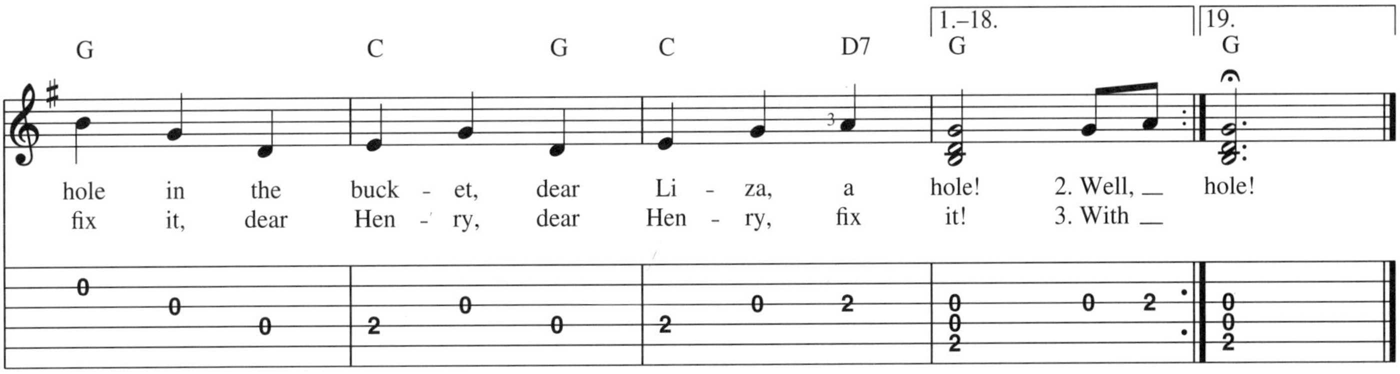

Additional Lyrics

3. With what shall I fix it, dear Liza, etc.
4. With a straw, dear Henry, etc.
5. But the straw is too long, dear Liza, etc.
6. Then cut it, dear Henry, etc.
7. With what shall I cut it, dear Liza, etc.
8. With a knife, dear Henry, etc.
9. But the knife is too dull, dear Liza, etc.
10. Then sharpen it, dear Henry, etc.
11. With what shall I sharpen it, dear Liza, etc.
12. With a stone, dear Henry, etc.
13. But the stone is too dry, dear Liza, etc.
14. Then wet it, dear Henry, etc.
15. With what shall I wet it, dear Liza, etc.
16. With water, dear Henry, etc.
17. In what shall I carry it, dear Liza, etc.
18. In a bucket, dear Henry, etc.
19. There's a hole in the bucket, dear Liza, etc.

There's a Hole in the Bottom of the Sea

Traditional

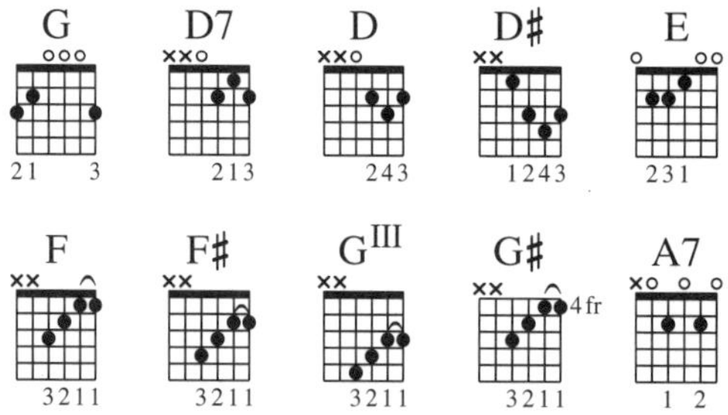

Strum Pattern: 3, 2
Pick Pattern: 3, 4

Verse
Moderately

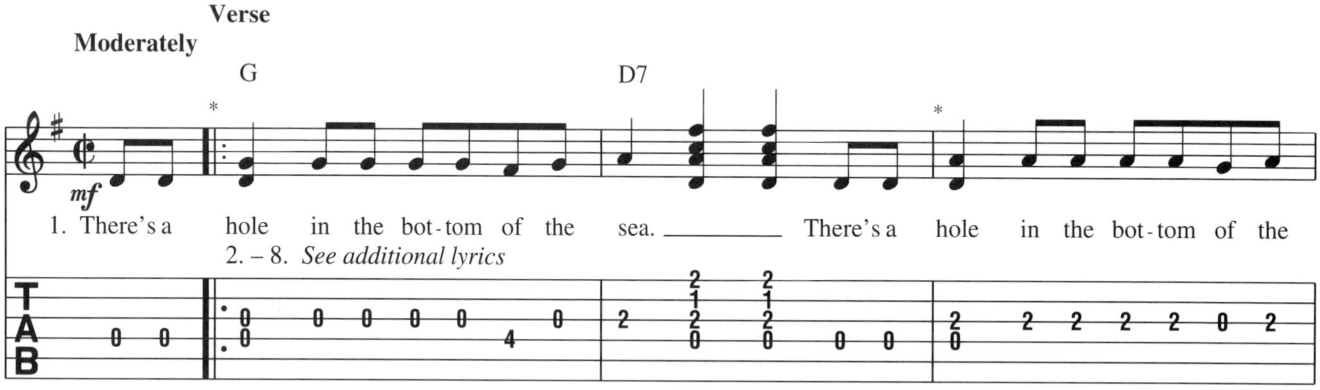

1. There's a hole in the bot-tom of the sea. _____ There's a hole in the bot-tom of the
2. – 8. *See additional lyrics*

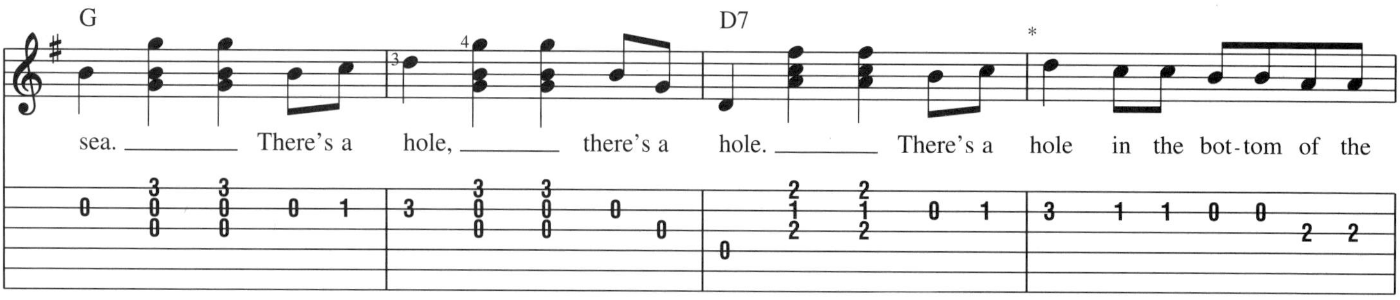

sea. _____ There's a hole, _____ there's a hole. _____ There's a hole in the bot-tom of the

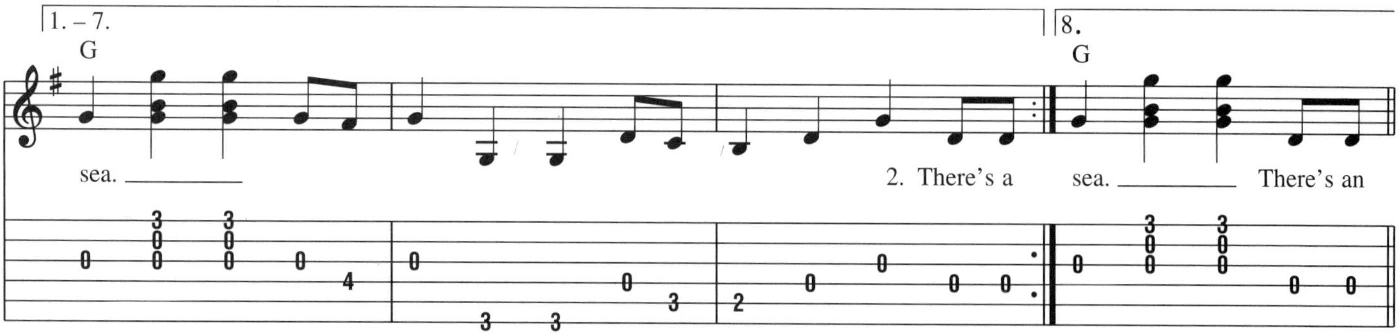

1. – 7.

sea. _____

8.

2. There's a sea. _____ There's an

Outro

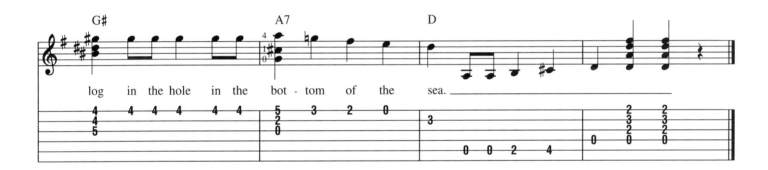

Additional Lyrics

For each new verse, add 2 extra beats (keep repeating the first 2 beats) to the measures that are marked with an asterisk. Extra beats are boldfaced italic below.

2. There's a *log in the* hole in the bottom of the sea.
   There's a *log in the* hole in the bottom of the sea.
   There's a log, there's a log.
   There's a *log in the* hole in the bottom of the sea.

3. There's a *bump on the log in the* hole in the bottom of the sea.
   There's a *bump on the log in the* hole in the bottom of the sea.
   There's a bump, there's a bump.
   There's a *bump on the log in the* hole in the bottom of the sea.

4. There's a *frog on the bump on the log*
   In the hole in the bottom of the sea.
   There's a *frog on the bump on the log*
   In the hole in the bottom of the sea.
   There's a frog, there's a frog.
   There's a *frog on the bump on the log*
   In the hole in the bottom of the sea.

5. There's a *fly on the frog on the bump on the log*
   In the hole in the bottom of the sea.
   There's a *fly on the frog on the bump on the log*
   In the hole in the bottom of the sea.
   There's a fly, there's a fly.
   There's a *fly on the frog on the bump on the log*
   In the hole in the bottom of the sea.

6. There's a *wing on the fly on the frog*
   On the bump on the log in the hole in the bottom of the sea.
   There's a *wing on the fly on the frog*
   On the bump on the log in the hole in the bottom of the sea.
   There's a wing, there's a wing.
   There's a *wing on the fly on the frog*
   On the bump on the log in the hole in the bottom of the sea.

7. There's a *flea on the wing on the fly on the frog*
   On the bump on the log in the hole in the bottom of the sea.
   There's a *flea on the wing on the fly on the frog*
   On the bump on the log in the hole in the bottom of the sea.
   There's a flea, there's a flea.
   There's a *flea on the wing on the fly on the frog*
   On the bump on the log in the hole in the bottom of the sea.

8. There's an *eye on the flea on the wing on the fly on the frog*
   On the bump on the log in the hole in the bottom of the sea.
   There's an *eye on the flea on the wing on the fly on the frog*
   On the bump on the log in the hole in the bottom of the sea.
   There's an eye, there's an eye.
   There's an *eye on the flea on the wing on the fly on the frog*
   On the bump on the log in the hole in the bottom of the sea.

This Little Light of Mine

African-American Spiritual

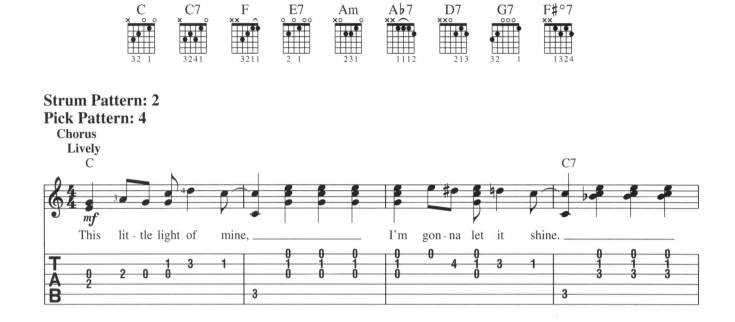

Strum Pattern: 2
Pick Pattern: 4

Chorus
Lively

This lit-tle light of mine, _____ I'm gon-na let it shine. _____

This lit-tle light of mine, _____ I'm gon-na let it shine. _____

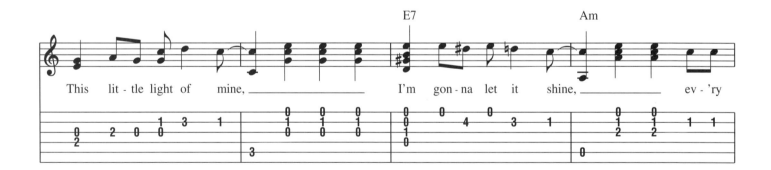

This lit-tle light of mine, _____ I'm gon-na let it shine, _____ ev-'ry

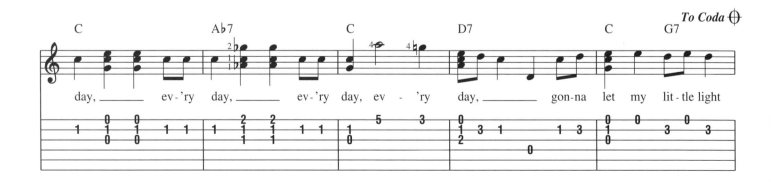

To Coda ⊕

day, _____ ev-'ry day, _____ ev-'ry day, ev-'ry day, _____ gon-na let my lit-tle light

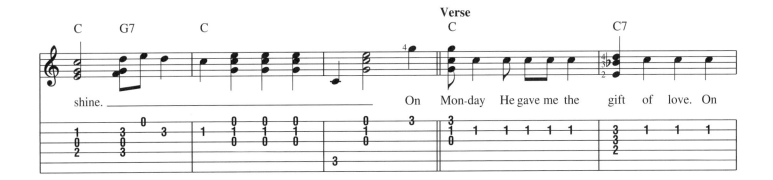

shine. _____ On Mon-day He gave me the gift of love. On

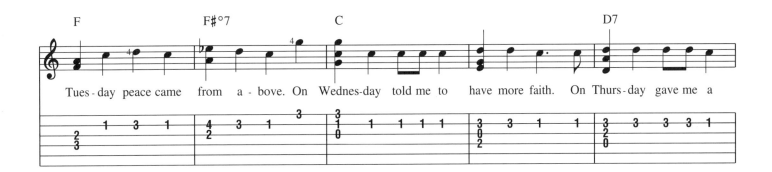

Tues-day peace came from a-bove. On Wednes-day told me to have more faith. On Thurs-day gave me a

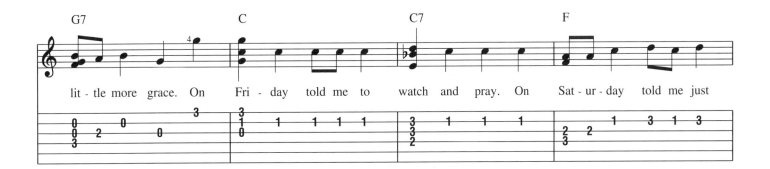

lit-tle more grace. On Fri-day told me to watch and pray. On Sat-ur-day told me just

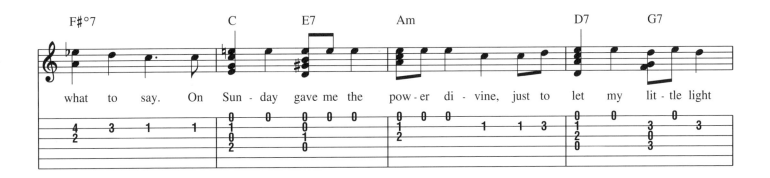

what to say. On Sun-day gave me the pow-er di-vine, just to let my lit-tle light

D.C. al Coda ⊕ **Coda**

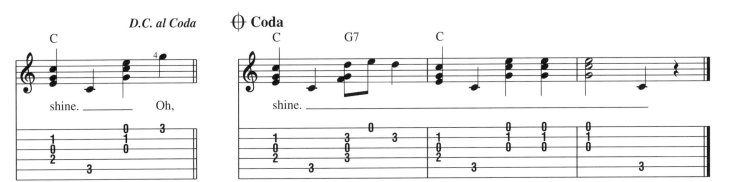

shine. _____ Oh,   shine. _____

This Old Man

Traditional

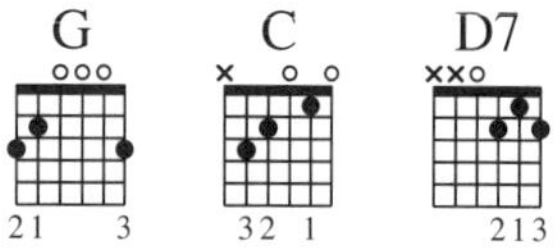

Strum Pattern: 4, 3
Pick Pattern: 3, 4

Verse
Lively

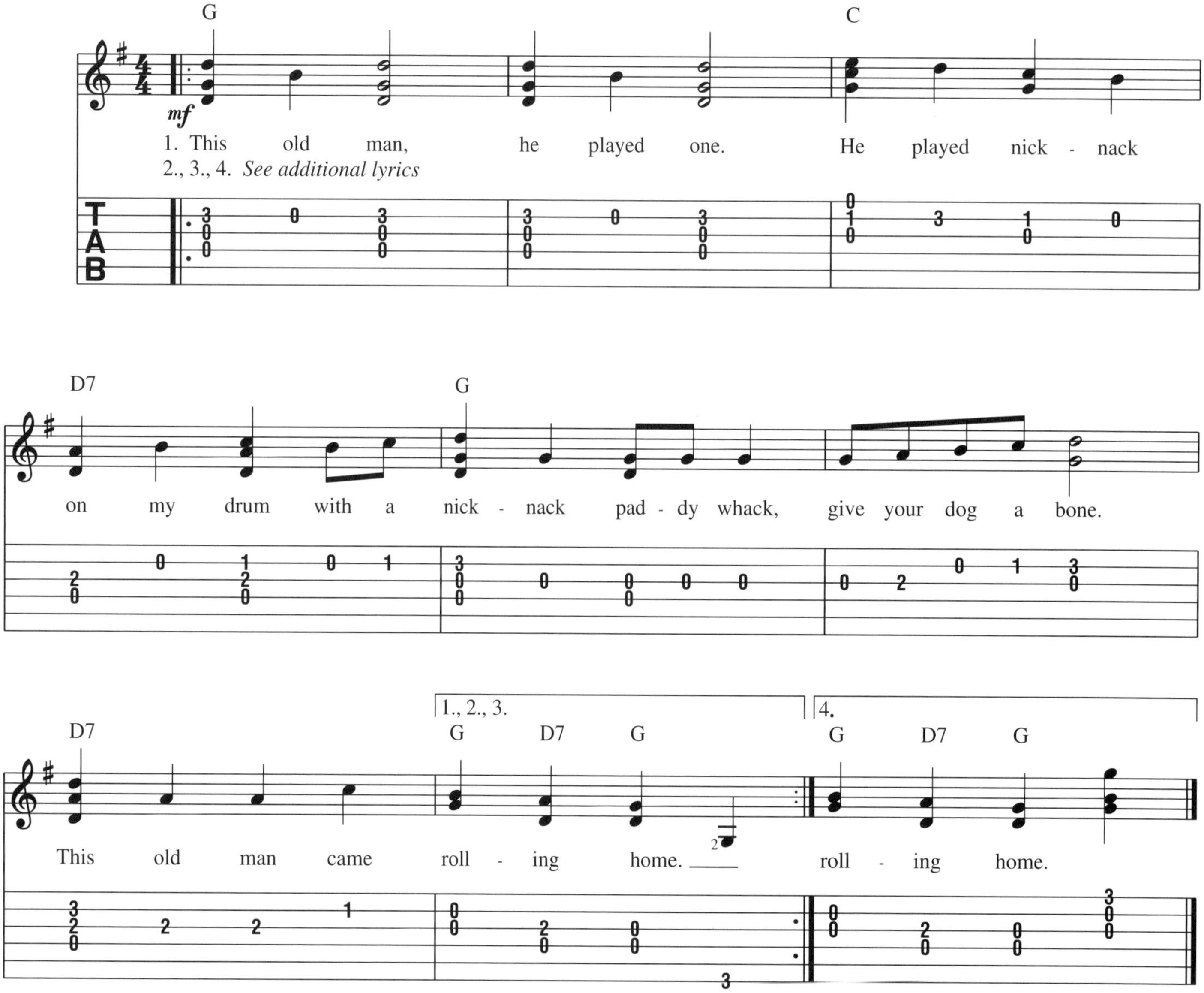

1. This old man, he played one. He played nick - nack
2., 3., 4. *See additional lyrics*

on my drum with a nick - nack pad - dy whack, give your dog a bone.

This old man came roll - ing home. roll - ing home.

Additional Lyrics

2. This old man, he played two.
He played nicknack on my shoe with a
Nicknack paddy whack, give your dog a bone.
This old man came rolling home.

3. This old man, he played three.
He played nicknack on my knee with a
Nicknack paddy whack, give your dog a bone.
This old man came rolling home.

4. This old man, he played four.
He played nicknack on my door with a
Nicknack paddy whack, give your dog a bone.
This old man came rolling home.

Three Blind Mice

Traditional

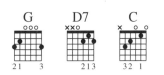

*Strum Pattern: 10
*Pick Pattern: 10

Moderately fast

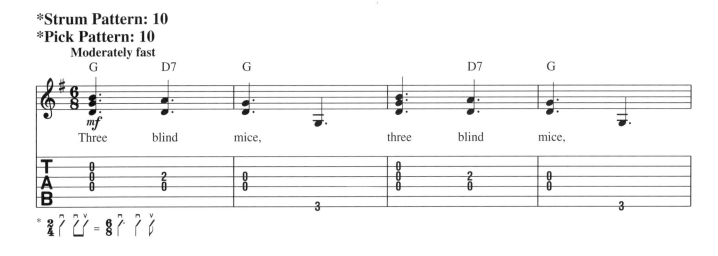

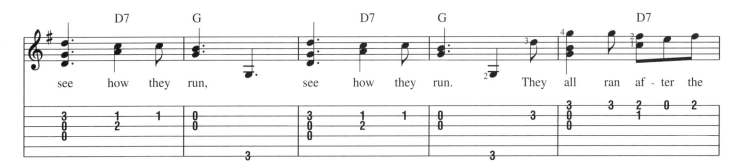

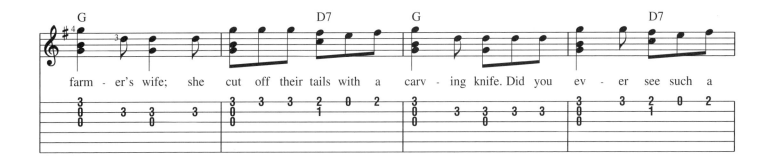

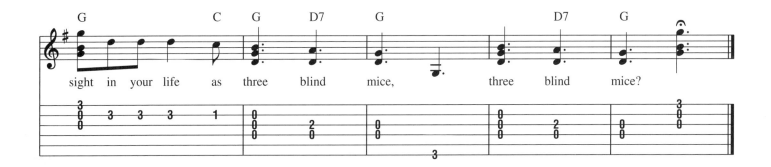

Three Little Kittens

Traditional

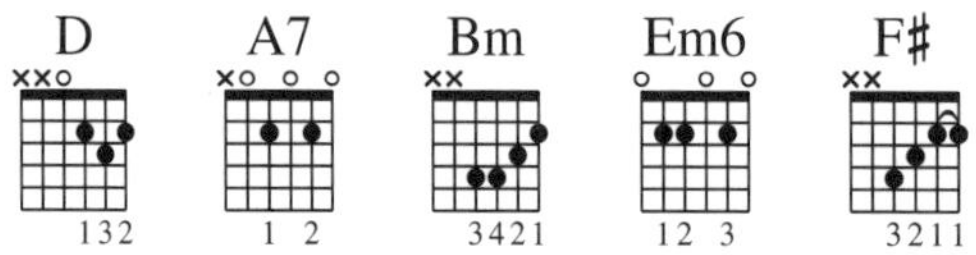

*Strum Pattern: 10
*Pick Pattern: 10

Verse
Moderately

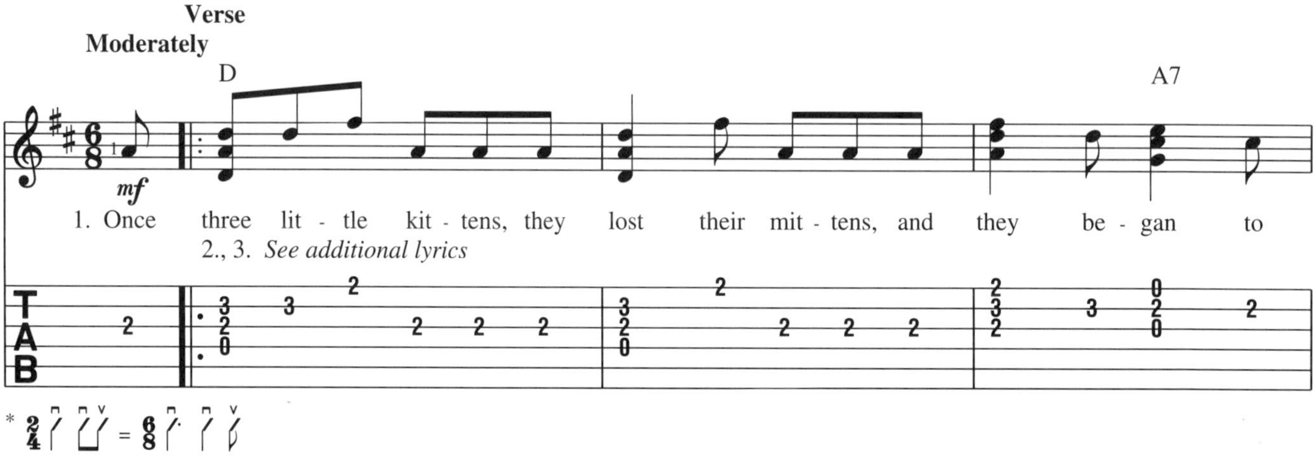

1. Once three lit-tle kit-tens, they lost their mit-tens, and they be-gan to
2., 3. *See additional lyrics*

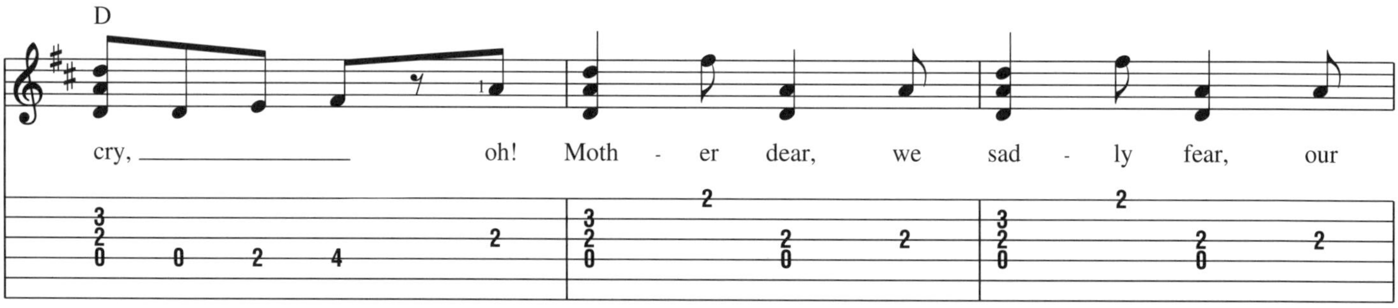

cry, _____ oh! Moth-er dear, we sad-ly fear, our

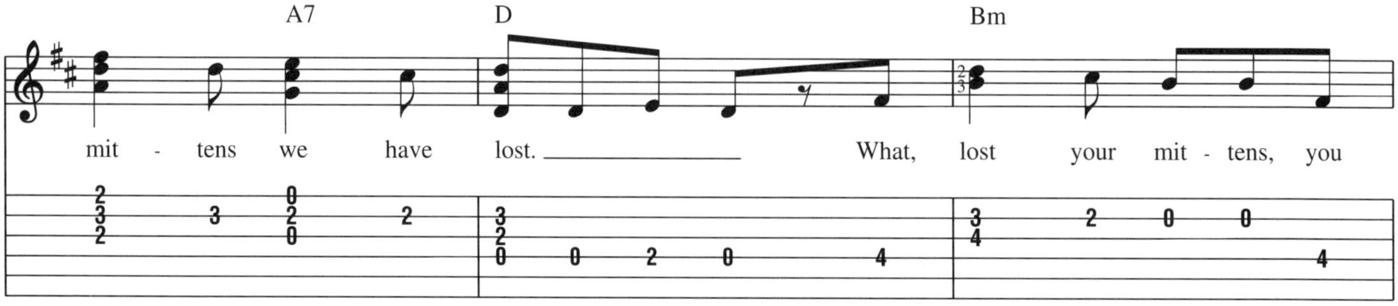

mit-tens we have lost. _____ What, lost your mit-tens, you

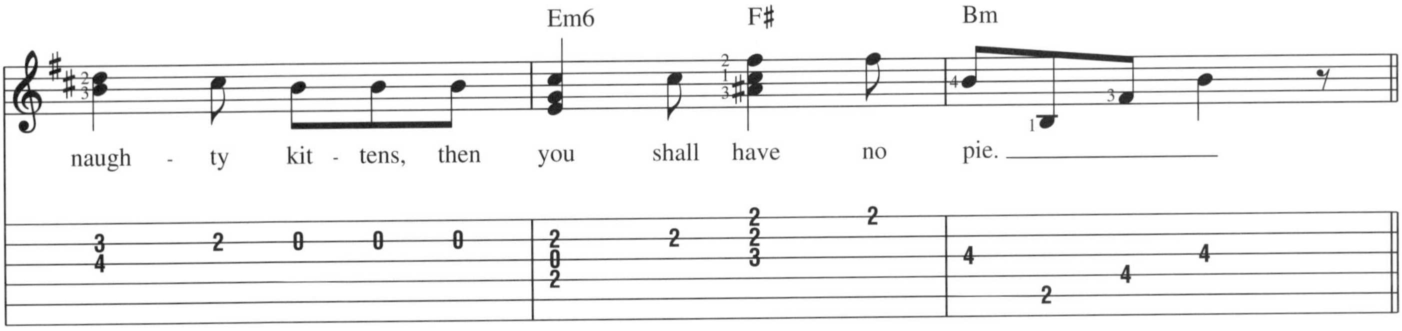

naugh - ty kit - tens, then you shall have no pie._____

Chorus

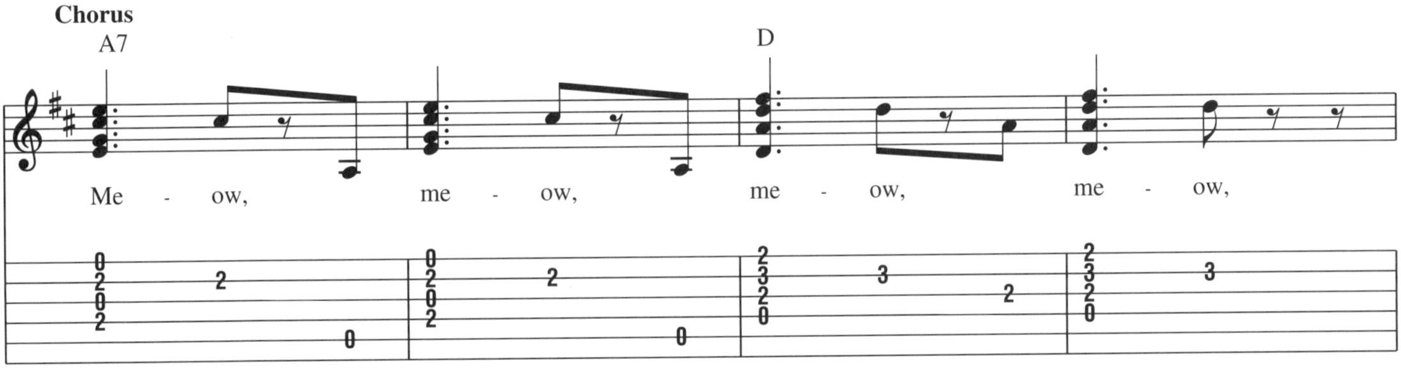

Me - ow, me - ow, me - ow, me - ow,

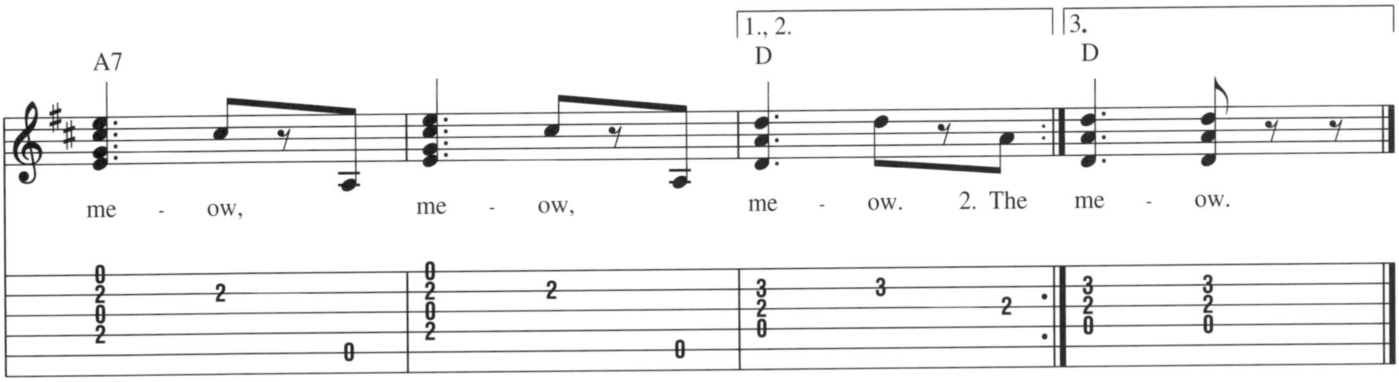

me - ow, me - ow, me - ow. 2. The me - ow.

Additional Lyrics

2. The three little kittens
   They found their mittens,
   And they began to cry,
   Oh! Mother dear, see here, see here,
   Our mittens we have found.
   What, found your mittens, you darling kittens,
   Then you shall have some pie.

3. The three little kittens
   Put on their mittens,
   And soon ate up the pie,
   Oh! Mother dear, we greatly fear,
   Our mittens we have soil'd.
   What, soil'd your mittens, you naughty kittens,
   Then they began to cry.

Tom, Tom, the Piper's Son

Traditional

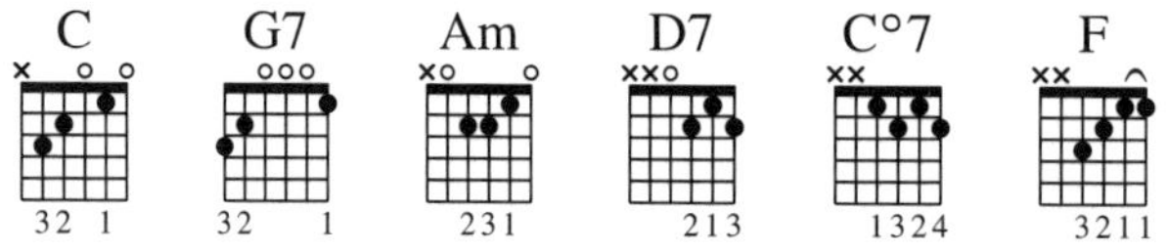

Strum Pattern: 10
Pick Pattern: 10

Verse
Moderately

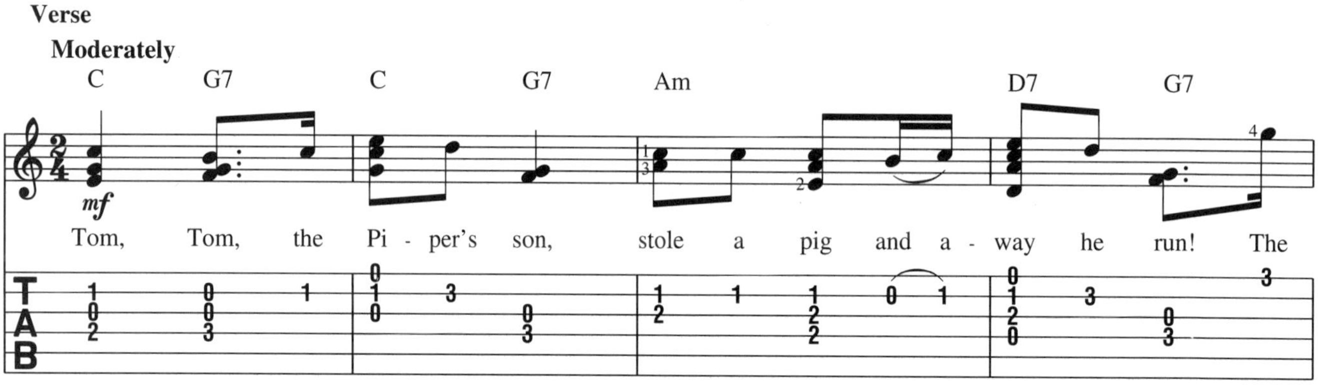

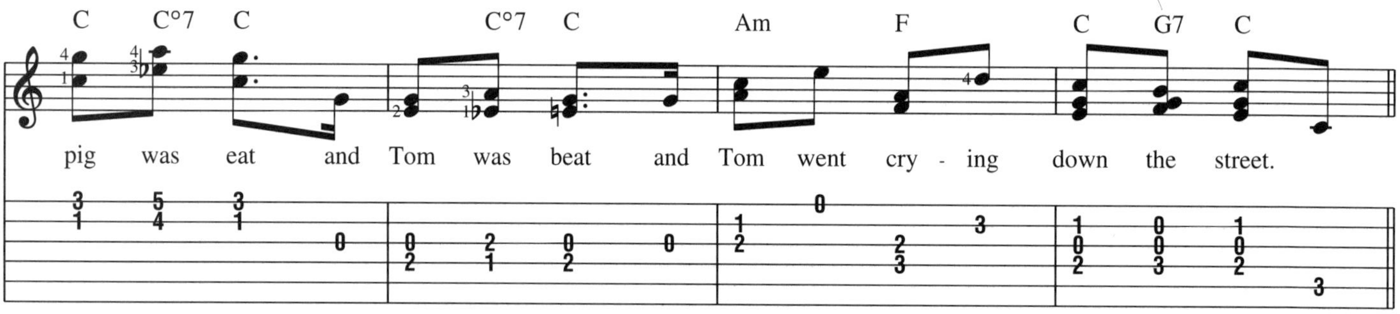

Outro

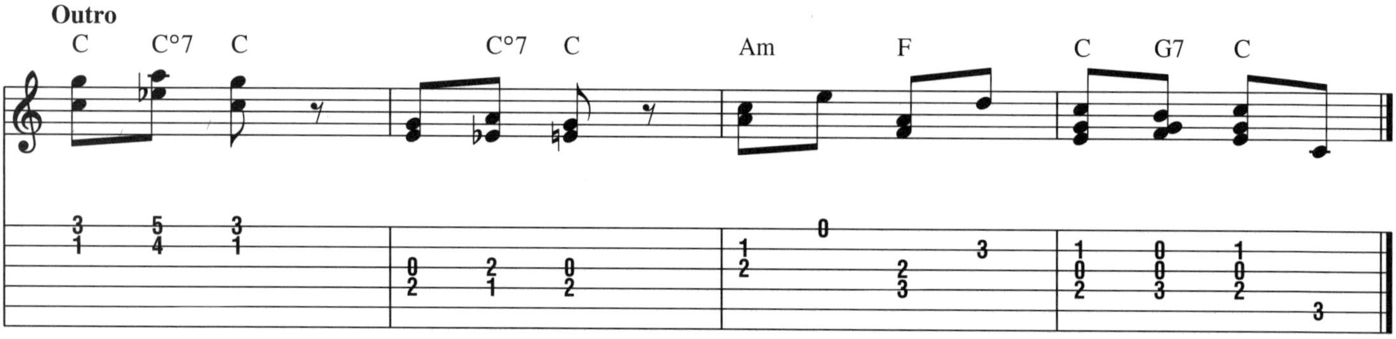

Twinkle, Twinkle Little Star

Traditional

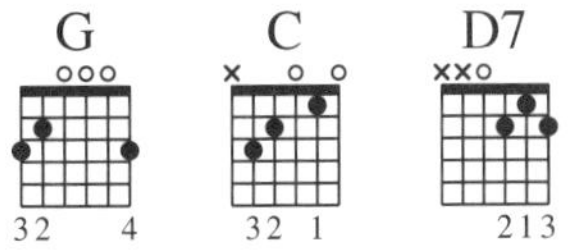

Strum Pattern: 3
Pick Pattern: 3, 4

Moderately

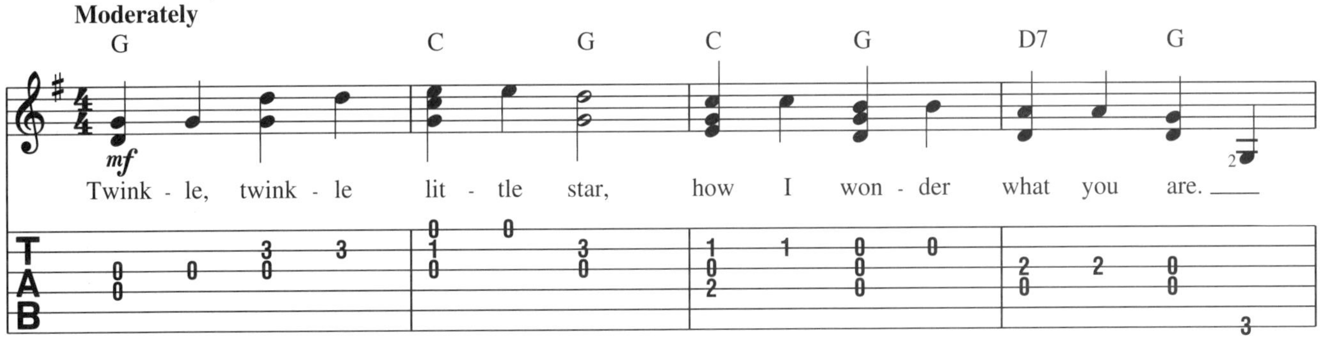

Twink - le, twink - le lit - tle star, how I won - der what you are. ____

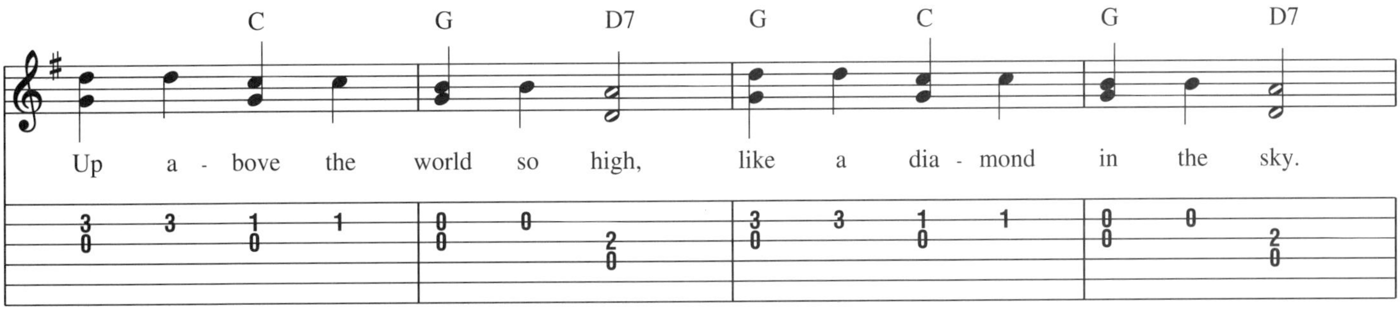

Up a - bove the world so high, like a dia - mond in the sky.

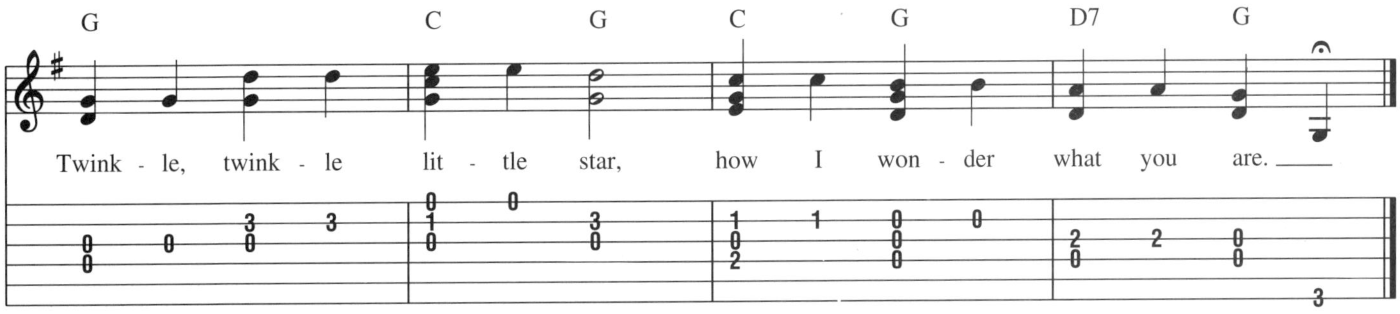

Twink - le, twink - le lit - tle star, how I won - der what you are. ____

When the Saints Go Marching In

Words by Katherine E. Purvis
Music by James M. Black

Strum Pattern: 1
Pick Pattern: 2

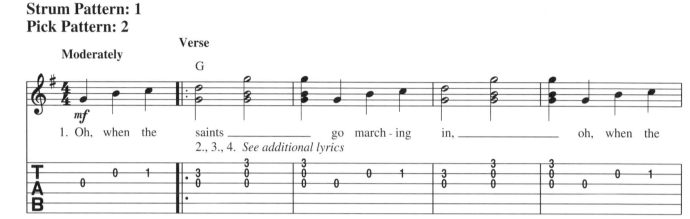

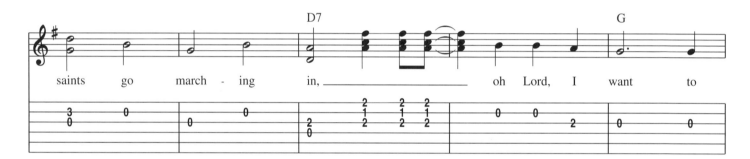

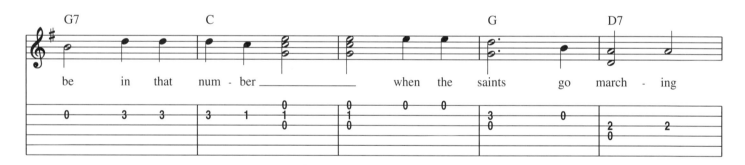

Additional Lyrics

2. Oh, when the sun refuse to shine,
Oh, when the sun refuse to shine,
Oh Lord, I want to be in that number,
When the sun refuse to shine.

3. Oh, when they crown Him Lord of all,
Oh, when they crown Him Lord of all,
Oh Lord, I want to be in that number,
When they crown Him Lord of all.

4. Oh, when they gather 'round the throne,
Oh, when they gather 'round the throne,
Oh Lord, I want to be in that number,
When they gather 'round the throne.

Yankee Doodle

Traditional

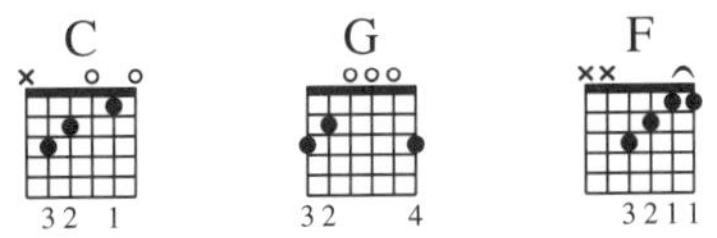

Strum Pattern: 10
Pick Pattern: 10

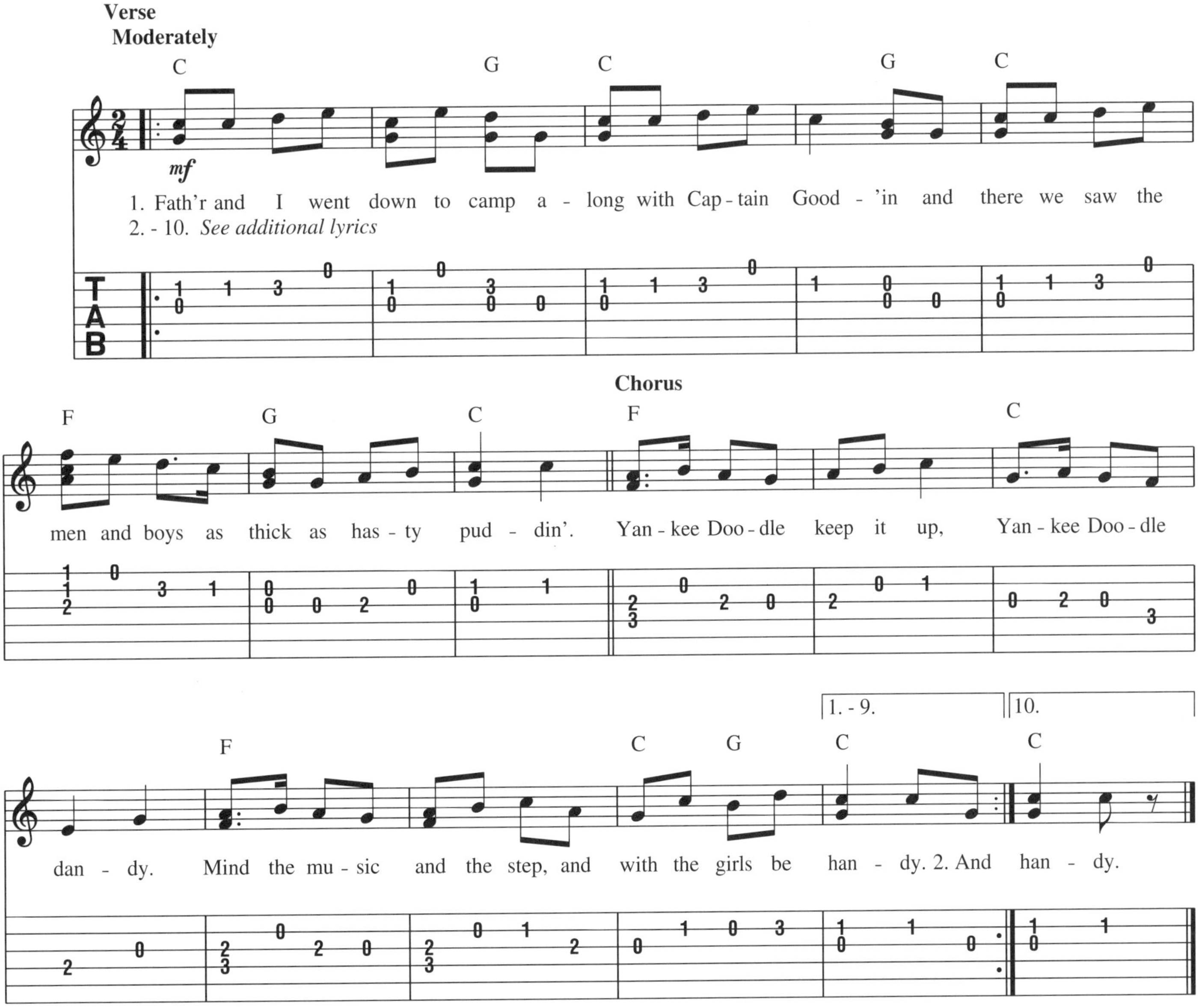

Additional Lyrics

2. And there we see a thousand men
   As rich as Squire David.
   And what they wasted ev'ry day
   I wish it could be saved.

3. And there was Captain Washington
   Upon a slapping stallion
   A-giving orders to his men,
   I guess there was a million.

4. And then the feathers on his hat,
   They looked so very fine, ah!
   I wanted peskily to get
   To give to my Jemima.

5. And there I see a swamping gun,
   Large as a log of maple,
   Upon a mighty little cart,
   A load for father's cattle.

6. And ev'ry time they fired it off,
   It took a horn of powder.
   It made a noise like father's gun,
   Only a nation louder.

7. An' there I see a little keg,
   Its head all made of leather.
   They knocked upon't with little sticks
   To call the folks together.

8. And Cap'n Davis had a gun,
   He kind o'clapt his hand on't
   And stuck a crooked stabbing-iron
   Upon the little end on't.

9. The troopers, too, would gallop up
   And fire right in our faces.
   It scared me almost half to death
   To see them run such races.

10. It scared me so I hooked it off
    Nor stopped, as I remember,
    Nor turned about till I got home,
    Locked up in mother's chamber.

You're a Grand Old Flag
Words and Music by George M. Cohan
G C D Bm D7 D°7 Am7 B7 Em A7 G7 E7
Strum Pattern: 10
Pick Pattern: 10
Verse
March
1. You're a (2.) grand old flag, you're a high fly - ing flag, and for - ev - er in peace may you wave. You're the
em - blem of the land I love, the home of the free and the brave. Ev - 'ry heart beats
true un - der red, white and blue, where there's nev - er a boast or brag. But, should auld ac -
quain - tance be for - got, keep your eye on the grand old flag. 2. You're a flag.

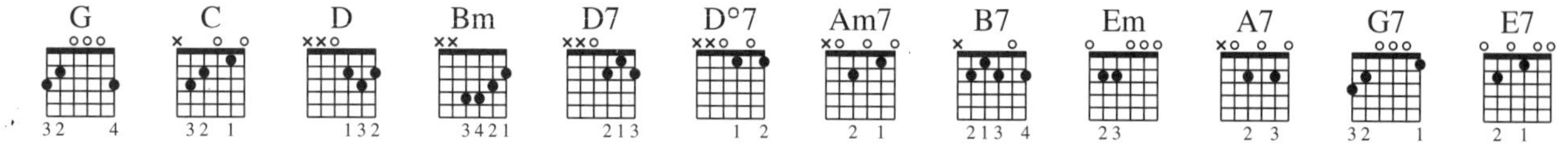

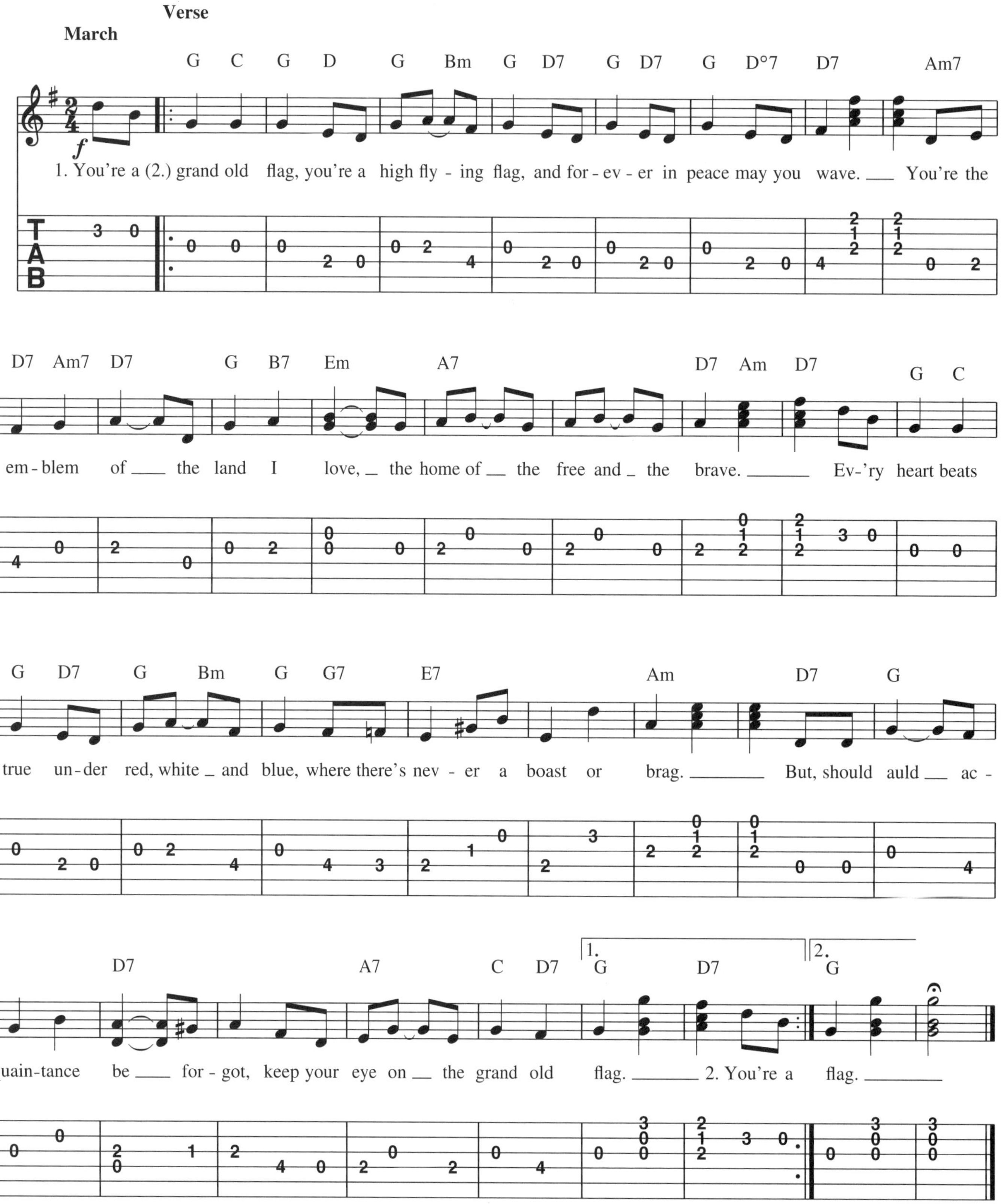

Zacchaeus

Traditional

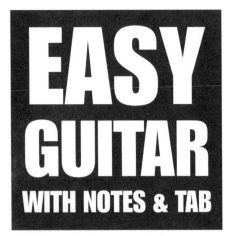

EASY GUITAR
WITH NOTES & TAB

This series features simplified arrangements with notes, TAB, chord charts, and strum and pick patterns.

00702002	Acoustic Rock Hits	$12.95
00702001	Best of Aerosmith	$12.95
00702040	Best of Allman Brothers	$9.95
00702166	All-Time Best Guitar Collection	$16.95
00702169	Best of The Beach Boys	$10.95
00702143	Best Chart Hits	$8.95
00702066	Best Contemporary Hits	$9.95
00702140	Best of Brooks and Dunn	$10.95
00702095	Best of Mariah Carey	$10.95
00702043	Best of Johnny Cash	$12.95
00702033	Best of Steven Curtis Chapman	$12.95
00702073	Steven Curtis Chapman – Favorites	$10.95
00702115	Blues Classics	$10.95
00385020	Broadway Songs for Kids	$9.95
00702149	Christian Children's Songbook	$7.95
00702090	Eric Clapton's Best	$10.95
00702086	Eric Clapton from "Unplugged"	$10.95
00702016	Classic Blues	$12.95
00702141	Classic Rock	$8.95
00702053	Best of Patsy Cline	$10.95
00702170	Contemporary Christian Christmas	$9.95
00702006	Contemporary Christian Favorites	$9.95
00702091	Contemporary Country Ballads	$9.95
00702089	Contemporary Country Pickin'	$9.95
00702065	Contemporary Women of Country	$9.95
00702121	Country from the Heart	$9.95
00702145	Best of Jim Croce	$10.95
00702085	Disney Movie Hits	$9.95
00702122	The Doors	$10.95
00702041	Favorite Hymns	$9.95
00702068	Forty Songs for a Better World	$10.95
00702159	Best of Genesis	$10.95
00702174	God Bless America and Other Songs for a Better Nation	$8.95
00702057	Golden Age of Rock	$8.95
00699374	Gospel Favorites	$14.95
00702099	Best of Amy Grant	$9.95
00702113	Grease Is Still the Word	$9.95
00702160	Great American Country Songbook	$12.95
00702050	Great Classical Themes	$6.95
00702131	Great Country Hits of the '90s	$8.95
00702116	Greatest Hymns for Guitar	$7.95
00702130	The Groovy Years	$9.95
00702136	Best of Merle Haggard	$10.95
00702037	Hits of the '50s	$10.95
00702035	Hits of the '60s	$10.95
00702046	Hits of the '70s	$8.95
00702047	Hits of the '80s	$8.95
00702054	Best of Hootie and the Blowfish	$9.95
00702059	Hunchback of Notre Dame & Hercules	$9.95
00702032	International Songs	$12.95
00702045	Jailhouse Rock, Kansas City and Other Hits by Leiber & Stoller	$10.95

00702021	Jazz Standards	$14.95
00702051	Jock Rock	$9.95
00702087	New Best of Billy Joel	$10.95
00702088	New Best of Elton John	$9.95
00702162	Jumbo Easy Guitar Songbook	$19.95
00702011	Best of Carole King	$12.95
00702112	Latin Favorites	$9.95
00702097	John Lennon – Imagine	$9.95
00699003	Lion King & Pocahontas	$9.95
00702005	Best of Andrew Lloyd Webber	$12.95
00702061	Love Songs of the '50s & '60s	$9.95
00702062	Love Songs of the '70s & '80s	$9.95
00702063	Love Songs of the '90s	$9.95
00702129	Songs of Sarah McLachlan	$12.95
00702138	Mellow Rock Hits	$10.95
00702147	Motown's Greatest Hits	$9.95
00702112	Movie Love Songs	$9.95
00702039	Movie Themes	$10.95
00702117	My Heart Will Go On & Other Top Hits	$9.95
00702096	Best of Nirvana	$14.95
00702026	'90s Rock	$12.95
00702067	The Nutcracker Suite	$5.95
00699261	Oasis	$14.95
00702030	Best of Roy Orbison	$12.95
00702158	Songs from Passion	$9.95
00702125	Praise and Worship for Guitar	$9.95
00702139	Elvis Country Favorites	$9.95
00702038	Elvis Presley – Songs of Inspiration	$10.95
00702004	Rockin' Elvis	$9.95
00699415	Best of Queen	$12.95
00702155	Rock Hits for Guitar	$9.95
00702128	Rockin' Down the Highway	$8.95
00702135	Rock'n'Roll Romance	$9.95
00702092	Best of the Rolling Stones	$10.95
00702093	Rolling Stones Collection	$17.95
00702101	17 Chart Hits	$9.95
00702137	Solid Gold Rock	$9.95
00702110	The Sound of Music	$8.95
00702010	Best of Rod Stewart	$12.95
00702049	Best of George Strait	$10.95
00702042	Today's Christian Favorites	$8.95
00702124	Today's Christian Rock	$8.95
00702171	Top Chart Hits for Guitar	$8.95
00702029	Top Hits of '95-'96	$12.95
00702034	Top Hits of '96-'97	$12.95
00702007	TV Tunes for Guitar	$12.95
00702108	Best of Stevie Ray Vaughan	$10.95
00702123	Best of Hank Williams	$9.95
00702111	Stevie Wonder – Guitar Collection	$9.95

E-Z PLAY GUITAR

EASY TO READ NOTES WITH TABLATURE

This series features your favorite songs in easy-to-play arrangements. The easy-to-read E-Z Play notes name themselves, while the TAB notation tells you where to play the notes on the guitar. The arrangements can be played solo or as a duet using the Strum and Picking patterns. E-Z Play Guitar books can be used to supplement ANY GUITAR METHOD Book 1!

BEATLES CLASSIC HITS
18 great songs from the Fab Four: Drive My Car • Get Back • Help! • I Saw Her Standing There • If I Fell • Love Me Do • Nowhere Man • Revolution • Twist and Shout • We Can Work It Out • more.
00702019 ....$9.95

BEATLES GREATEST HITS
19 songs: Can't Buy Me Love • Eleanor Rigby • A Hard Day's Night • Hey Jude • Let It Be • Penny Lane • She Loves You • Ticket to Ride • Yesterday • and more.
00702072 ....$9.95

CHRISTMAS TIDINGS
23 Christmas favorites, including: Blue Christmas • The Chipmunk Song • Feliz Navidad • Grandma Got Run Over by a Reindeer • Happy Holiday • I'll Be Home for Christmas • Rudolph the Red-Nosed Reindeer • Silver Bells • and more.
00699123 ....$9.95

CLASSIC ROCK FOR GUITAR
16 songs, including: All Right Now • Angie • Born to Be Wild • Free Bird • Iron Man • My Generation • Nights in White Satin • Rock and Roll All Nite • and more.
00702036 ....$9.95

CLASSICAL THEMES
20 beloved classical themes: Air on the G String • Ave Maria • Für Elise • In the Hall of the Mountain King • Jesu, Joy of Man's Desiring • Largo • Ode to Joy • Pomp and Circumstance • and more. Ideal for beginning or vision-impaired players.
00699272 ....$8.95

COUNTRY FAVORITES
20 songs, including: Green Green Grass of Home • Hey, Good Lookin' • Jambalaya (On the Bayou) • Make the World Go Away • Your Cheatin' Heart • and more.
00702077 ....$8.95

THE CREAM OF CLAPTON
19 hits from his early years, including: Crossroads • I Shot the Sheriff • Knockin' on Heaven's Door • Layla • White Room • Wonderful Tonight • and more.
00702024 ....$10.95

NEIL DIAMOND SMASH HITS
19 songs, including: America • Heartlight • Hello Again • Love on the Rocks • September Morn • Song Sung Blue • Sweet Caroline • Love Me Two Times • You Don't Bring Me Flowers • and more.
00702082 ....$9.95

THE DOORS
Features 16 of The Doors' greatest hits, including: Break on Through (To the Other Side) • Crystal Ship • Five to One • Hello, I Love You • L.A. Woman • Light My Fire • Love Her Madly • Love Me Two Times • People Are Strange • Riders on the Storm • Touch Me • Twentieth Century Fox • more.
00699176 ....$8.95

EARLY ROCK 'N' ROLL
17 songs: All Shook Up • At the Hop • Blue Suede Shoes • Hound Dog • Put Your Head on My Shoulder • Sixteen Candles • Wake Up Little Susie • and more.
00702078 ....$9.95

FAVORITE CHILDREN'S SONGS
28 songs: The Alphabet Song • The Farmer in the Dell • Jack and Jill • Oh, Susanna • Old MacDonald Had a Farm • This Old Man • Three Blind Mice • and more.
00702079 ....$8.95

GLORIOUS HYMNS
30 inspirational hymns: Abide with Me • Amazing Grace • Blessed Assurance • Come Christians Join to Sing • In the Garden • Jacob's Ladder • Rock of Ages • What a Friend We Have in Jesus • Wondrous Love • more.
00699192 ....$8.95

GOSPEL SONGS TO LIVE BY
20 songs, including: Amazing Grace • At Calvary • At the Cross • Blessed Assurance • Count Your Blessings • Do Lord • Footsteps of Jesus • Higher Ground • I Surrender All • Just as I Am • O Happy Day • Rock of Ages • This Little Light of Mine • What a Friend We Have in Jesus • more.
00699236 ....$7.95

GREAT ACOUSTIC HITS
Features 15 of the best acoustic songs: Barely Breathing • Best of My Love • Blackbird • Dust in the Wind • Fast Car • Love Song • Mr. Jones • Name • Only Wanna Be with You • Patience • Silent Lucidity • Tears in Heaven • Wanted Dead or Alive • Wonderwall • You Were Meant for Me.
00699127 ....$8.95

HITS OF THE '80S
13 songs: Every Breath You Take • Every Rose Has Its Thorn • Fast Car • Somewhere Out There • Time After Time • With or Without You • and more.
00702076 ....$8.95

BEST OF BILLY JOEL
11 songs: Just the Way You Are • Only the Good Die Young • Piano Man • Uptown Girl • and more.
00702081 ....$9.95

THE BEST OF ELTON JOHN
15 songs: Candle in the Wind • Bennie and the Jets • Your Song • Rocket Man • and more.
00702080 ....$9.95

KIDS' GUITAR SONGBOOK
A big collection of 38 favorites: Alphabet Song • A Bicycle Built for Two • Bingo • Eensy Weensy Spider • The Farmer in the Dell • Home on the Range • Jesus Loves Me • Old MacDonald • Sailing, Sailing • Twinkle, Twinkle Little Star • Yankee Doodle • more.
00702102 ....$7.95

LOVE SONGS
20 romantic favorites: All for Love • And I Love Her • Can You Feel the Love Tonight • Can't Help Falling in Love • How Am I Supposed to Live Without You • How Deep Is Your Love • Love Me Tender • Lovefool • My Heart Will Go On (Love Theme from *Titanic*) • Stand by Me • Wonderful Tonight • Your Song • more.
00699133 ....$9.95

OLD TIME GOSPEL SONGS
23 songs, including: Amazing Grace • Because He Lives • How Great Thou Art • Just a Closer Walk with Thee • (There'll Be) Peace in the Valley (For Me) • Rock of Ages • Sweet By and By • Will the Circle Be Unbroken • and more.
00702022 ....$9.95

POP/ROCK HITS
15 recognizable favorites, including: Come Sail Away • Fields of Gold • Good Vibrations • Let It Be • Louie, Louie • Mony, Mony • Tears in Heaven • and more.
00699513 ....$9.95

THE BEST OF ELVIS PRESLEY
18 of the King's best, including: All Shook Up • Blue Suede Shoes • Hound Dog • Heartbreak Hotel • (Let Me Be Your) Teddy Bear • and more.
00702083 ....$9.95

SUNDAY SCHOOL SONGS
31 wonderful songs of inspiration, including: Amazing Grace • The B-I-B-L-E • Deep and Wide • Go Tell It on the Mountain • Hallelu, Hallelujah! • I Am a C-H-R-I-S-T-I-A-N • Jesus Loves Me • Kum Ba Yah • This Little Light of Mine • and more.
00699220 ....$7.95

25 CHRISTMAS FAVORITES
25 songs: Away in a Manger • The Conventry Carol • Deck the Hall • Jolly Old St. Nicholas • Joy to the World • Up on the Housetop • and more.
00702075 ....$8.95

Prices, availability and contents subject to change without notice.

For more information contact your local music dealer or:

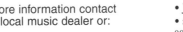

7777 W. BLUEMOUND RD. P.O. BOX 13819 MILWAUKEE, WI 53213

Visit Hal Leonard Online at
www.halleonard.com

0502

STRUM IT GUITAR

• AUTHENTIC CHORDS • ORIGINAL KEYS • COMPLETE SONGS •

The *Strum It* series lets players strum the chords and sing along with their favorite hits. Each song has been selected because it can be played with regular open chords, barre chords, or other moveable chord types. Guitarists can simply play the rhythm, or play and sing along through the entire song. All songs are shown in their original keys complete with chords, strum patterns, melody and lyrics. Wherever possible, the chord voicings from the recorded versions are notated.

Acoustic Classics

Play along with the recordings of 21 acoustic classics. Songs include: And I Love Her • Angie • Barely Breathing • Free Fallin' • Maggie May • Melissa • Mr. Jones • Only Wanna Be with You • Patience • Signs • Teach Your Children • Wonderful Tonight • Wonderwall • Yesterday • and more.
00699238 $10.95

The Beatles Favorites

Features 23 classic Beatles hits, including: Can't Buy Me Love • Eight Days a Week • Hey Jude • I Saw Her Standing There • Let It Be • Nowhere Man • She Loves You • Something • Yesterday • You've Got to Hide Your Love Away • and more.
00699249 $14.95

Celtic Guitar Songbook

Features 35 complete songs in their original keys, with authentic chords, strum patterns, melody and lyrics. Includes: Black Velvet Band • Cockles and Mussels (Molly Malone) • Danny Boy (Londonderry Air) • Finnegan's Wake • Galway Bay • I'm a Rover and Seldom Sober • The Irish Washerwoman • Kerry Dance • Killarney • McNamara's Band • My Wild Irish Rose • The Rose of Tralee • Sailor's Hornpipe • Whiskey in the Jar • Wild Rover • and more. 00699265 $9.95

Christmas Songs for Guitar

Over 40 Christmas favorites, including: The Christmas Song (Chestnuts Roasting on an Open Fire) • Feliz Navidad • Frosty the Snow Man • Grandma Got Run Over by a Reindeer • The Greatest Gift of All • I'll Be Home for Christmas • It's Beginning to Look Like Christmas • Rockin' Around the Christmas Tree • Silver Bells • and more. 00699247 $9.95

Christmas Songs with Three Chords

30 all-time favorites: Angels We Have Heard on High • Away in a Manger • Deck the Hall • Go, Tell It on the Mountain • Here We Come A-Wassailing • I Heard the Bells on Christmas Day • Jolly Old St. Nicholas • Silent Night • Up on the Housetop • and more. 00699487 $8.95

Country Strummin'

Features 24 songs: Achy Breaky Heart • Adalida • Ain't That Lonely Yet • Blue • The Beaches of Cheyenne • A Broken Wing • Gone Country • I Fall to Pieces • My Next Broken Heart • She and I • Unchained Melody • What a Crying Shame • and more. 00699119 $8.95

Jim Croce - Classic Hits

Authentic chords to 22 great songs from Jim Croce, including: Bad, Bad Leroy Brown • I'll Have to Say I Love You in a Song • Operator (That's Not the Way It Feels) • Time in a Bottle • and more. 00699269 $10.95

Disney Favorites

A great collection of 34 easy-to-play Disney favorites. Includes: Can You Feel the Love Tonight • Circle of Life • Cruella De Vil • Friend Like Me • It's a Small World • Some Day My Prince Will Come • Under the Sea • Whistle While You Work • Winnie the Pooh • Zero to Hero • and more. 00699171 $10.95

Disney Greats

Easy arrangements with guitar chord frames and strum patterns for 39 wonderful Disney classics including: Arabian Nights • The Aristocats • Beauty and the Beast • Colors of the Wind • Go the Distance • Hakuna Matata • Heigh-Ho • Kiss the Girl • A Pirate's Life • When You Wish Upon a Star • Zip-A-Dee-Doo-Dah • Theme from Zorro • and more. 00699172 $10.95

Best of The Doors

Strum along with more than 25 of your favorite hits from The Doors. Includes: Been Down So Long • Hello I Love You • Won't You Tell Me Your Name? • Light My Fire • Riders on the Storm • Touch Me • and more. 00699177 $10.95

Favorite Songs with 3 Chords

27 popular songs that are easy to play, including: All Shook Up • Blue Suede Shoes • Boot Scootin' Boogie • Evil Ways • Great Balls of Fire • Lay Down Sally • Semi-Charmed Life • Surfin' U.S.A. • Twist and Shout • Wooly Bully • and more. 00699112 $8.95

Favorite Songs with 4 Chords

22 tunes in this great collection, including: Beast of Burden • Don't Be Cruel • Get Back • Gloria • I Fought the Law • La Bamba • Last Kiss • Let Her Cry • Love Stinks • Peggy Sue • 3 AM • Wild Thing • and more. 00699270 $8.95

Irving Berlin's God Bless America

25 patriotic anthems: Amazing Grace • America, the Beautiful • Battle Hymn of the Republic • From a Distance • God Bless America • Imagine • The Lord's Prayer • The Star Spangled Banner • Stars and Stripes Forever • This Land Is Your Land • United We Stand • You're a Grand Old Flag • and more. 00699508 $9.95

Great '50s Rock

28 of early rock's biggest hits, including: At the Hop • Blueberry Hill • Bye Bye Love • Hound Dog • Rock Around the Clock • That'll Be the Day • and more. 00699187 $8.95

Great '60s Rock

Features the chords, strum patterns, melody and lyrics for 27 classic rock songs, all in their original keys. Includes: And I Love Her • Crying • Gloria • Good Lovin' • I Fought the Law • Mellow Yellow • Return to Sender • Runaway • Surfin' U.S.A. • The Twist • Twist and Shout • Under the Boardwalk • Wild Thing • and more. 00699188 $8.95

Great '70s Rock

Strum the chords to 21 classic '70s hits! Includes: Band on the Run • Burning Love • If • It's a Heartache • Lay Down Sally • Let It Be • Love Hurts • Maggie May • New Kid in Town • Ramblin' Man • Time for Me to Fly • Two Out of Three Ain't Bad • Wild World • and more. 00699262 $8.95

Great '80s Rock

23 arrangements that let you play along with your favorite recordings from the 1980s, such as: Back on the Chain Gang • Centerfold • Crazy Little Thing Called Love • Free Fallin' • Got My Mind Set on You • Kokomo • Should I Stay or Should I Go • Uptown Girl • Waiting for a Girl Like You • What I Like About You • and more. 00699263 $8.95

Best of Woody Guthrie

20 of the Guthrie's most popular songs, including: Do Re Mi • The Grand Coulee Dam • I Ain't Got No Home • Ramblin' Round • Roll On, Columbia • So Long It's Been Good to Know Yuh (Dusty Old Dust) • Talking Dust Bowl • This Land Is Your Land • Tom Joad • and more. 00699496 $12.95

The John Hiatt Collection

This collection includes 17 classics: Angel Eyes • Feels Like Rain • Have a Little Faith in Me • Memphis in the Meantime • Perfectly Good Guitar • A Real Fine Love • Riding with the King • Thing Called Love (Are You Ready for This Thing Called Love) • The Way We Make a Broken Heart • and more. 00699398 $12.95

Hymn Favorites

Includes: Amazing Grace • Battle Hymn of the Republic • Down by the Riverside • Holy, Holy, Holy • Just as I Am • Rock of Ages • This Is My Father's World • What a Friend We Have in Jesus • and more. 00699271 $9.95

Best of Sarah McLachlan

20 of Sarah's most popular hits for guitar, including: Adia • Angel • Building a Mystery • I Will Remember You • Ice Cream • Sweet Surrender • and more. 00699231 $10.95

A Merry Christmas Songbook

Easy arrangements for 51 holiday hits: Away in a Manger • Deck the Hall • Fum, Fum, Fum • The Holly and the Ivy • Jolly Old St. Nicholas • O Christmas Tree • Star of the East • The Twelve Days of Christmas • and more! 00699211 $8.95

Pop-Rock Guitar Favorites

31 songs, including: Angie • Brown Eyed Girl • Crazy Little Thing Called Love • Eight Days a Week • Fire and Rain • Free Bird • Gloria • Hey Jude • Let It Be • Maggie May • New Kid in Town • Surfin' U.S.A. • Wild Thing • Wonderful Tonight • and more. 00699088 $8.95

Best of George Strait

Strum the chords to 20 great Strait hits! Includes: Adalida • All My Ex's Live in Texas • The Best Day • Blue Clear Sky • Carried Away • The Chair • Does Fort Worth Ever Cross Your Mind • Lovebug • Right or Wrong • Write This Down • and more. 00699235 $10.95

Best of Hank Williams Jr.

24 of Hank's signature standards. Includes: Ain't Misbehavin' • All My Rowdy Friends Are Coming Over Tonight • Attitude Adjustment • Family Tradition • Honky Tonkin' • Texas Women • There's a Tear in My Beer • Whiskey Bent and Hell Bound • and more. 00699224 $10.95

Women of Rock

22 hits from today's top female artists. Includes: Bitch • Don't Speak • Galileo • Give Me One Reason • I Don't Want to Wait • Insensitive • Lovefool • Mother Mother • Stay • Torn • You Oughta Know • You Were Meant for Me • Zombie • and more. 00699183 $9.95

FOR MORE INFORMATION, SEE YOUR LOCAL MUSIC DEALER, OR WRITE TO:

HAL•LEONARD® CORPORATION
7777 W. BLUEMOUND RD. P.O. BOX 13819 MILWAUKEE, WI 53213

www.halleonard.com

Prices, contents & availability subject to change without notice. Disney characters & artwork ©Disney Enterprises, Inc.

0102